Learning PowerCLI

A practical guide to get you started with automating
VMware vSphere via PowerCLI

Robert van den Nieuwendijk

[PACKT] enterprise
PUBLISHING   professional expertise distilled

BIRMINGHAM - MUMBAI

Learning PowerCLI

First published: February 2014

Production Reference: 1050214

Published by Packt Publishing Ltd.
Livery Place
35 Livery Street
Birmingham B3 2PB, UK.

ISBN 978-1-78217-016-7

www.packtpub.com

Cover Image by John M. Quick (john.m.quick@gmail.com)

Credits

Author
Robert van den Nieuwendijk

Reviewers
Chris Halverson
Timothy J. Patterson
Victoria Peterson
Philip Sellers
Brian Wuchner

Acquisition Editors
Sam Birch
Gregory Wild

Content Development Editor
Madhuja Chaudhari

Technical Editors
Tanvi Bhatt
Akashdeep Kundu
Shiny Poojary

Copy Editors
Roshni Banerjee
Brandt D'Mello
Adithi Shetty

Project Coordinator
Joel Goveya

Proofreader
Stephen Copestake

Indexers
Monica Ajmera Mehta
Rekha Nair
Tejal Soni

Graphics
Yuvraj Mannari
Abhinash Sahu

Production Coordinator
Manu Joseph

Cover Work
Manu Joseph

About the Author

Robert van den Nieuwendijk is an IT veteran from the Netherlands with over 25 years of experience in the IT industry. He holds a bachelor's degree in Software Engineering. After working for a few years as a programmer of air traffic control and vessel traffic management systems for a company that is now called HITT, he started his own company Van den Nieuwendijk Informatica in 1988. Since then he has worked as a freelance systems administrator for OpenVMS, Windows Server, Linux, and VMware vSphere systems, mainly for Dutch governmental organizations. Currently, he is a VMware vSphere administrator at Wageningen UR (University and Research centre). During winter, he is also a ski and snowboard instructor at an indoor ski school.

With his background as a programmer, he always tries to make his job easier by writing programs or scripts to perform repetitive tasks. In the past, he used the C programming language, OpenVMS DCL, Visual Basic Script, and KiXtart to do this. Since Windows PowerShell 1.0, he uses Windows PowerShell and VMware vSphere PowerCLI for all of his scripting work.

Robert is a member of the Dutch VMware User group (VMUG) Customer Council and a frequent contributor and moderator at the VMware VMTN Communities. In 2012 and 2013, VMware awarded him the vExpert title for his "significant contributions to the community and a willingness to share his expertise with others".

He has his own blog at `http://rvdnieuwendijk.com` where he has shared his knowledge since 2011. He writes mainly about VMware vSphere PowerCLI, Windows PowerShell, and VMware vSphere.

If you want to get in touch with Robert, you can find him on Twitter. His username is `@rvdnieuwendijk`.

I would like to thank my wife, Ali, for supporting me in writing this book and all the hours she had to spend alone while I was writing.

About the Reviewers

Chris Halverson is the co-leader of his local VMUG and the principal consultant at Darus Consulting (`www.darus.ca`). He has been working in the IT industry for over 14 years and specifically 7 years in virtualization. He has worked hard to increase his skill in the automation and cloud realm over that point of time, thanks to his enjoyment in the PowerShell scripting arena. He excels in architecture and design space helping others conceptualize and design the ideal layout and performance for the company's infrastructure. In his spare time, he enjoys spending time with his wife and four children and participating in his local Tae Kwon Do Dojang.

Timothy J. Patterson is a Cloud and Virtualization Systems Engineer, currently working at ProQuest based in Ann Arbor, Michigan. Focused primarily on Amazon Web Services and VMware technologies, he is currently in possession of the VCAP5-DCA, VCAP5-DCD, VCP5-DCV technical certifications from VMware, as well as the AWS Certified Solutions Architect certification from Amazon. Additionally, he is a Bachelor of Science from Saginaw Valley State University in Computer Information Systems and is a Novell Certified Linux Engineer.

Throughout his career, Tim has gained over 10 years of direct hands-on experience working with VMware products and AWS with a passion towards cloud architecture, design, and automation technologies. He is currently a VCDX hopeful and is always looking ahead for the next challenge.

I would like to thank my wife, Danielle, for her never-ending support and love. I also want to mention my two little girls, Molly and Amelia, because without them I would not be complete. My family serves as a constant source of inspiration, driving me to succeed in both my personal and professional goals.

Additionally, I would like to take this opportunity to thank the individuals I have had the pleasure of working with throughout my professional career. I have learned a lot from each and every one of you. I look forward to what the future has in store for us as the technology we work with every day continues to evolve.

Victoria Peterson is originally from Scotland and is now based in the Netherlands. She has more than 15 years of experience in the IT industry.

Her expertise is mainly focused on systems monitoring, automation, and integration. She has extensive knowledge and experience of design and implementation of monitoring solutions and development of custom monitoring based on System Center Operations Manager. She is currently a System Center Monitoring Specialist at Wageningen UR.

Her product skill set includes technologies such as SCOM, SCCM, SCSM, Windows Server, Active Directory, SQL, Citrix XenApp, VMware vSphere, Unicenter NSM, and automation of various tasks using PowerShell scripting.

Victoria has MCSE (legacy) and MCDBA certifications and she additionally holds other non-Microsoft certifications such as Citrix Certified Administrator (XenApp 6.5) and Certified Unicenter Specialist Engineer for Unicenter NSM.

Philip Sellers is a Senior Systems Administrator based in Myrtle Beach, South Carolina, with 15 years of experience. Primarily focused in Microsoft and VMware technologies, he is the virtualization lead for Horry Telephone Cooperative (HTC) and works extensively with core technology platforms such as vSphere, Active Directory, and Exchange. Prior to his current role, he served as a trusted IT consultant for medical, legal, and hospitality companies administering their infrastructure and systems.

Philip is an active blogger, covering vSphere, Microsoft software, and HP hardware platforms. He is a VMware vExpert for 2013, and he has recognizing contributions to the VMware community and advocacy of the vSphere platform. He also participates with the VMware User Groups in his area.

To find out more about Philip, you may follow his blog at `http://tech.philipsellers.com` and on Twitter, `@pbsellers`.

Brian Wuchner is a Senior Systems Administrator for a government agency. He has over 10 years of industry experience with specialties in infrastructure automation, directory services, and data center virtualization. Brian holds the VCA-Cloud, VCA-WM, and VCP5-DCV certifications and was awarded the vExpert title from VMware for 2011-2013. He can be contacted on LinkedIn (`http://www.linkedin.com/in/bwuch`), Twitter (`@bwuch`), or through his blog at `http://enterpriseadmins.org`.

www.PacktPub.com

Support files, eBooks, discount offers and more

You might want to visit www.PacktPub.com for support files and downloads related to your book.

Did you know that Packt offers eBook versions of every book published, with PDF and ePub files available? You can upgrade to the eBook version at www.PacktPub.com and as a print book customer, you are entitled to a discount on the eBook copy. Get in touch with us at service@packtpub.com for more details.

At www.PacktPub.com, you can also read a collection of free technical articles, sign up for a range of free newsletters and receive exclusive discounts and offers on Packt books and eBooks.

http://PacktLib.PacktPub.com

Do you need instant solutions to your IT questions? PacktLib is Packt's online digital book library. Here, you can access, read and search across Packt's entire library of books.

Why Subscribe?

- Fully searchable across every book published by Packt
- Copy and paste, print and bookmark content
- On demand and accessible via web browser

Free Access for Packt account holders

If you have an account with Packt at www.PacktPub.com, you can use this to access PacktLib today and view nine entirely free books. Simply use your login credentials for immediate access.

Instant Updates on New Packt Books

Get notified! Find out when new books are published by following @PacktEnterprise on Twitter, or the *Packt Enterprise* Facebook page.

Table of Contents

Preface

VMware vSphere PowerCLI is a command-line automation and scripting tool that provides a Windows PowerShell interface to the VMware vSphere and vCloud products.

Learning PowerCLI shows you how to install and use PowerCLI to automate the management of your VMware vSphere environment. With lots of examples, this book will teach you how to manage vSphere from the command line and how to create advanced PowerCLI scripts.

What this book covers

Chapter 1, Introduction to PowerCLI, gets you started using PowerCLI. First, you will see how to download and install PowerCLI. Then, you will learn to connect to and disconnect from the vCenter and ESXi servers and retrieve a list of all of your hosts and virtual machines.

Chapter 2, Learning Basic PowerCLI Concepts, introduces the Get-Help, Get-Command, and Get-Member cmdlets. It explains the difference between PowerShell Providers and PSDrives. You will see how you can use the raw vSphere API objects from PowerCLI and how to use the New-VIProperty cmdlet to extend a PowerCLI object.

Chapter 3, Working with Objects in PowerShell, concentrates on objects, properties, and methods. This chapter shows how you can use the pipeline to use the output of one command as the input of another command. You will learn how to use the PowerShell object cmdlets and how to create your own PowerShell objects.

Chapter 4, Managing vSphere Hosts with PowerCLI, covers the management of the vSphere ESXi servers. You will see how to add hosts to the vCenter server and how to remove them. You will work with host profiles, host services, Image Builder, and Auto Deploy, as well as with the esxcli command and the vSphere CLI commands from PowerCLI.

Chapter 5, Managing Virtual Machines with PowerCLI, examines the lifecycle of virtual machines—from creating to removing them. Creating templates, updating VMware Tools and upgrading virtual hardware, running commands in the guest OS, and configuring fault tolerance are some of the topics discussed in this chapter.

Chapter 6, Managing Virtual Networks with PowerCLI, walks you through vSphere Standard Switches and vSphere Distributed Switches, port groups, and network adapters. It shows you how to configure host networking and how to configure the network of a virtual machine.

Chapter 7, Managing Storage with PowerCLI, explores creating and removing datastores and Datastore Clusters, working with Raw Device Mapping, configuring software iSCSI initiators, Storage I/O Control, and Storage DRS.

Chapter 8, Managing High Availability and Clustering with PowerCLI, covers HA and DRS clusters, DRS rules and DRS groups, resource pools, and Distributed Power Management.

Chapter 9, Managing vCenter with PowerCLI, shows you how to work with privileges, work with roles and permissions, manage licenses, configure alarm definitions, alarm action triggers, and retrieve events.

Chapter 10, Reporting with PowerCLI, concentrates on retrieving log files and log bundles, performance reporting, exporting reports to CSV files, generating HTML reports, sending reports by e-mail, and reporting the health of your vSphere environment with the vCheck script.

What you need for this book

To run the example PowerCLI scripts given in this book, you need the following software:

- VMware vSphere PowerCLI
- Windows PowerShell 2.0 or Windows PowerShell 3.0
- VMware vCenter Server
- VMware ESXi

The scripts in this book are tested using VMware vSphere PowerCLI 5.5 Release 1, VMware vCenter Server 5.5, and VMware ESXi 5.5.

Windows PowerShell and VMware vSphere PowerCLI are free. You can download a free 60-day evaluation of VMware vCenter Server and VMware ESXi from the VMware website. It is not possible to modify the settings on the free VMware vSphere Hypervisor using PowerCLI.

Who this book is for

This book is written for VMware vSphere administrators who want to automate their vSphere environment using PowerCLI. It is assumed that you have at least a basic knowledge of VMware vSphere. If you are not a vSphere administrator, but you are interested in learning more about PowerCLI, then this book will also give you some basic knowledge of vSphere.

Conventions

In this book, you will find a number of styles of text that distinguish between different kinds of information. Here are some examples of these styles, and an explanation of their meaning.

Code words in text are shown as follows: "The -Name parameter is required."

A block of code is set as follows:

```
$Cluster = Get-Cluster -Name Cluster01
New-VM -Name VM1 -ResourcePool $Cluster
```

Any command-line input or output is written as follows:

```
PowerCLI C:\> New-VM -Name VM1 -ResourcePool (Get-Cluster -Name
Cluster01)
```

New terms and **important words** are shown in bold. Words that you see on the screen, in menus or dialog boxes for example, appear in the text like this: "clicking the **Next** button moves you to the next screen".

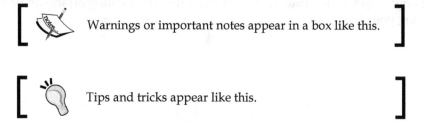

Warnings or important notes appear in a box like this.

Tips and tricks appear like this.

Reader feedback

Feedback from our readers is always welcome. Let us know what you think about this book—what you liked or may have disliked. Reader feedback is important for us to develop titles that you really get the most out of.

To send us general feedback, simply send an e-mail to feedback@packtpub.com, and mention the book title via the subject of your message. If there is a topic that you have expertise in and you are interested in either writing or contributing to a book, see our author guide on www.packtpub.com/authors.

Customer support

Now that you are the proud owner of a Packt book, we have a number of things to help you to get the most from your purchase.

Downloading the example code

You can download the example code files for all Packt books you have purchased from your account at http://www.packtpub.com. If you purchased this book elsewhere, you can visit http://www.packtpub.com/support and register to have the files e-mailed directly to you.

Errata

Although we have taken every care to ensure the accuracy of our content, mistakes do happen. If you find a mistake in one of our books—maybe a mistake in the text or the code—we would be grateful if you would report this to us. By doing so, you can save other readers from frustration and help us improve subsequent versions of this book. If you find any errata, please report them by visiting http://www.packtpub.com/submit-errata, selecting your book, clicking on the **errata submission form** link, and entering the details of your errata. Once your errata are verified, your submission will be accepted and the errata will be uploaded on our website, or added to any list of existing errata, under the Errata section of that title. Any existing errata can be viewed by selecting your title from http://www.packtpub.com/support.

Piracy

Piracy of copyright material on the Internet is an ongoing problem across all media. At Packt, we take the protection of our copyright and licenses very seriously. If you come across any illegal copies of our works, in any form, on the Internet, please provide us with the location address or website name immediately so that we can pursue a remedy.

Please contact us at copyright@packtpub.com with a link to the suspected pirated material.

We appreciate your help in protecting our authors, and our ability to bring you valuable content.

Questions

You can contact us at questions@packtpub.com if you are having a problem with any aspect of the book, and we will do our best to address it.

1
Introduction to PowerCLI

Have you ever had to create 100 virtual machines in a really short period of time, change a setting on all of your hosts, or make an advanced report for your boss to show how full the hard disks of your virtual machines are? If you have, you know that performing these tasks using the vSphere client will take a lot of time. This is where automation can make your job easier. **VMware vSphere PowerCLI** is a powerful tool that can perform these tasks and much more. And the best thing is that it is free!

VMware vSphere PowerCLI is a **command-line interface** distributed as a Microsoft Windows PowerShell snap-in. You can use PowerCLI to automate your vSphere hosts, virtual machines, virtual networks, storage, clusters, vCenter Servers, and more.

In this chapter, you will learn:

- Downloading and installing PowerCLI
- Modifying the PowerShell execution policy
- Connecting and disconnecting servers
- Using the credential store
- Retrieving a list of all of your virtual machines
- Retrieving a list of all of your hosts

Downloading and installing PowerCLI

Before you can install PowerCLI, you have to download the PowerCLI installer from the VMware website. You will need a My VMware account to do this.

Downloading PowerCLI

Perform the following steps to download PowerCLI:

1. Visit `http://www.vmware.com/go/powercli`. On this page, you will find a **Resources** section.

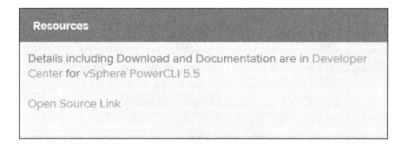

2. Click on the **vSphere PowerCLI 5.5** link in the **Resources** section to go to the download page.
3. Click on the **Download** button to download PowerCLI.
4. You have to log in with a My VMware account. If you don't have a **My VMware** account, you can register for free.

5. After you log in, you will be taken to the **vSphere PowerCLI 5.5** download page. Click on the **Download Now** button to start downloading PowerCLI.

6. You have to agree to and accept the terms and conditions outlined in the VMware End User License Agreement. Check the tick box in front of **I agree to the terms and conditions outlined in the End User License Agreement** and click on **Accept** to download the PowerCLI installer.

7. Save the PowerCLI installation file on your local hard disk.

Installing PowerCLI

Perform the following steps to install PowerCLI:

1. Run the PowerCLI installer that you just downloaded.

2. Click on **Yes** in the **User Account Control** window to accept the **Do you want to allow the following program to make changes to this computer?** option.

3. PowerCLI requires VMware Remote Console Plug-In and VMware VIX to be installed on your computer. Click on **Install** to install these products.

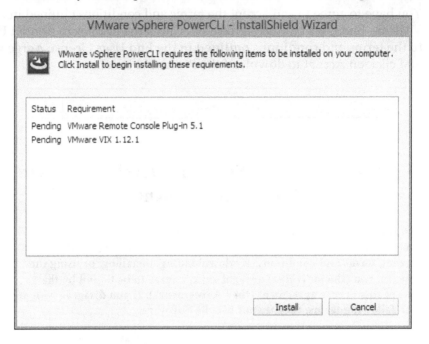

4. Click on **Next** on the **Welcome to the InstallShield Wizard for VMware vSphere PowerCLI** window.

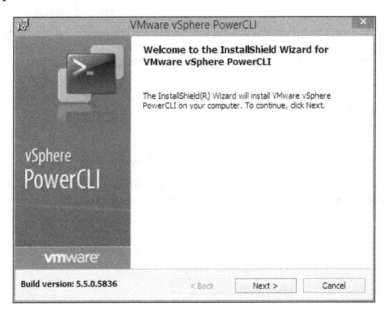

5. Select **I accept the terms in the license agreement** and click on **Next**.

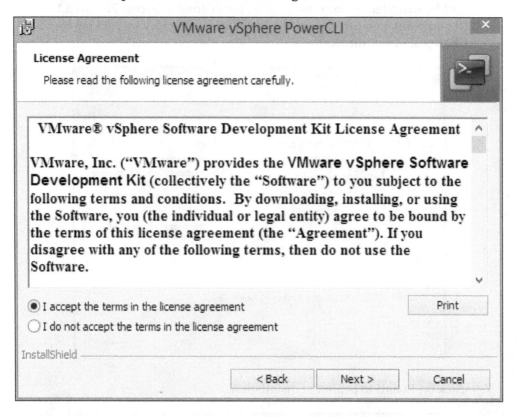

6. If you are using **VMware vCloud Director**, you can select **This feature will be installed on local hard drive** for **vCloud Director PowerCLI**. (If you want, you can change the installation directory by clicking on **Change....**) Click on **Next**.

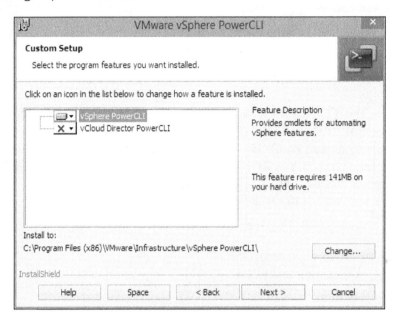

7. Click on **Install** to begin the installation.

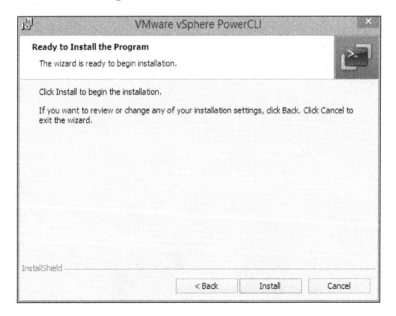

8. Click on **Finish** to exit the installation wizard.

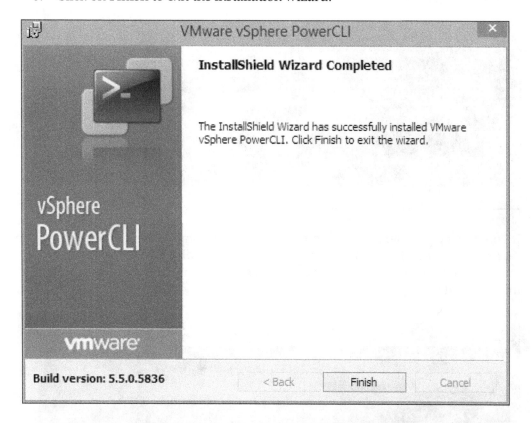

After installing PowerCLI, you will have a **VMware vSphere PowerCLI** icon on your desktop. If you installed PowerCLI on a 64-bit computer, you will also have a **VMware vSphere PowerCLI (32-Bit)** icon. Some PowerCLI commands only work in the 32-bit version of PowerCLI. So install both versions.

Besides starting PowerCLI from the icon on your desktop, you can also start PowerCLI from the Start menu. Go to **All Programs | VMware | VMware vSphere PowerCLI** to launch **VMware vSphere PowerCLI** or **VMware vSphere PowerCLI (32-Bit)**.

When you start PowerCLI, you will get the following screen:

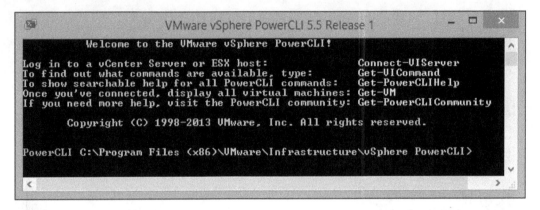

If you didn't get the text from the screenshot but got some red error messages saying that files **cannot be loaded because running scripts is disabled on this system**, read the following section to solve this problem. The following screenshot shows the error message that will be displayed:

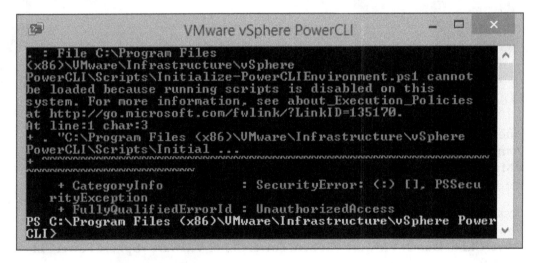

Modifying the PowerShell execution policy

If this is the first time that you are using Windows PowerShell on the computer on which you installed PowerCLI, you have to change the **execution policy** to be able to start PowerCLI.

The Windows PowerShell execution policies define when you can run scripts or load configuration files. The possible values for the execution policy are: Restricted, AllSigned, RemoteSigned, Unrestricted, Bypass, and Undefined.

Policy	Description
Restricted	This is the default execution policy. It allows you to run commands at the command prompt but disables the execution of scripts. It will also disable the start of PowerCLI.
AllSigned	With the AllSigned execution policy, scripts can run but must be signed by a trusted publisher. If you run a script by a publisher that is not trusted yet, you will see a prompt asking whether you trust the publisher of the script.
RemoteSigned	The RemoteSigned execution policy allows you to run scripts that you have written on the local computer. Any script downloaded from the Internet must be signed by a trusted publisher or must be unblocked.
Unrestricted	When the execution policy is set to Unrestricted, unsigned scripts can run. If you run a script that has been downloaded from the Internet, you will get a security warning saying that this script can potentially harm your computer and asking whether you want to run this script.
Bypass	The Bypass execution policy blocks nothing and displays no warnings or prompts. This execution policy is designed for configurations in which a Windows PowerShell script is built into a larger application that has its own security model.
Undefined	The Undefined execution policy removes the execution policy from the current scope. If the execution policy in all scopes is Undefined, the effective execution policy is Restricted, which is the default execution policy. The Undefined execution policy will not remove an execution policy that is set in a **Group Policy** scope.

You can check the current execution policy setting with the following command:

```
PowerCLI C:\> Get-ExecutionPolicy
```

`Get-ExecutionPolicy` is a Windows PowerShell **commandlet (cmdlet)**. Cmdlets are commands built into PowerShell or PowerCLI. They follow a verb-noun naming convention. The **get cmdlets** receives information about the item that is specified as the noun part of the cmdlet.

Set the execution policy to `RemoteSigned` to be able to start PowerCLI and run scripts written on the local computer with the `Set-ExecutionPolicy -ExecutionPolicy RemoteSigned` command, as shown in the next screenshot.

> You have to run the `Set-ExecutionPolicy -ExecutionPolicy RemoteSigned` command from a PowerShell or PowerCLI session that you started using the **Run as Administrator** option, or you will get the following error message:
>
> ```
> Set-ExecutionPolicy : Access to the registry key
> 'HKEY_LOCAL_MACHINE\SOFTWARE\Microsoft\PowerShell\1\
> ShellIds\Microsoft.PowerShell' is denied.
> ```
>
> If you are using both the 32-bit and the 64-bit versions of PowerCLI, you have to run this command in both versions.

In the next screenshot of the PowerCLI console, you will see the output of the `Set-ExecutionPolicy -ExecutionPolicy RemoteSigned` command if you run this command in a PowerCLI session started with "**Run as Administrator**".

```
Administrator: VMware vSphere PowerCLI                      _  □  ×
PS C:\WINDOWS\system32>
PS C:\WINDOWS\system32> Set-ExecutionPolicy -ExecutionPolicy RemoteSigned

Execution Policy Change
The execution policy helps protect you from scripts that you do not trust.
Changing the execution policy might expose you to the security risks described
in the about_Execution_Policies help topic at
http://go.microsoft.com/fwlink/?LinkID=135170. Do you want to change the
execution policy?
[Y] Yes   [N] No   [S] Suspend   [?] Help (default is "Y"):
PS C:\WINDOWS\system32> Get-ExecutionPolicy
RemoteSigned
PS C:\WINDOWS\system32>
```

You can get more information about execution policies by typing the following command:

```
PowerCLI C:\> Get-Help about_Execution_Policies
```

To get more information about signing your scripts, type the following command:

```
PowerCLI C:\> Get-Help about_signing
```

Connecting and disconnecting servers

Before you can do useful things with PowerCLI, you have to connect to a vCenter Server or an ESXi server. And if you are finished, it is a good practice to disconnect your session. We will discuss how to do this in the following sections.

Connecting to a server

If you are not connected to a vCenter or an ESXi server, you will get an error message if you try to run a PowerCLI cmdlet. Let's try to retrieve a list of all of your datacenters using the following command:

```
PowerCLI C:\> Get-Datacenter
```

The output of the preceding command is as follows:

```
Get-Datacenter : 12/19/2013 7:29:36 PM    Get-Datacenter        You
 are not currently connected to any servers. Please connect first
 using a Connect cmdlet.

At line:1 char:1

+ Get-Datacenter

+ ~~~~~~~~~~~~~~

    + CategoryInfo          : ResourceUnavailable: (:)
[Get-Datacenter], ViServerConnectionException

    + FullyQualifiedErrorId :
Core_BaseCmdlet_NotConnectedError,
VMware.VimAutomation.ViCore.Cmdlets.Commands.GetDatacenter
```

You see that this gives an error message. You first have to connect to a vCenter Server or an ESXi server using the Connect-VIServer cmdlet. If you have a vCenter Server, you only need to connect to the vCenter Server and not to the individual ESXi servers. It is possible to connect to multiple vCenter Servers or ESXi servers at once. The Connect-VIServer cmdlet has the following syntax:

```
Connect-VIServer [-Server] <String[]> [-Port <Int32>] [-Protocol
<String>] [-Credential <PSCredential>] [-User <String>] [-Password
<String>] [-Session <String>] [-NotDefault] [-SaveCredentials]
[-AllLinked] [-Force] [<CommonParameters>]

Connect-VIServer -Menu [<CommonParameters>]
```

As you can see, the Connect-VIserver cmdlet has two parameter sets: Default and Menu. In the Default parameter set, the -Server parameter is required. In the Menu parameter set, the -Menu parameter is required. You cannot combine parameters from the Default parameter set with the Menu parameter set.

Let's first try to connect to a vCenter Server with the following cmdlet:

```
PowerCLI C:\> Connect-VIServer -Server 192.168.0.132
```

`192.168.0.132` is the IP address of the vCenter Server in my home lab. Replace this IP address with the IP address or DNS name of your vCenter or ESXi server.

The preceding command will pop up a window in which you have to specify server credentials to connect to your server if your Windows session credentials don't have rights on your server. Enter values for **User name** and **Password** and click on **OK**.

If you specified valid credentials, you will get output similar to the following:

```
Name                           Port  User
----                           ----  ----
192.168.0.132                  443   root
```

You can also specify a username and password on the command line as follows:

```
PowerCLI C:\> Connect-VIServer -Server 192.168.0.132 -User admin
-Password pass
```

You can also save the credentials in a variable with the following command:

```
PowerCLI C:\> $Credential = Get-Credential
```

The preceding command will pop up a window in which you can type the username and password.

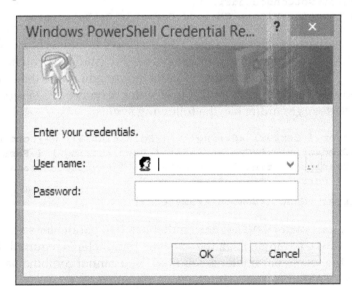

You can now use the `$Credential` variable to connect to a server using the –`Credential` parameter, as follows:

```
PowerCLI C:\> Connect-VIServer -Server 192.168.0.132 -Credential
 $Credential
```

You can also use the PowerCLI **credential store**. This will be discussed in a later section in this chapter.

The default protocol that the `Connect-VIServer` cmdlet uses is HTTPS. If you want to make a connection with the HTTP protocol, you can do that with the following command:

```
PowerCLI C:\> Connect-VIServer -Server 192.168.0.132 -Protocol http
```

If you have multiple vCenter Servers in **Linked Mode**, you can use the `Connect-VIServer -AllLinked` parameter to connect all of these vCenter Servers at once, as follows:

```
PowerCLI C:\> Connect-VIserver -Server 192.168.0.132 -Credential
 $Credential -AllLinked
```

The `Connect-VIServer -Menu` command gives you a list of previously connected servers from which you can pick one, as shown in the following command line:

```
PowerCLI C:\> Connect-VIServer -Menu
Select a server from the list (by typing its number and
 pressing Enter):
[1] 192.168.0.132
[2] 192.168.0.133
```

Type the number of the server you want to connect to.

Connecting to multiple servers

It is possible in PowerCLI to connect to multiple servers at once. You can do this by specifying more than one server, as follows:

```
PowerCLI C:\> Connect-VIServer -Server vCenter1,vCenter2
```

The first time you try to do this, you will get the following message:

```
Working with multiple default servers?


    Select [Y] if you want to work with more than one default
servers. In this case, every time when you connect to a different
server using Connect-VIServer, the new server connection is stored
in an array variable together with the previously connected servers.
 When you run a cmdlet and the target servers cannot be determined
from the specified parameters, the cmdlet runs against all servers
stored in the array variable.
    Select [N] if you want to work with a single default server. In
this case, when you run a cmdlet and the target servers cannot be
determined from the specified parameters, the cmdlet runs against the
last connected server.


    WARNING: WORKING WITH MULTIPLE DEFAULT SERVERS WILL BE ENABLED BY
 DEFAULT IN A FUTURE RELEASE. You can explicitly set your own
preference at any time by using the DefaultServerMode parameter of
Set-PowerCLIConfiguration.


[Y] Yes  [N] No  [S] Suspend  [?] Help (default is "Y"):
```

Press *Enter* or type *Y* to work with multiple default servers.

As the message says, you can always connect to multiple servers but your commands will only work against the last server you connected to unless you have enabled working with multiple servers.

You can see the current value of `DefaultServerMode` with the `Get-PowerCLIConfiguration` cmdlet:

```
PowerCLI C:\> Get-PowerCLIConfiguration
```

If you want to change the DefaultServerMode from single to multiple, you can do that with the `Set-PowerCLIConfiguration` cmdlet. The cmdlet has the following syntax:

```
Set-PowerCLIConfiguration [-ProxyPolicy <ProxyPolicy>]
 [-DefaultVIServerMode <DefaultVIServerMode>]
 [-InvalidCertificateAction <BadCertificateAction>]
[-DisplayDeprecationWarnings [<Boolean>]]
[-WebOperationTimeoutSeconds <Int32>]
[-VMConsoleWindowBrowser <String>]
[-Scope <ConfigurationScope>]  [-WhatIf]
[-Confirm]  [<CommonParameters>]
```

Change the DefaultServerMode from single to multiple with the following command:

```
PowerCLI C:\> Set-PowerCLIConfiguration -DefaultVIServerMode Multiple
 -Scope User
```

All of the servers that you are currently connected to are stored in the variable $global:DefaultVIServers. If DefaultVIServerMode is set to multiple, your PowerCLI cmdlets will run against all servers stored in the $global:DefaultVIServers variable.

The last server you are connected to is stored in the variable $global:DefaultVIServer. If DefaultVIServerMode is set to single, your PowerCLI cmdlets will only run against the server stored in the $global:DefaultVIServer variable.

Suppressing certificate warnings

If your vCenter Server does not have valid server certificates, the Connect-VIserver cmdlet will display some warning messages, as shown in the following screenshot:

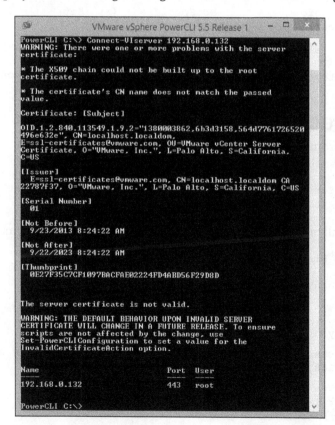

It is a good practice is to supply your vCenter Server and ESXi servers with valid certificates. You can find information on how to do this in the VMware Knowledge Base article, *Implementing CA signed SSL certificates with vSphere 5.x (2034833)* at `http://kb.vmware.com/kb/2034833`.

If you don't have valid certificates, you can easily suppress the warning messages using the `Set-PowerCLIConfiguration` cmdlet with the following command:

```
PowerCLI C:\ > Set-PowerCLIConfiguration -InvalidCertificateAction Ignore
```

This will modify `InvalidCertificationAction` in the `AllUsers` scope. You have to run this command using the **Run as Administrator** PowerCLI session. Otherwise, you will get the following error message:

```
Set-PowerCLIConfiguration : Only administrators can change settings for
all users.

At line:1 char:1

+ Set-PowerCLIConfiguration -InvalidCertificateAction Ignore

+ ~~~~~~~~~~~~~~~~~~~~~~~~~~~~~~~~~~~~~~~~~~~~~~~~~~~~~~~~~~~~~

    + CategoryInfo          : NotSpecified: (:) [Set-
PowerCLIConfiguration], InvalidArgument

    + FullyQualifiedErrorId : VMware.VimAutomation.ViCore.Types.
V1.ErrorHandling.InvalidArgument
,VMware.VimAutomation.ViCore.Cmdlets.Commands.SetVIToolkitConfiguration
```

Disconnecting from a server

To disconnect from a vSphere server, you have to use the `Disconnect-VIServer` cmdlet. The `Disconnect-VIServer` cmdlet has the following syntax:

```
Disconnect-VIServer [[-Server] <VIServer[]>] [-Force] [-WhatIf]
 [-Confirm] [<CommonParameters>]
```

To disconnect all of your server connections, type the following command:

```
PowerCLI C:\> Disconnect-VIServer -Server * -Force
```

The output of the preceding command is as follows:

```
Confirm

Are you sure you want to perform this action?

Performing operation "Disconnect VIServer" on Target "User: root,
 Server: 192.168.0.132, Port: 443".

[Y] Yes  [A] Yes to All  [N] No  [L] No to All  [S] Suspend  [?]
 Help (default is "Y"):
```

Type *Y* or *Enter* to disconnect from the server.

If you don't want to be prompted with **Are you sure you want to perform this action?**, you can use the -Confirm:$false option as follows:

```
PowerCLI C:\> Disconnect-VIServer -Server * -Force -Confirm:$false
```

It may be that you want to disconnect only one session and not all. In that case, specify the server name or IP address of the server you want to disconnect. The following command only disconnects the latest session from server 192.168.0.132:

```
PowerCLI C:\> Disconnect-VIServer -Server 192.168.0.132
```

Disconnecting one or more sessions will also change the value of the $global:DefaultVIServers and $global:DefaultVIServer variables.

Retrieving the PowerCLI configuration

To see the current setting of InvalidCertificationAction, you can use the Get-PowerCLIConfiguration cmdlet. The syntax of this cmdlet is as follows:

```
Get-PowerCLIConfiguration [-Scope <ConfigurationScope>]
[<CommonParameters>]
```

The following example will retrieve the PowerCLI configuration and shows the InvalidCertificateAction value for all scopes:

```
PowerCLI C:\> Get-PowerCLIConfiguration |
>> Select-Object -Property Scope,InvalidCertificateAction,DisplayDeprecat
ionWarnings |
>> Format-Table -AutoSize
>>

    Scope InvalidCertificateAction DisplayDeprecationWarnings
    ----- ------------------------ --------------------------
  Session                   Ignore                       True
     User                   Ignore                       True
 AllUsers                    Unset
```

As you can see in the output, there are three different scopes for which you can modify the PowerCLI configuration: Session, User, and AllUsers. The Set-PowerCLIConfiguration cmdlet will modify the AllUser scope if you don't specify a scope.

The DisplayDeprecationWarnings property shown in the preceding output will be discussed in a later section in this chapter.

Using the credential store

If you are logged in to your computer with a domain account, you can use your Windows session credentials to connect to a vCenter or ESXi server. If you are not logged in to your computer with a domain account or your domain account has no rights in vSphere, you have to supply account information every time you connect to a vCenter or ESXi server.

To prevent you from having to do this, you can store credentials in the credential store. These stored credentials will be used as default if you connect to a server that is stored in the credential store. You can use the `-SaveCredentials` parameter of the `Connect-VIServer` cmdlet to indicate that you want to save the specified credentials in the local credential store, as follows:

```
PowerCLI C:\> Connect-VIServer -Server 192.168.0.132 -User admin
 -Password pass -SaveCredentials
```

You can also create a new entry in the credential store with the `New-VICredentialStoreItem` cmdlet:

```
PowerCLI C:\> New-VICredentialStoreItem -Host 192.168.0.132
 -User Admin -Password pass
```

You can not only store credentials for vCenter Servers but also for ESXi servers, using the following command:

```
PowerCLI C:\> New-VICredentialStoreItem -Host ESX1
 -User root -Password vmware
```

To get a listing of all of your stored credentials, type the following command:

```
PowerCLI C:\> Get-VICredentialStoreItem
```

And to remove a stored credential you can use the following command:

```
PowerCLI C:\> Remove-VICredentialStoreItem -Host ESX1 -User root
```

The stored credentials are stored in a file on your computer. The default credential store file location is: `%APPDATA%\VMware\credstore\vicredentials.xml`. But it is also possible to create other credential store files. You can see the contents of the default credential store file with the following command:

```
PowerCLI C:\> Get-Content -Path $env:APPDATA\VMware\credstore\
vicredentials.xml
```

The passwords stored in a credential store file are encrypted. But you can easily retrieve the stored passwords with the following command:

```
PowerCLI C:\> Get-VICredentialStoreItem |
>> Select-Object -Property Host,User,Password
```

So, if your computer is also used by other users and you are not sure that the information in the credential store file cannot be read by other people, it might be better not to use this feature.

Retrieving a list of all of your virtual machines

Now that we know how to connect to a server, let's do something useful with PowerCLI. Most of the people who begin using PowerCLI create reports, so create a list of all of your virtual machines as your first report. You have to use the Get-VM cmdlet to retrieve a list of your virtual machines. The syntax of the Get-VM cmdlet is as follows:

```
Get-VM [[-Name] <String[]>] [-Server <VIServer[]>]
[-Datastore <StorageResource[]>] [-Location <VIContainer[]>]
 [-Tag <Tag[]>] [-NoRecursion] [<CommonParameters>]

Get-VM [[-Name] <String[]>] [-Server <VIServer[]>]
[-DistributedSwitch <DistributedSwitch[]>] [-Tag <Tag[]>]
 [<CommonParameters>]

Get-VM [-Server <VIServer[]>] -Id <String[]> [<CommonParameters>]

Get-VM -RelatedObject <VmRelatedObjectBase[]> [<CommonParameters>]
```

As you can see, the Get-VM cmdlet has four different parameter sets. The names of these parameter sets are: Default, DistributedSwitch, ById, and RelatedObject. You can use these parameter sets to filter the virtual machines based on name, server, data store, location, distributed switch, ID, or related object.

Create your first report with the following command:

```
PowerCLI C:\> Get-VM
```

This will create a list of all of your virtual machines. You will see the name, power state, number of CPU's, and the amount of memory in GB for each virtual machine, as shown in the following command-line output:

```
Name                  PowerState Num CPUs MemoryGB

----                  ---------- -------- --------

Dc1                   PoweredOn  2        8.000

VM1                   PoweredOn  1        0.250

DNS1                  PoweredOn  2        8.000
```

The `Name`, `PowerState`, `NumCPU`, and `MemoryGB` properties are the properties that you will see by default if you use the `Get-VM` cmdlet. However, the virtual machine object in PowerCLI has a lot of other properties that are not shown by default. You can see them all by piping the output of the `Get-VM` cmdlet to the `Format-List` cmdlet using the pipe character '|'. The `Format-List` cmdlet displays object properties and their values in a list format, as shown in the following command-line output:

```
PowerCLI C:\> Get-VM -Name DC1 | Format-List -Property *


PowerState            : PoweredOn

Version               : v10

Description           : Domain controller

Notes                 : Domain controller

Guest                 : DC1: Microsoft Windows Server 2012 (64-bit)

NumCpu                : 2

MemoryMB              : 8192

MemoryGB              : 8

HardDisks             : {Hard disk 1, Hard disk 2}

NetworkAdapters       : {Network adapter 1}

UsbDevices            : {}

CDDrives              : {CD/DVD drive 1}

FloppyDrives          : {}

Host                  : ESX1.blackmilktea.com

HostId                : HostSystem-host-10

VMHostId              : HostSystem-host-10

VMHost                : ESX1.blackmilktea.com

VApp                  :

FolderId              : Folder-group-v9
```

```
Folder                     : Discovered virtual machine
ResourcePoolId             : ResourcePool-resgroup-8
ResourcePool               : Resources
PersistentId               : 50289ad0-a545-1299-5a75-811049f98276
UsedSpaceGB                : 71.2685827957466244469757080078
ProvisionedSpaceGB         : 78.2041296707466244469757080078
DatastoreIdList            : {Datastore-datastore-14}
HARestartPriority          : ClusterRestartPriority
HAIsolationResponse        : AsSpecifiedByCluster
DrsAutomationLevel         : AsSpecifiedByCluster
VMSwapfilePolicy           : Inherit
VMResourceConfiguration    : CpuShares:Normal/2000 MemShares:Normal/81920
Name                       : DC1
CustomFields               : {[Application code, ], [CreatedBy, Unknown],
[CreatedOn, Unknown], [Function, ]...}
ExtensionData              : VMware.Vim.VirtualMachine
Id                         : VirtualMachine-vm-16
Uid                        : /VIServer=blackteamilk\admin@192.168.0.132:443/
VirtualMachine=Virtual
Machine-vm-16/
Client                     :
VMware.VimAutomation.ViCore.Impl.V1.VimClient
```

You can select specific properties with the `Select-Object` cmdlet. Say you want to make a report that shows the `Name`, `Notes`, `VMHost`, and `Guest` properties for all your virtual machines. You can do that with the following command:

```
PowerCLI C:\> Get-VM | Select-Object -Property Name,Notes,VMHost,Guest
```

The output of the preceding command is as follows:

```
Name            Notes        VMHost         Guest
----            -----        ------         -----
DC1                          192.168.0.133 DC1:
VM1                          192.168.0.134 VM1:
DNS1            DNS Server   192.168.0.134 DNS1:
```

Suppressing displaying deprecated warnings

You will probably have also seen the following warning messages:

```
WARNING: The 'Description' property of VirtualMachine type is
deprecated. Use the 'Notes' property instead.
WARNING: The 'HardDisks' property of VirtualMachine type is
deprecated. Use 'Get-HardDisk' cmdlet instead.
WARNING: The 'NetworkAdapters' property of VirtualMachine type is
deprecated. Use 'Get-NetworkAdapter' cmdlet instead.
WARNING: The 'UsbDevices' property of VirtualMachine type is
deprecated. Use 'Get-UsbDevice' cmdlet instead.
WARNING: The 'CDDrives' property of VirtualMachine type is
deprecated. Use 'Get-CDDrive' cmdlet instead.
WARNING: The 'FloppyDrives' property of VirtualMachine type is
deprecated. Use 'Get-FloppyDrive' cmdlet instead.
WARNING: The 'Host' property of VirtualMachine type is deprecated.
Use the 'VMHost' property instead.
WARNING: The 'HostId' property of VirtualMachine type is deprecated.
Use the 'VMHostId' property instead.
WARNING: PowerCLI scripts should not use the 'Client' property. The
property will be removed in a future release.
```

These warning messages show the properties that should not be used in your scripts because they are deprecated and might be removed in a future PowerCLI release. Personally, I like these warnings because they remind me of the properties that I should not use anymore. But if you don't like these warnings, you can stop them from appearing with the following command:

```
PowerCLI C:\> Set-PowerCLIConfiguration -DisplayDeprecationWarnings
$false -Scope User
```

Using wildcard characters

You can also use **wildcard characters** to select specific virtual machines. To display only the virtual machines that have names that start with an "A" or "a", type the following command:

```
PowerCLI C:\> Get-VM -Name A*
```

Parameter values are not case-sensitive. The asterisk (*) is a wildcard character that matches zero or more characters, starting at the specified position. Another wildcard character is the question mark (?) which matches any character at the specified position. To get all virtual machines with a three-letter name that ends with an "e", use the following command:

```
PowerCLI C:\> Get-VM -Name ??e
```

You can also specify some specific characters, as shown in the following command:

```
PowerCLI C:\> Get-VM -Name [bc]*
```

The preceding command displays all the virtual machines that have names starting with "b" or "c". You can also specify a range of characters, as shown in the following command:

```
PowerCLI C:\> Get-VM -Name *[0-4]
```

The preceding command lists all the virtual machines that have names ending with 0, 1, 2, 3, or 4.

Filtering objects

If you want to filter properties that don't have their own Get-VM parameter, you can pipe the output of the Get-VM cmdlet to the Where-Object cmdlet. Using the Where-Object cmdlet, you can set the filter on any property. Let's display a list of all of your virtual machines that have more than one virtual CPU using the following command:

```
PowerCLI C:\> Get-VM | Where-Object {$_.NumCPU -gt 1}
```

In this example, the Where-Object cmdlet has a PowerShell scriptblock as a parameter. A **scriptblock** is a PowerShell script surrounded by braces. In this scriptblock, you see $_. When using commands in the pipeline, $_ represents the current object. In the preceding example, $_ represents the virtual machine object that is passed through the pipeline. $_.NumCPU is the NumCPU property of the current virtual machine in the pipeline. -gt means greater than, so the preceding command shows all virtual machines' objects where the NumCPU property has a value greater than 1.

PowerShell v3 introduced a new, easier syntax for the Where-Object cmdlet. You don't have to use a scriptblock anymore. You can now use the following command:

```
PowerCLI C:\> Get-VM | Where-Object NumCPU -gt 1
```

Isn't the preceding command much more like simple English?

> In the rest of this book, the PowerShell v2 syntax will be used by default because the v2 syntax will also work in PowerShell v3. If PowerShell v3 syntax is used anywhere, it will be specifically mentioned.

Using comparison operators

In the previous section, you saw an example of the -gt comparison operator. In the following table, we will show you all of the PowerShell comparison operators:

Operator	Description
-eq, -ceq, and -ieq	Equals
-ne, -cne, and -ine	Not equals
-gt, -cgt, and -igt	Greater than
-ge, -cge, and -ige	Greater than or equal to
-lt, -clt, and -ilt	Less than
-le, -cle, and -ile	Less than or equal to

In the preceding table, you see three different operators for all functions. So what is the difference? The c variant is case-sensitive. The two-letter variant and the i variant are case-insensitive. The i variant is made to make it clear that you want to use the case-insensitive operator.

Using aliases

The Where-Object cmdlet has an alias, ?. Therefore, both the following commands will display a list of all your virtual machines that have more than one virtual CPU:

- PowerCLI C:\> Get-VM | ? {$_.NumCPU -gt 1}
- PowerCLI C:\> Get-VM | Where-Object NumCPU -gt 1

Using aliases will save you from the trouble of typing in the PowerCLI console. However, it is good practice to use the full cmdlet names when you write a script. This will make the script much more readable and easier to understand. To see a list of all of the aliases that are defined for cmdlets, type the following command:

```
PowerCLI C:\> Get-Alias
```

You can create your own aliases using the `New-Alias` cmdlet. For example, to create an alias `childs` for the `Get-ChildItem` cmdlet, you can use the following command:

```
PowerCLI C:\> New-Alias -Name childs -Value Get-ChildItem
```

Retrieving a list of all of your hosts

Similar to the `Get-VM` cmdlet, which retrieves your virtual machines, is the `Get-VMHost` cmdlet, which displays your hosts. The `Get-VMHost` cmdlet has the following syntax:

```
Get-VMHost [[-Name] <String[]>] [-NoRecursion] [-Datastore
<StorageResource[]>] [-State <VMHostState[]>] [-Location
<VIContainer[]>] [-Tag <Tag[]>] [-Server <VIServer[]>]
[<CommonParameters>]

Get-VMHost [[-Name] <String[]>] [-DistributedSwitch
<DistributedSwitch[]>] [-Tag <Tag[]>] [-Server <VIServer[]>]
[<CommonParameters>]

Get-VMHost [[-Name] <String[]>] [-NoRecursion]
[-VM <VirtualMachine[]>] [-ResourcePool <ResourcePool[]>]
[-Datastore <StorageResource[]>] [-Location <VIContainer[]>]
[-Tag <Tag[]>] [-Server <VIServer[]>] [<CommonParameters>]

Get-VMHost -Id <String[]> [-Server <VIServer[]>] [<CommonParameters>]
```

You see that there are four different parameter sets. They are named: `Default`, `DistributedSwitch`, `SecondaryParameterSet`, and `ById`. Don't mix parameters from different sets or you will get an error as follows:

```
PowerCLI C:\> Get-VMHost -Id HostSystem-host-22 -Name 192.168.0.133
Get-VMHost : Parameter set cannot be resolved using the specified
 named parameters.
At line:1 char:1
+ Get-VMHost -Id HostSystem-host-22 -Name 192.168.0.133
+ ~~~~~~~~~~~~~~~~~~~~~~~~~~~~~~~~~~~~~~~~~~~~~~~~~~~~~~~~
    + CategoryInfo          : InvalidArgument: (:) [Get-VMHost]
, ParameterBindingException
```

```
    + FullyQualifiedErrorId :
AmbiguousParameterSet,
VMware.VimAutomation.ViCore.Cmdlets.Commands.GetVMHost
```

To get a list of all of your hosts, type the following command:

```
PowerCLI C:\> Get-VMHost
```

By default, only the `Name`, `ConnectionState`, `PowerState`, `NumCPU`, `CpuUsageMhz`, `CpuTotalMhz`, `MemoryUsageGB`, `MemoryTotalGB`, and `Version` properties are shown. To get a list of all of the properties, type the following command:

```
PowerCLI C:\> Get-VMHost | Format-List -Property *
```

```
State                   : Connected
ConnectionState         : Connected
PowerState              : PoweredOn
VMSwapfileDatastoreId   :
VMSwapfilePolicy        : Inherit
ParentId                : ClusterComputeResource-domain-c7
IsStandalone            : False
Manufacturer            : VMware, Inc.
Model                   : VMware Virtual Platform
NumCpu                  : 2
CpuTotalMhz             : 4588
CpuUsageMhz             : 54
LicenseKey              : 00000-00000-00000-00000-00000
MemoryTotalMB           : 2047.48828125
MemoryTotalGB           : 1.999500274658203125
MemoryUsageMB           : 965
MemoryUsageGB           : 0.9423828125
ProcessorType           : Intel(R) Core(TM) i5-2415M CPU @ 2.30GHz
HyperthreadingActive    : False
TimeZone                : UTC
Version                 : 5.5.0
Build                   : 1331820
Parent                  : Cluster01
VMSwapfileDatastore     :
StorageInfo             : HostStorageSystem-storageSystem-22
```

```
NetworkInfo              : localhost:sitecomwl306
DiagnosticPartition      : mpx.vmhba1:C0:T0:L0
FirewallDefaultPolicy    : VMHostFirewallDefaultPolicy:HostSystem-host-22
ApiVersion               : 5.5
Name                     : 192.168.0.133
CustomFields             : {[AutoDeploy.MachineIdentity, ]}
ExtensionData            : VMware.Vim.HostSystem
Id                       : HostSystem-host-22
Uid                      : /VIServer=root@192.168.0.132:443/
VMHost=HostSystem-host-22/
Client                   : VMware.VimAutomation.ViCore.Impl.V1.VimClient
DatastoreIdList          : {Datastore-datastore-23}
```

You can use the Get-VMHost parameters or the Where-Object cmdlet to filter the hosts you want to display, as we did with the Get-VM cmdlet.

Displaying the output in a grid view

Instead of displaying the output of your PowerCLI commands in the PowerCLI console, you can also display the output in a grid view. A grid view is a pop up that looks like a spreadsheet with rows and columns. To display the output of the Get-VMHost cmdlet in a grid view, type the following command:

```
PowerCLI C:\> Get-VMHost | Out-GridView
```

The preceding command opens the window of the following screenshot:

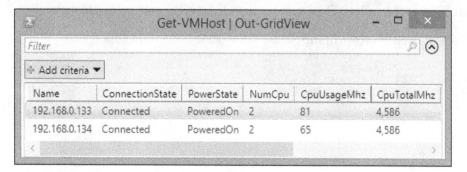

You can create filters to display only certain rows, and you can sort columns by clicking on the column header. You can also reorder columns by dragging and dropping them. In the next screenshot, we created a filter to show only the hosts with a CpuUsageMhz value greater than or equal to 70. We also changed the order of the **ConnectionState** and **PowerState** columns.

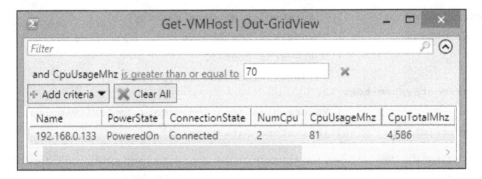

Isn't that cool?

Summary

In this chapter, we looked at downloading and installing PowerCLI and modified the PowerShell execution policy to be able to start PowerCLI. Then we covered how to connect to and disconnect from a server and introduced the credential store to save you from having to specify credentials when you connect to a server. You also learned how to get a list of your virtual machines or hosts and how to stop deprecated warnings. You learned all of the PowerShell comparison operators and found out about aliases for cmdlets. Finally, we concluded the chapter with grid views.

In the next chapter, we will introduce some basic PowerCLI concepts.

2
Learning Basic PowerCLI Concepts

While learning something new, you always have to learn the basics first. In this chapter, you will learn some basic PowerShell and PowerCLI concepts. Knowing these concepts will make it easier for you to learn the advanced topics. We will cover the following topics in this chapter:

- Using the `Get-Command`, `Get-Help`, and `Get-Member` cmdlets
- Using providers and PSDrives
- Using arrays and hash tables
- Creating calculated properties
- Using raw API objects with `ExtensionData` or `Get-View`
- Extending PowerCLI objects with the `New-VIProperty` cmdlet
- Working with vSphere folders

Using the Get-Command, Get-Help, and Get-Member cmdlets

There are some PowerShell cmdlets that everyone should know. Knowing these cmdlets will help you to discover other cmdlets, their functions, parameters, and returned objects.

Using Get-Command

The first cmdlet that you should know is Get-Command. This cmdlet returns all of the commands that are installed on your computer. The Get-Command cmdlet has the following syntax:

```
Get-Command [[-ArgumentList] <Object[]>] [-All] [-ListImported]
[-Module <String[]>] [-Noun <String[]>] [-ParameterName <String[]>]
[-ParameterType <PSTypeName[]>] [-Syntax] [-TotalCount <Int32>] [-Verb
<String[]>] [<CommonParameters>]

Get-Command [[-Name] <String[]>] [[-ArgumentList] <Object[]>] [-All]
[-CommandType <CommandTypes>] [-ListImported] [-Module <String[]>]
[-ParameterName <String[]>] [-ParameterType <PSTypeName[]>] [-Syntax]
[-TotalCount <Int32>] [<CommonParameters>]
```

> **Downloading the example code**
>
> You can download the example code files for all Packt books you have purchased from your account at http://www.packtpub.com. If you purchased this book elsewhere, you can visit http://www.packtpub.com/support and register to have the files e-mailed directly to you.

The first parameter set is called CmdletSet and the second parameter set is called AllCommandSet.

If you type the following command then you will get a list of commands installed on your computer including cmdlets, aliases, functions, workflows, filters, scripts, and applications:

```
PowerCLI C:\> Get-Command
```

You can also specify the name of a specific cmdlet to get information about that cmdlet as shown in the following command:

```
PowerCLI C:\> Get-Command -Name Get-VM
```

This will return the following information about the Get-VM cmdlet:

```
CommandType Name     ModuleName

----------- ----     ----------

Cmdlet      Get-VM VMware.VimAutomation.Core
```

You see that the command returns the command type and the name of the module that contains the Get-VM cmdlet. CommandType, Name, and ModuleName are the properties that the Get-VM cmdlet returns by default. You will get more properties if you pipe the output to the Format-List cmdlet:

```
PowerCLI C:\> Get-Command -Name Get-VM | Format-List *


HelpUri                : http://www.vmware.com/support/developer/PowerCLI/
PowerCLI55R1/html/Get-VM.html
DLL                    : C:\Program Files (x86)\VMware\Infrastructure\
vSphere PowerCLI\VMware.VimAutomation.ViCore.Cmdlets.dll
Verb                   : Get
Noun                   : VM
HelpFile               : VMware.VimAutomation.ViCore.Cmdlets.dll-Help.xml
PSSnapIn               : VMware.VimAutomation.Core
ImplementingType       : VMware.VimAutomation.ViCore.Cmdlets.Commands.GetVM
Definition             :

                         Get-VM [[-Name] <string[]>] [-Server <VIServer[]>]
[-Datastore <StorageResource[]>] [-Location <VIContainer[]>] [-Tag
<Tag[]>] [-NoRecursion] [<CommonParameters>]


                         Get-VM [[-Name] <string[]>] [-Server
<VIServer[]>] [-DistributedSwitch <DistributedSwitch[]>] [-Tag <Tag[]>]
[<CommonParameters>]


                         Get-VM [-Server <VIServer[]>] [-Id <string[]>]
[<CommonParameters>]


                         Get-VM -RelatedObject <VmRelatedObjectBase[]>
[<CommonParameters>]


DefaultParameterSet : Default
OutputType          : { VMware.VimAutomation.ViCore.Types.V1.Inventory.
VirtualMachine}
Options             : ReadOnly
Name                : Get-VM
CommandType         : Cmdlet
Visibility          : Public
ModuleName          : VMware.VimAutomation.Core
```

```
Module               :
RemotingCapability   : PowerShell
Parameters                  : {[Name, System.Management.Automation.
ParameterMetadata], [Server, System.Management.Automation.
ParameterMetadata], [Datastore,
System.Management.Automation.ParameterMetadata], [DistributedSwitch,
System.Management.Automation.ParameterMetadata...}
ParameterSets          : {[[-Name] <string[]>] [-Server <VIServer[]>]
[-Datastore <StorageResource[]>] [-Location <VIContainer[]>] [-Tag
<Tag[]>] [-NoRecursion] [<CommonParameters>], [[-Name] <string[]>]
[-Server <VIServer[]>] [-DistributedSwitch <DistributedSwitch[]>]
[-Tag <Tag[]>] [<CommonParameters>], [-Server <VIServer[]>] [-Id
<string[]>] [<CommonParameters>], -RelatedObject <VmRelatedObjectBase[]>
[<CommonParameters>]}
```

You can use the Get-Command cmdlet to search for cmdlets. For example, if you want search for the cmdlets that are used for vSphere hosts, type:

```
PowerCLI C:\> Get-Command -Name *VMHost*
```

If you are searching for the cmdlets to work with networks, type:

```
PowerCLI C:\> Get-Command -Name *network*
```

Using Get-VICommand

PowerCLI has a cmdlet Get-VICommand that is similar to the Get-Command cmdlet. The Get-VICommand cmdlet is actually a function that creates a filter on the Get-Command output and returns only PowerCLI commands. Type the following command to list all of the PowerCLI commands:

```
PowerCLI C:\> Get-VICommand
```

The Get-VICommand cmdlet has only one parameter –Name. So you can also type, for example, the following command to get information only about the Get-VM cmdlet

```
PowerCLI C:\> Get-VICommand –Name Get-VM
```

Using Get-Help

To discover more information about cmdlets, you can use the Get-Help cmdlet. For example:

```
PowerCLI C:\> Get-Help Get-VM
```

will display the following information about the Get-VM cmdlet:

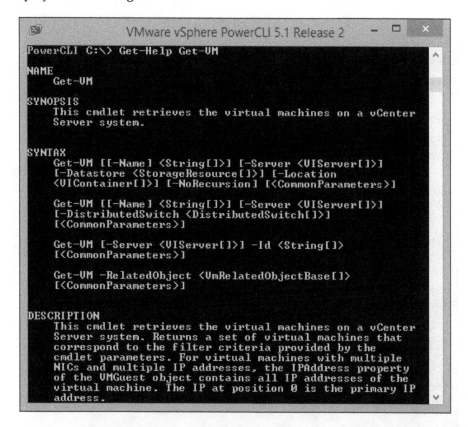

The Get-Help cmdlet has some parameters that you can use to get more information. The -examples parameter shows examples of the cmdlet. The -detailed parameter adds parameter descriptions and examples to the basic help display. The -full parameter displays all of the information available about the cmdlet. And the -online parameter retrieves online help information available about the cmdlet and displays it in a web browser. In PowerShell v3, there is a new Get-Help parameter -ShowWindow. This displays the output of Get-Help in a new window.

The Get-Help Get-Help -ShowWindow command opens the following screenshot:

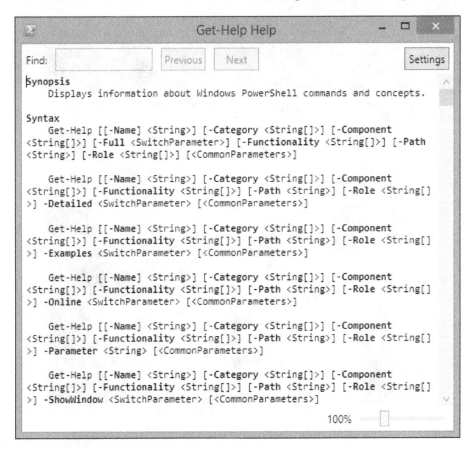

Using Get-PowerCLIHelp

The PowerCLI Get-PowerCLIHelp cmdlet opens a separate help window for PowerCLI cmdlets, PowerCLI objects, and articles. This is a very useful tool if you want to browse through the PowerCLI cmdlets or PowerCLI objects.

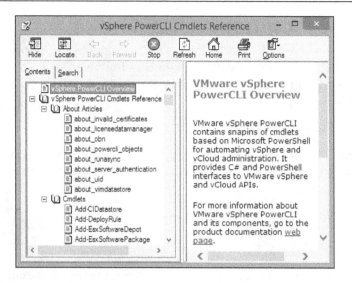

Using Get-PowerCLICommunity

If you have a question about PowerCLI and you can't find the answer in this book, use the Get-PowerCLICommunity cmdlet to open the VMware vSphere PowerCLI section of the VMware VMTN Communities. You can log in to the VMware VMTN Communities using the same **My VMware** account that you used to download PowerCLI. First, search the community for an answer to your question. If you still can't find the answer, go to the **Discussions** tab and ask your question by clicking on the **Start a discussion** button. You might receive an answer to your question in a few minutes.

Using Get-Member

In PowerCLI, you work with objects. Even a string is an object. An object contains properties and methods; these are called members in PowerShell. To see which members an object contains, you can use the Get-Member cmdlet. To see the members of a string, type:

```
PowerCLI C:\> "Learning PowerCLI" | Get-Member
```

Pipe an instance of a PowerCLI object to Get-Member to retrieve the members of that PowerCLI object. For example, to see the members of a virtual machine object, you can type:

```
PowerCLI C:\> Get-VM | Get-Member
```

```
   TypeName:
VMware.VimAutomation.ViCore.Impl.V1.Inventory.VirtualMachineImpl


Name                    MemberType Definition

----                    ---------- ----------

ConvertToVersion        Method     T VersionedObjectInterop.Conver...

Equals                  Method     bool Equals(System.Object obj)

GetHashCode             Method     int GetHashCode()

GetType                 Method     type GetType()

IsConvertableTo         Method     bool VersionedObjectInterop.IsC...

LockUpdates             Method     void ExtensionData.LockUpdates()

ObtainExportLease       Method     VMware.Vim.ManagedObjectReferen...

ToString                Method     string ToString()

UnlockUpdates           Method     void ExtensionData.UnlockUpdates()

CDDrives                Property   VMware.VimAutomation.ViCore.Typ...

Client                  Property   VMware.VimAutomation.ViCore.Int...

CustomFields            Property   System.Collections.Generic.IDic...

DatastoreIdList         Property   string[] DatastoreIdList {get;}

Description             Property   string Description {get;}

DrsAutomationLevel      Property   System.Nullable[VMware.VimAutom...

ExtensionData           Property   System.Object ExtensionData {get;}

FloppyDrives            Property   VMware.VimAutomation.ViCore.Typ...

Folder                  Property   VMware.VimAutomation.ViCore.Typ...

FolderId                Property   string FolderId {get;}
```

Guest	Property	VMware.VimAutomation.ViCore.Typ...
HAIsolationResponse	Property	System.Nullable[VMware.VimAutom...
HardDisks	Property	VMware.VimAutomation.ViCore.Typ...
HARestartPriority	Property	System.Nullable[VMware.VimAutom...
Host	Property	VMware.VimAutomation.ViCore.Typ...
HostId	Property	string HostId {get;}
Id	Property	string Id {get;}
MemoryGB	Property	decimal MemoryGB {get;}
MemoryMB	Property	decimal MemoryMB {get;}
Name	Property	string Name {get;}
NetworkAdapters	Property	VMware.VimAutomation.ViCore.Typ...
Notes	Property	string Notes {get;}
NumCpu	Property	int NumCpu {get;}
PersistentId	Property	string PersistentId {get;}
PowerState	Property	VMware.VimAutomation.ViCore.Typ...
ProvisionedSpaceGB	Property	decimal ProvisionedSpaceGB {get;}
ResourcePool	Property	VMware.VimAutomation.ViCore.Typ...
ResourcePoolId	Property	string ResourcePoolId {get;}
Uid	Property	string Uid {get;}
UsbDevices	Property	VMware.VimAutomation.ViCore.Typ...
UsedSpaceGB	Property	decimal UsedSpaceGB {get;}
VApp	Property	VMware.VimAutomation.ViCore.Typ...
Version	Property	VMware.VimAutomation.ViCore.Typ...
VMHost	Property	VMware.VimAutomation.ViCore.Typ...
VMHostId	Property	string VMHostId {get;}
VMResourceConfiguration	Property	VMware.VimAutomation.ViCore.Typ...
VMSwapfilePolicy	Property	System.Nullable[VMware.VimAutom...

The command returns the full type name of the VirtualMachineImpl object and all its methods and properties. Remember that the properties are objects themselves. You can also use Get-Member to get the members of the properties. For example, the following command line will give you the members of the VMGuestImpl object:

```
PowerCLI C:\> $VM = Get-VM -Name vCenter

PowerCLI C:\> $VM.Guest | Get-Member
```

Using providers and PSDrives

Until now, you have only seen cmdlets. Cmdlets are PowerShell commands. However, PowerShell has another import concept named **providers**. Providers are accessed through named drives or **PSDrives**. In the following sections, providers and PSDrives will be explained.

Using providers

A PowerShell provider is a piece of software that makes data stores look like filesystems. PowerShell providers are usually part of a snap-in or a module-like PowerCLI. The advantage of providers is that you can use the same cmdlets for all of the providers. These cmdlets have the following nouns: Item, ChildItem, Content, and ItemProperty. You can use the Get-Command cmdlet to get a list of all of the cmdlets with these nouns:

```
PowerCLI C:> Get-Command -Noun Item,ChildItem,Content,ItemProperty
```

CommandType	Name	ModuleName
Cmdlet	Add-Content	Microsoft.PowerShell.Management
Cmdlet	Clear-Content	Microsoft.PowerShell.Management
Cmdlet	Clear-Item	Microsoft.PowerShell.Management
Cmdlet	Clear-ItemProperty	Microsoft.PowerShell.Management
Cmdlet	Copy-Item	Microsoft.PowerShell.Management
Cmdlet	Copy-ItemProperty	Microsoft.PowerShell.Management
Cmdlet	Get-ChildItem	Microsoft.PowerShell.Management
Cmdlet	Get-Content	Microsoft.PowerShell.Management
Cmdlet	Get-Item	Microsoft.PowerShell.Management
Cmdlet	Get-ItemProperty	Microsoft.PowerShell.Management
Cmdlet	Invoke-Item	Microsoft.PowerShell.Management
Cmdlet	Move-Item	Microsoft.PowerShell.Management
Cmdlet	Move-ItemProperty	Microsoft.PowerShell.Management
Cmdlet	New-Item	Microsoft.PowerShell.Management
Cmdlet	New-ItemProperty	Microsoft.PowerShell.Management
Cmdlet	Remove-Item	Microsoft.PowerShell.Management
Cmdlet	Remove-ItemProperty	Microsoft.PowerShell.Management

```
Cmdlet     Rename-Item         Microsoft.PowerShell.Management
Cmdlet     Rename-ItemProperty Microsoft.PowerShell.Management
Cmdlet     Set-Content         Microsoft.PowerShell.Management
Cmdlet     Set-Item            Microsoft.PowerShell.Management
Cmdlet     Set-ItemProperty    Microsoft.PowerShell.Management
```

To display a list of all of the providers in your PowerCLI session, you can use the `Get-PSProvider` cmdlet:

```
PowerCLI C:\> Get-PSProvider
```

```
Name         Capabilities                          Drives

----         ------------                          ------

Alias        ShouldProcess                         {Alias}

Environment  ShouldProcess                         {Env}

FileSystem   Filter, ShouldProcess, Credentials    {C, H, D}

Function     ShouldProcess                         {Function}

Registry     ShouldProcess, Transactions           {HKLM, HKCU}

Variable     ShouldProcess                         {Variable}

Certificate  ShouldProcess                         {Cert}

WSMan        Credentials                           {WSMan}

VimDatastore ShouldProcess                         {vmstores, vmstore}

VimInventory Filter                                {vis, vi}
```

The `VimDatastore` and `VimInventory` providers are part of PowerCLI. You will soon learn more about the `VimDatastore` and `VimInventory` providers.

Using PSDrives

Each provider has one or more drives. For example, the `FileSystem` provider has drives named `C`, `H`, and `D`, which are hard disks on my PC. You can use the drives to access the providers. Microsoft calls these drives PSDrives to prevent confusing the drives with physical drives in your computer. For instance, to get a listing of all of the files and folders in the root of `C:` on your PC, type:

```
PowerCLI C:\> Get-ChildItem C:\
```

The `Get-ChildItem` cmdlet has aliases `dir`, `gci`, and `ls` that give you the same result:

```
PowerCLI C:\> dir C:\
PowerCLI C:\> ls C:\
```

You can use the same `Get-ChildItem` cmdlet to get a list of all of your cmdlet aliases by typing:

```
PowerCLI C:\> Get-ChildItem alias:
```

Using the vSphere PowerCLI Inventory Provider

The **Inventory Provider** gives you a filesystem-like view of the inventory items from a vCenter Server or an ESXi server. You can use this provider to view, move, rename, or delete objects by running PowerCLI commands.

When you connect to a server with the `Connect-VIServer` cmdlet, two PSDrives are created: `vi` and `vis`. The `vi` PSDrive contains the inventory of the last connected server. The `vis` PSDrive contains the inventory of all currently connected servers in your PowerCLI session.

You can set the location to the `vis` PSDrive using the `Set-Location` cmdlet:

```
PowerCLI C:\> Set-Location vis:
PowerCLI vis:\>
```

Use the `Get-ChildItem` cmdlet to display the items in the current location of the `vis` PSDrive:

```
PowerCLI vis:\> Get-ChildItem
```

Name	Type	Id
vCenter@443	VIServer	/VIServer=b1...

Use the `Get-ChildItem -Recurse` parameter to display all of the items in the Inventory Provider:

```
PowerCLI vis:\> Get-ChildItem -Recurse
```

Using the vSphere PowerCLI Datastore Provider

The **Datastore Provider** gives you access to the content of your vSphere datastores.

When you connect to a server with the `Connect-VIServer` cmdlet, two PSDrives are created: `vmstore` and `vmstores`. The `vmstore` PSDrive contains the datastores of the last connected server. The `vmstores` PSDrive contains the datastores of all the currently connected servers in your PowerCLI session. You can use these two default PSDrives or you can create custom PSDrives using the `New-PSDrive` cmdlet.

Set the location to the `vmstore` PSDrive with the following command:

```
PowerCLI C:\> Set-Location vmstore:
PowerCLI vmstore:\>
```

Display the content of the root directory of the `vmstore` PSDrive with the following command:

```
PowerCLI vmstore:\> Get-ChildItem
```

Name	Type	Id
YourDatacenter	Datacenter	Datacenter-d...

You have to go one level deeper to get a listing of your datastores:

```
PowerCLI vmstore:\> Set-Location YourDatacenter
PowerCLI vmstore:\ YourDatacenter > Get-ChildItem
```

You can also create a custom PSDrive for a datastore using the `New-PSDrive` cmdlet. Start with getting a datastore object and save it in the `$Datastore` variable:

```
PowerCLI C:\> $Datastore = Get-Datastore –Name Datastore1
```

Create a new PowerShell PSDrive named `ds` that maps to the `$Datastore` variable:

```
PowerCLI C:\> New-PSDrive -Location $Datastore -Name ds -PSProvider
VimDatastore -Root "\"
```

Now, you can change your location into the PowerShell PSDrive using the `Set-Location` cmdlet:

```
PowerCLI C:\> Set-Location ds:
```

You can get a listing of the files and directories on the datastore using the
`Get-ChildItem` cmdlet:

```
PowerCLI ds:\> Get-ChildItem
```

You will see an output similar to:

```
Datastore path: [Datastore1]
```

LastWriteTime		Type	Length	Name
12/22/2013	3:14 PM	Folder		.dvsData
12/20/2013	8:14 PM	Folder		.naa.600a0b800011...
12/21/2013	10:06 AM	Folder		ISOfiles
12/21/2013	2:05 PM	Folder		vCenter Mobile Ac...
12/22/2013	1:24 PM	Folder		.vSphere-HA

Copying files between a datastore and your PC

You can use the vSphere Datastore Provider to copy files between a datastore and
your PC using the `Copy-DatastoreItem` cmdlet.

Change the location to a subfolder using the `Set-Location` cmdlet with the help of
the following command line:

```
PowerCLI ds:\> Set-Location "virtualmachine1"
```

Copy a file or directory to the destination using the `Copy-DatastoreItem` cmdlet
as follows:

```
PowerCLI ds:\virtualmachine1> Copy-DatastoreItem -Item ds:\
virtualmachine1\virtualmachine1.vmx -Destination c:\virtualmachine1\
```

Now, you can view the content of the `virtualmachine1.vmx` file with:

```
PowerCLI C:\> Get-Content c:\virtualmachine1\virtualmachine1.vmx
```

Files cannot be copied directly between vSphere datastores in different
vCenter Servers using `Copy-DatastoreItem`. Copy the files to the
PowerCLI host's local filesystem temporarily, and then copy them to
the destination.

Using arrays and hash tables

In PowerCLI, you can create a list of objects. For example, `"red"`, `"white"`, `"blue"` is a list of strings. In PowerShell, a list of terms is called an **array**. An array can have zero or more objects. You can create an empty array and assign it to a variable:

```
PowerCLI C:\> $Array = @()
```

You can fill the array during creation using the following command line:

```
PowerCLI C:\> $Array = @("red","white")
```

You can use the `+=` operator to add an element to an array:

```
PowerCLI C:\> $Array += "blue"
PowerCLI C:\> $Array
red
white
blue
```

If you want to retrieve a specific element of an array, you can use an index starting with `0` for the first element, `1` for the second element, and so on. If you want to retrieve an element from the tail of the array, you have to use `-1` for the last element, `-2` for the second to last, and so on. You have to use square brackets around the index number. In the next example, the first element of the array is retrieved using the following command line:

```
PowerCLI C:\> $Array[0]
Red
```

If you want to test whether an object is an array, you can use:

```
PowerCLI C:\> $Array -is [array]
True
```

There is a different kind of an array called a **hash table**. In a hash table, you map a set of keys to a set of values. You can create an empty hash table using the following command line:

```
PowerCLI C:\> $HashTable = @{}
```

You can fill the hash table during creation using the following command line:

```
PowerCLI C:\> $HashTable = @{LastName='Doe';FirstName='John'}
```

To add a key-value pair to a hash table, you can use the following command line:

```
PowerCLI C:\> $HashTable["Company"]='VMware'
```

To show the contents of the hash table, just display the variable:

```
PowerCLI C:\> $HashTable
```

Name	Value
Company	VMware
FirstName	John
LastName	Doe

If you want to retrieve a specific key-value pair, you can use:

```
PowerCLI C:\> $HashTable["FirstName"]
John
```

To retrieve all of the hash table's keys, you can use the Keys property:

```
PowerCLI C:\> $HashTable.Keys
Company
FirstName
LastName
```

To retrieve all of the values in the hash table, you can use the Values property:

```
PowerCLI C:\> $HashTable.Values
VMware
John
Doe
```

If you want to test whether an object is a hash table, you can use:

```
PowerCLI C:\> $HashTable -is [hashtable]
True
```

In the next section, hash tables will be used to create calculated properties.

Creating calculated properties

You can use the Select-Object cmdlet to select certain properties of the objects that you want to return. For example, you can use the following code to return the name and the used space, in GB, of your virtual machines:

```
PowerCLI C:\> Get-VM | Select-Object -Property Name,UsedSpaceGB
```

But what if you want to return the used space in MB? The PowerCLI `VirtualMachineImpl` object has no `UsedSpaceMB` property. This is where you can use a **calculated property**. A calculated property is a PowerShell hash table with two elements: `Name` and `Expression`. The `Name` element contains the name that you want to give the calculated property. The `Expression` element contains a scriptblock with PowerCLI code to calculate the value of the property. To return the name and the used space in MB for all of your virtual machines, run the following command:

```
PowerCLI C:\> Get-VM |
>> Select-Object -Property Name,
>> @{Name="UsedSpaceMB";Expression={1KB*$_.UsedSpaceGB}}
>>
```

The hash table contains two key-value pairs. In the first element, the key is `Name` and the value is `UsedSpaceMB`. In the other element, the key is `Expression` and the value is `{1KB*$_.UsedSpaceGB}`. The special variable `$_` is used to represent the current object in the pipeline. `1KB` is a PowerShell constant that has the value `1024`. In calculated properties, you can abbreviate the `Name` and `Expression` names to `N` and `E`.

Another example of a calculated property shows you how to return the aliases of all of the cmdlets that are the same for all of the providers:

```
PowerCLI C:\> Get-Command -Noun Item,ChildItem,Content,ItemProperty |
>> Select-Object -Property Name,
>> @{Name="Aliases";Expression={Get-Alias -Definition $_.Name}}
>>
```

Name	Aliases
Add-Content	ac
Clear-Content	clc
Clear-Item	cli
Clear-ItemProperty	clp
Copy-Item	{copy, cp, cpi}
Copy-ItemProperty	cpp
Get-ChildItem	{dir, gci, ls}
Get-Content	{cat, gc, type}
Get-Item	gi
Get-ItemProperty	gp
Invoke-Item	ii

Move-Item	{mi, move, mv}
Move-ItemProperty	mp
New-Item	ni
New-ItemProperty	
Remove-Item	{del, erase, rd, ri...}
Remove-ItemProperty	rp
Rename-Item	{ren, rni}
Rename-ItemProperty	rnp
Set-Content	sc
Set-Item	si
Set-ItemProperty	sp

The first command is the Get-Command statement that you have seen before; this returns the cmdlets that are the same for all of the providers. In the calculated property, the Get-Alias cmdlet is used to get the aliases of these commands.

Using raw API objects with ExtensionData or Get-View

PowerCLI makes it easy to use the VMware vSphere **application programming interface (API)**. There are two ways to do this. The first one is by using the ExtensionData property that most of the PowerCLI objects have. The Extensiondata property is a direct link to the vSphere API object related to the PowerCLI object. The second way is by using the Get-View cmdlet to retrieve the vSphere API object related to a PowerCLI object. Both these ways will be discussed in the following sections.

Using the ExtensionData property

Most PowerCLI objects, such as VirtualMachineImpl and VMHostImpl, have a property called ExtensionData. This property is a reference to a view of a VMware vSphere object as described in the "VMware vSphere API Reference Documentation". For example, the ExtensionData property of the PowerCLI's VirtualMachineImpl object links to a vSphere VirtualMachine object view. ExtensionData is a very powerful property because it allows you to use all of the properties and methods of the VMware vSphere API. For example, to see if the VMware Tools are running in your virtual machines, you can run the following command:

```
PowerCLI C:\> Get-VM |
>> Select-Object -Property Name,
```

```
>> @{Name = "ToolsRunningStatus"
>>    Expression = {$_.ExtensionData.Guest.ToolsRunningStatus}
>> }
>>
```

If VMware Tools are not installed in a virtual machine, the `ExtensionData.Guest.ToolsStatus` property will have the value `toolsNotInstalled`. You can check the tools' status with:

```
PowerCLI C:\> Get-VM |
>> Select-Object -Property Name,
>> @{Name = "ToolsStatus"
>>    Expression = {$_.ExtensionData.Guest.ToolsStatus}
>> }
>>
```

Name	ToolsStatus
VM1	toolsNotInstalled
DNS1	toolsOk
DC1	toolsNotRunning
WindowsServer2012	toolsOld

Using the Get-View cmdlet

Another way to get the vSphere API objects is by using the `Get-View` cmdlet. This cmdlet returns a vSphere object view, which is the same object you can retrieve via the `ExtensionData` property. For example, the following two PowerCLI commands will give you the same result:

```
PowerCLI C:\> (Get-VM -Name vCenter).ExtensionData
PowerCLI C:\> Get-VIew -VIObject (Get-VM -Name vCenter)
```

The `Get-View` cmdlet has the following syntax:

```
Get-View [-VIObject] <VIObject[]> [-Property <String[]>]
[<CommonParameters>]
```

```
Get-View [-Server <VIServer[]>] [-SearchRoot <ManagedObjectReference>]
-ViewType <Type> [-Filter <Hashtable>] [-Property <String[]>]
[<CommonParameters>]
```

```
Get-View [-Server <VIServer[]>] [-Id] <ManagedObjectReference[]>
[-Property <String[]>] [<CommonParameters>]
Get-View [-Property <String[]>] -RelatedObject <ViewBaseMirroredObject[]>
[<CommonParameters>]
```

The names of the parameter sets are: `GetViewByVIObject`, `GetEntity`, `GetView`, and `GetViewByRelatedObject`. The second parameter set, `GetEntity`, is very powerful and will allow you to create PowerCLI commands or scripts that are optimized for speed. For example, the following command will give you the vSphere object views of all virtual machines and templates:

```
PowerCLI C:\> Get-View -ViewType VirtualMachine
```

Possible argument values for the `-ViewType` parameter are: `ClusterComputeResource`, `ComputeResource`, `Datacenter`, `Datastore`, `DistributedVirtualPortgroup`, `DistributedVirtualSwitch`, `Folder`, `HostSystem`, `Network`, `OpaqueNetwork`, `ResourcePool`, `StoragePod`, `VirtualApp`, `VirtualMachine`, and `VmwareDistributedVirtualSwitch`.

If you want only the virtual machines and not the templates, you need to specify a filter:

```
PowerCLI C:\> Get-View -ViewType VirtualMachine -Filter @{" Config.
Template" = "false"}
```

The filter is in the form of a hash table in which you specify that the value of the `Config.Template` property needs to be false to get only the virtual machines.

To make your command run faster, you need to specify the properties that you want to return. Otherwise all of the properties are returned and that will make your command run slower.

Let's retrieve only the name and the overall status of your virtual machines:

```
PowerCLI C:\>  Get-View -ViewType VirtualMachine -Filter @{"Config.
Template" = "false"} -Property Name,OverallStatus |
>> Select-Object -Property Name,OverAllStatus
>>
```

This command runs in my test environment about 23 times faster than the equivalent:

```
PowerCLI C:\>  Get-VM | Select-Object -Property Name,
@{Name="OverallStatus";Expression={$_.ExtensionData.OverallStatus}}
```

The conclusion is: if you need your script to run faster, try to find a solution using the Get-View cmdlet.

> You should always make a trade-off between the time it takes you to write a script and the time it takes you to run the script. If you spend 10 minutes to create a script that takes one hour to run, you will have your work done in 70 minutes. If you spend two hours to create a faster script that runs in 10 minutes, you will have your work done in 130 minutes. I would prefer the first solution. Of course, if you intend to run the script more than once, the time you spend to improve the speed of your script is spent better.

Using Managed Object References

If you look at a vSphere object view using the Get-Member cmdlet, you will see that a lot of properties are from type VMware.Vim.ManagedObjectReference:

```
PowerCLI C:\> Get-VM -Name vCenter | Get-View | Get-Member |
>> Where-Object {$_.Name -eq 'Parent'}
>>


    TypeName: VMware.Vim.VirtualMachine


Name    MemberType Definition
----    ---------- ----------
Parent Property    VMware.Vim.ManagedObjectReference Parent {get;}
```

A **Managed Object Reference (MoRef)** is a unique value that is generated by the vCenter Server and is guaranteed to be unique for a given entity in a single vCenter instance.

> The vSphere object views returned by the ExtensionData property or by the Get-View cmdlet are not the actual vSphere objects. The objects returned are copies or views of the actual objects that represent the actual objects at the time the view was made.

Using the Get-VIObjectByVIView cmdlet

The `Get-View` cmdlet gives you a way to go from a PowerCLI object to a vSphere object view. If you want to go back from a vSphere object view to a PowerCLI object, you can use the `Get-VIObjectByVIView` cmdlet. For example:

```
PowerCLI C:\> $VMView = Get-VM -Name vCenter | Get-View
PowerCLI C:\> $VM = $VMView | Get-VIObjectByVIView
```

In the previous example, the first line will give you a vSphere object view from a PowerCLI `VirtualMachineImpl` object. The second line will convert the vSphere object view back to a PowerCLI `VirtualMachineImpl` object.

The `Get-VIObjectByVIView` cmdlet has the following syntax:

```
Get-VIObjectByVIView [-VIView] <ViewBase[]> [<CommonParameters>]

Get-VIObjectByVIView [-Server <VIServer[]>] [-MORef]
<ManagedObjectReference[]> [<CommonParameters>]
```

You can see that the `Get-VIObjectByVIView` cmdlet has two parameter sets. The first parameter set contains the `-VIView` parameter. The second parameter set contains the `-Server` and `-MORef` parameters. Remember that parameters from different parameter sets cannot be mixed in one command.

If you are connected to multiple vCenter Servers, the `Get-VIObjectByVIView` cmdlet might return objects from multiple vCenter Servers because MoRefs are only unique on a single vCenter Server instance. You can use the `-Server` parameter of the `Get-VIObjectByVIView` cmdlet to solve this problem by specifying the vCenter Server for which you want to return objects. Because the `-Server` parameter is in a different parameter set from the `-VIView` parameter, you cannot use the `-VIView` parameter that is used in the pipeline. You have to use the `ForEach-Object` cmdlet and the `-MORef` parameter of the `Get-VIObjectByVIView` cmdlet:

```
PowerCLI C:\> $VMView |
>> ForEach-Object {
>>    Get-VIObjectByVIView -Server vCenter1 -MoRef $_.MoRef
>> }
>>
```

In the name of the `Get-VIObjectByVIView` cmdlet, you can see
a piece of the history of PowerCLI. VMware vSphere was named
VMware Infrastructure before VMware vSphere 4. The earlier VMware
vSphere PowerCLI versions were called VI Toolkit. In the name of this
cmdlet, you see that a PowerCLI object is still called a VIObject and a
vSphere object view is called a VIView.

Extending PowerCLI objects with the New-VIProperty cmdlet

Sometimes you can have the feeling that a PowerCLI object is missing a property.
Although the VMware PowerCLI team tried to include the most useful properties
in the objects, you can have the need for an extra property. Luckily, PowerCLI has
a way to extend a PowerCLI object using the `New-VIProperty` cmdlet. This cmdlet
has the following syntax:

```
New-VIProperty [-Name] <String> [-ObjectType] <String[]> [-Value]
<ScriptBlock> [-Force] [-BasedOnExtensionProperty <String[]>] [-WhatIf]
[-Confirm] [<CommonParameters>]

New-VIProperty [-Name] <String> [-ObjectType] <String[]> [-Force]
[-ValueFromExtensionProperty] <String> [-WhatIf] [-Confirm]
[<CommonParameters>]
```

Let's start with an example. You will add the VMware Tools' running statuses
used in a previous example to the `VirtualMachineImpl` object using the `New-VIProperty` cmdlet:

```
PowerCLI C:\> New-VIProperty -ObjectType VirtualMachine -Name
ToolsRunningStatus -ValueFromExtensionProperty 'Guest.ToolsRunningStatus'
```

Name	RetrievingType	DeclaringType	Value
ToolsRunning... ToolsRunningStatus	VirtualMachine	VirtualMachine	Guest.

Now you can get the tools' running statuses of all of your virtual machines with:

```
PowerCLI C:\> Get-VM | Select-Object -Property Name, ToolsRunningStatus
```

Isn't this much easier?

In the next example, you will add the `vCenterServer` property to the `VirtualMachineImpl` object. The name of the vCenter Server is part of the `VirtualMachineImpl` `Uid` property. The `Uid` property is a string that looks like `/VIServer=domain\account@vCenter:443/VirtualMachine=VirtualMachine-vm-239/`

You can use the `Split()` method to split the string. For example, the following command splits the string `192.168.0.1` into an array with four elements:

```
PowerCLI C:\> "192.168.0.1".Split('.')
192
168
0
1
```

The first element is `192`, the second element `168`, the third element `0`, and the fourth and last element `1`. If you assign the array to a variable then you can use an index to specify a certain element of the array:

```
PowerCLI C:\> $Array = "192.168.0.1".Split('.')
```

The index is `0` for the first element, `1` for the second element, and so on. If you want to specify the last element of the array, you can use the index `-1`. For example:

```
PowerCLI C:\> $Array[0]
192
```

In the `Uid` property, the name of the vCenter Server is between the `@` sign and the colon. So you can use those two characters to split the string. First you split the string at the colon and take the part before the colon. That is the first element of the resulting array:

```
PowerCLI C:\> $Uid = '/VIServer=domain\account@vCenter:443/
VirtualMachine=VirtualMachine-vm-239/'
PowerCLI C:\> $Uid.Split(':')[0]
/VIServer=domain\account@vCenter
```

Split the resulting part at the `@` sign and take the second element of the resulting array to get the name of the vCenter Server:

```
PowerCLI C:\> $String = '/VIServer=domain\account@vCenter'
PowerCLI C:\> $String.Split('@')[1]
vCenter
```

You can do this splitting with one line of code:

```
PowerCLI C:\> $Uid = '/VIServer=domain\account@vCenter:443/
VirtualMachine=VirtualMachine-vm-239/'
PowerCLI C:\> $Uid.Split(':')[0].Split('@')[1]
vCenter
```

Use the -Value parameter of the New-VIProperty cmdlet to specify a scriptblock. In this scriptblock, $Args[0] is the object with which you want to retrieve the name of the vCenter Server:

```
PowerCLI C:\> New-VIProperty -Name vCenterServer -ObjectType
VirtualMachine -Value {$Args[0].Uid.Split(":")[0].Split("@")[1]} -Force
```

The New-VIProperty -Force parameter indicates that you want to create the new property even if another property with the same name already exists for the specified object type.

Now you can get a list of all of your virtual machines and their vCenter Servers with:

```
PowerCLI C:\> Get-VM | Select-Object -Property Name,vCenterServer
```

Working with vSphere folders

In a VMware vSphere environment, you can use folders to organize your infrastructure. In the vSphere web client, you can create folders in the Hosts and Clusters, VMs and Templates, Storage, and Networking inventories. The following screenshot shows an example of folders in the VMs and Templates inventory.

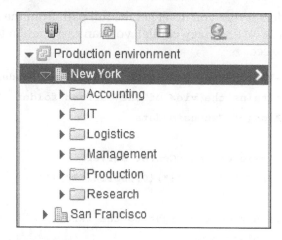

You can browse through these folders using the vSphere PowerCLI Inventory Provider. PowerCLI also has a set of cmdlets to work with these folders: `Get-Folder`, `Move-Folder`, `New-Folder`, `Remove-Folder`, and `Set-Folder`.

You can use the `Get-Folder` cmdlet to get a list of all of your folders:

```
PowerCLI C:\> Get-Folder
```

Or you can select specific folders by name using the following command line:

```
PowerCLI C:\> Get-Folder -Name "Accounting"
```

All folders are organized in a tree structure under the root folder. You can retrieve the root folder with:

```
PowerCLI C:\> Get-Folder -NoRecursion
```

Name	Type
Datacenters	Datacenter

The root folder is always called `Datacenters`. In this folder, you can only create subfolders or datacenters.

Folders in vSphere are of a certain type. Valid folder types are `VM`, `HostAndCluster`, `Datastore`, `Network`, and `Datacenter`. You can use this to specify the type of folders you want to retrieve. For example, to retrieve only folders of type VM, use:

```
PowerCLI C:\> Get-Folder -Type VM
```

A problem with folders is that you don't get the full path from the root if you retrieve a folder. Using the `New-VIProperty` cmdlet, you can easily add a `Path` property to a PowerCLI `Folder` object:

```
PowerCLI C:\> New-VIProperty -Name Path -ObjectType Folder -Value {
  # $FolderView contains the view of the current folder object
  $FolderView = $Args[0].Extensiondata

  # $Server is the name of the vCenter server
  $Server = $Args[0].Uid.Split(":")[0].Split("@")[1]

  # We build the path from the right to the left
  # Start with the folder name
  $Path = $FolderView.Name
```

```
# While we are not at the root folder
while ($FolderView.Parent){
  # Get the parent folder
  $FolderView = Get-View -Id $FolderView.Parent -Server $Server

  # Extend the path with the name of the parent folder
  $Path = $FolderView.Name + "\" + $Path
}


# Return the path
$Path
} -Force # Create the property even if a property with this name exists
```

In this example, you see that the # character in PowerShell is used to comment.

Using the new Path property, you can now get the path for all of the folders with:

```
PowerCLI C:\> Get-Folder | Select-Object -Property Name,Path
```

You can use the `Path` property to find a folder by its complete path. For example:

```
PowerCLI C:\> Get-Folder |
>> Where-Object {$_.Path -eq 'Datacenters\Dallas\vm\Templates'}
>>
```

Summary

In this chapter, you looked at the Get-Help, Get-Command, and Get-Member cmdlets. You learned how to use providers and PSDrives. You also saw how to create a calculated property. Using the raw API objects with the ExtensionData property or the Get-View cmdlet was discussed, and you looked at extending PowerCLI objects with the New-VIProperty cmdlet. At the end, you learned to work with folders and you saw how you can use the New-VIProperty cmdlet to extend the Folder object of PowerCLI with a Path property.

In the next chapter, you will learn more about working with objects in PowerCLI.

3
Working with Objects in PowerShell

PowerShell is an object-oriented shell. Don't let this scare you because knowing how to work with PowerShell objects will make your life much easier. Objects in PowerShell have properties and methods, just as with objects in real life. For example, let's take a computer and try to see it as an object. It has properties such as the manufacturer, the number of CPUs, the amount of memory, and the computer type (for example, server, workstation, desktop, or laptop). The computer also has methods. For example, you can switch the computer on and off. Properties and methods together are called **members** in PowerShell. In *Chapter 2, Learning Basic PowerCLI Concepts*, you already saw the `Get-Member` cmdlet that lists the properties and methods of a PowerShell object. In this chapter, you will learn all of the ins and outs of PowerShell objects. We will focus on the following topics:

- Using objects, properties, and methods
- Expanding variables and subexpressions in strings
- Using here-strings
- Using the pipeline
- Using the PowerShell object cmdlets
- Creating your own objects
- Using COM objects

Using objects, properties, and methods

In PowerCLI, even a string is an object. You can list the members of a string object using the Get-Member cmdlet that you have seen before. Let's go back to our example in *Chapter 2, Learning Basic PowerCLI Concepts*. First, we create a string "Learning PowerCLI" and put it in a variable called $String. Then, we take this $String variable and execute the Get-Member cmdlet using the $String variable as the input:

```
PowerCLI C:\> $String = "Learning PowerCLI"
PowerCLI C:\> Get-Member -Inputobject $String
```

You can also use the pipeline and do it in a single line, as follows:

```
PowerCLI C:\> "Learning PowerCLI" | Get-Member
```

The output will be the following:

```
    TypeName: System.String
```

Name	MemberType	Definition
Clone	Method	System.Object Clone(), Syst...
CompareTo	Method	int CompareTo(System.Object...
Contains	Method	bool Contains(string value)
CopyTo	Method	void CopyTo(int sourceIndex...
EndsWith	Method	bool EndsWith(string value)...
Equals	Method	bool Equals(System.Object o...
GetEnumerator	Method	System.CharEnumerator GetEn...
GetHashCode	Method	int GetHashCode()
GetType	Method	type GetType()
GetTypeCode	Method	System.TypeCode GetTypeCode...
IndexOf	Method	int IndexOf(char value), in...
IndexOfAny	Method	int IndexOfAny(char[] anyOf...
Insert	Method	string Insert(int startInde...
IsNormalized	Method	bool IsNormalized(), bool I...
LastIndexOf	Method	int LastIndexOf(char value)...
LastIndexOfAny	Method	int LastIndexOfAny(char[] a...
Normalize	Method	string Normalize(), string ...

PadLeft	Method	string PadLeft(int totalWid...
PadRight	Method	string PadRight(int totalWi...
Remove	Method	string Remove(int startInde...
Replace	Method	string Replace(char oldChar...
Split	Method	string[] Split(Params char[...
StartsWith	Method	bool StartsWith(string valu...
Substring	Method	string Substring(int startI...
ToBoolean	Method	bool IConvertible.ToBoolean...
ToByte	Method	byte IConvertible.ToByte(Sy...
ToChar	Method	char IConvertible.ToChar(Sy...
ToCharArray	Method	char[] ToCharArray(), char[...
ToDateTime	Method	datetime IConvertible.ToDat...
ToDecimal	Method	decimal IConvertible.ToDeci...
ToDouble	Method	double IConvertible.ToDoubl...
ToInt16	Method	int16 IConvertible.ToInt16(...
ToInt32	Method	int IConvertible.ToInt32(Sy...
ToInt64	Method	long IConvertible.ToInt64(S...
ToLower	Method	string ToLower(), string To...
ToLowerInvariant	Method	string ToLowerInvariant()
ToSByte	Method	sbyte IConvertible.ToSByte(...
ToSingle	Method	float IConvertible.ToSingle...
ToString	Method	string ToString(), string T...
ToType	Method	System.Object IConvertible....
ToUInt16	Method	uint16 IConvertible.ToUInt1...
ToUInt32	Method	uint32 IConvertible.ToUInt3...
ToUInt64	Method	uint64 IConvertible.ToUInt6...
ToUpper	Method	string ToUpper(), string To...
ToUpperInvariant	Method	string ToUpperInvariant()
Trim	Method	string Trim(Params char[] t...
TrimEnd	Method	string TrimEnd(Params char[...
TrimStart	Method	string TrimStart(Params cha...
Chars	ParameterizedProperty	char Chars(int index) {get;}
Length	Property	int Length {get;}

You see that a string has a lot of methods, one property, and a special type of property called `ParameterizedProperty`. Let's first use the `Length` property. To use a property, type the object name or the name of the variable containing the object; then type a dot; finally, type the property name. For the string, you could use both of the following command lines:

```
PowerCLI C:\> "Learning PowerCLI".Length
17
PowerCLI C:\> $String.Length
17
```

You see that the `Length` property contains the number of characters of the string `"Learning PowerCLI"`, 17 in this case.

Property names in PowerShell are not case-sensitive, so you could type the following command and still get the same results:

```
PowerCLI C:\> $String.length
17
```

`ParameterizedProperty` is a property that accepts a parameter value. The `ParameterizedProperty` property's `Chars` can be used to return the character at a specific position in the string. You have to specify the position, also called the index, as a parameter to `Chars`. Indexes in PowerShell start with 0. Therefore, to get the first character of the string, type the following command:

```
PowerCLI C:\> $String.Chars(0)
L
```

To get the second character of the string, type the following command:

```
PowerCLI C:\> $String.Chars(1)
e
```

You cannot use -1 to get the last character of the string as you can do with indexing in a PowerShell array. You have to calculate the last index yourself; this is calculated by subtracting 1 from the length of the string. Therefore, to get the last character of the string, you can type the following command:

```
PowerCLI C:\> $String.Chars($String.Length - 1)
I
```

PowerShell has more types of properties, such as `AliasProperty`, `CodeProperty`, `NoteProperty`, and `ScriptProperty`.

- `AliasProperty` is an alias name for an existing property
- `CodeProperty` is a property that maps to a static method on a .NET class
- `NoteProperty` is a property that contains data
- `ScriptProperty` is a property whose value is returned from executing a PowerShell scriptblock

Using methods

Using methods is as easy as using properties. You type the object name, or the name of a variable containing the object; then you type a dot; and, after the dot, you type the name of the method. For methods, you always have to use parentheses after the method name. For example, to modify a string to all uppercase letters, type in the following command:

```
PowerCLI C:\> $String.ToUpper()
LEARNING POWERCLI
```

Some methods require parameters. For example, to find the index of the P character in the string, you can use the following command:

```
PowerCLI C:\> $String.IndexOf('P')
9
```

The character P is the tenth character in the `"Learning PowerCLI"` string. But because indexes in PowerShell start with 0 and not 1, the index of the P character in the string is 9 and not 10.

One very useful method is `Replace`, which you can use to replace a character or a substring with another character or string or with nothing. For example you can replace all instances of the e characters in the string with the u character, as follows:

```
PowerCLI C:\> $String.Replace('e','u')
Luarning PowurCLI
```

The characters in the method are case-sensitive. If you use an uppercase `'E'`, it won't find the letter and will replace nothing:

```
PowerCLI C:\> $String.Replace('E','U')
Learning PowerCLI
```

You can also replace a substring with another string. Let's replace the word
`"PowerCLI"` with `"VMware vSphere PowerCLI"`:

```
PowerCLI C:\> $String.Replace('PowerCLI','VMware vSphere PowerCLI')
Learning VMware vSphere PowerCLI
```

There is also a `-Replace` operator in PowerShell. You can use the `-Replace` operator
to carry out a regular expression-based text substitution on a string or a collection of
strings as shown in the following command line:

```
PowerCLI C:\> $string -Replace 'e','u'
Luarning PowurCLI
```

Although both have the same name, the string `Replace` method and the `-Replace`
operator are two different things. There is no `-ToUpper` operator; as you can see in
the following example, this gives an error message:

You can use more than one method in the same command. Say you want to replace
`Learning` with `Gaining` and that you want to remove the characters `C`, `L`, and `I` from
the end of the string using the `TrimEnd` method. For this, you can use the following
command:

```
PowerCLI C:\> $String.Replace('Learning','Gaining').TrimEnd('CLI')
Gaining Power
```

Expanding variables and subexpressions in strings

In PowerShell, you can define a string with single or double quotes. There is a
difference between these two methods. In a string with single quotes, variables and
subexpressions are not expanded; while in a string with double quotes, variables
and subexpressions are expanded.

Let's look at an example of variable expansion in a double-quoted string:

```
PowerCLI C:\> $Number = 3
PowerCLI C:\> "The number is: $Number"
The number is: 3
```

In the preceding example, the string is defined with double quotes and the $Number variable is expanded. Let's see what happens if you use single quotes:

```
PowerCLI C:\> $Number = 3
PowerCLI C:\> 'The number is: $Number'
The number is: $Number
```

Using a single-quoted string, PowerShell doesn't expand the $Number variable. Let's try to put the number of virtual CPUs of a virtual machine in a double-quoted string:

```
PowerCLI C:\> $vm = Get-VM -Name dc1
PowerCLI C:\> "The number of vCPU's of the vm is: $vm.NumCpu"
The number of vCPU's of the vm is: dc1.NumCpu
```

The output is not what you intended. What happened? The $ in front of a variable name tells PowerShell to evaluate the variable. In the string used in the preceding example, $vm evaluates the variable vm but does not evaluate $vm.NumCpu. To evaluate $vm.NumCpu, you have to use another $ sign before and parentheses around the code that you want to evaluate, like so: $($vm.NumCpu). This is called a **subexpression** notation.

In the corrected example, you will get the number of virtual CPUs:

```
PowerCLI C:\> $vm = Get-VM -Name dc1
PowerCLI C:\> "The number of vCPU's of the vm is: $($vm.NumCpu)"
The number of vCPU's of the vm is: 2
```

You can use subexpression evaluation to evaluate any PowerShell code. In the next example, you will use PowerShell to calculate the sum of 3 and 4:

```
PowerCLI C:\> "3 + 4 = $(3+4)"
3 + 4 = 7
```

Understanding what expands a string

A string will be expanded when it is assigned to a variable. It will not be reevaluated when the variable is used later. The following example shows this behavior:

```
PowerCLI C:\> $Number = 3
PowerCLI C:\> $String = "The number is: $Number"
PowerCLI C:\> $String
The number is: 3
PowerCLI C:\> $Number = 4
PowerCLI C:\> $String
The number is: 3
```

As you can see, $String is assigned before $Number gets the value 4. The $String variable stays "The number is: 3".

Expanding a string when it is used

Want to know how to delay the expansion of the string until you use it? PowerShell has a predefined variable called $ExecutionContext. You can use the InvokeCommand.ExpandString() method of this variable to expand the string:

```
PowerCLI C:\> $Number = 3
PowerCLI C:\> $String = 'The number is: $Number'
PowerCLI C:\> $ExecutionContext.InvokeCommand.ExpandString($String)
The number is: 3
PowerCLI C:\> $Number = 4
PowerCLI C:\> $ExecutionContext.InvokeCommand.ExpandString($String)
The number is: 4
```

The preceding example defines $String as a single-quoted string, so $Number is not expanded at the assignment of $String. The $ExecutionContext. InvokeCommand.ExpandString($String) command expands the string every time the command is executed.

Using here-strings

Until now, you have only seen single-line strings in this book. PowerShell has a so-called **here-string** that spans multiple lines. You use @" or @' to start the here-string and "@ or '@ to finish the here-string. The @"or @' must be at the end of a line and the "@ or '@ must be at the beginning of the line that terminates the here-string. As in single-line strings, variables and subexpressions are expanded in double-quoted here-strings and are not expanded in single-quoted here-strings.

The following command creates a here-string that spans two lines and puts the here-string in the variable $s:

```
PowerCLI C:\> $s = @"
>> Learning PowerCLI
>> is a lot of fun!
>> "@
>> $s
>>
Learning PowerCLI
is a lot of fun!
```

Using the pipeline

In PowerShell, you can use the output of one command as input for another command by using the vertical bar (|) character. This is called using the pipeline. The vertical bar character is called the **pipe** character. In PowerShell, complete objects pass through the pipeline. This is different from cmd.exe or a Linux shell where only strings pass through the pipeline. The advantage of passing complete objects through the pipeline is that you don't have to perform string manipulation to retrieve property values.

Using the ByValue parameter binding

You have already seen some examples of using the pipeline in previous sections of this book, for example:

```
PowerCLI C:\> Get-VM | Get-Member
```

In this example, the output of the Get-VM cmdlet is used as the input for the Get-Member cmdlet. This is much simpler than the following command, which gives you the same result:

```
PowerCLI C:\> Get-Member -InputObject (Get-VM)
```

You can see that the Get-Member cmdlet accepts input from the pipeline if you look at the help content for the Get-Member parameter –InputObject parameter using the following command:

```
PowerCLI C:\> Get-Help Get-Member -Parameter InputObject
```

The output will be the following:

```
-InputObject <PSObject>
```

Specifies the object whose members are retrieved.

Using the InputObject parameter is not the same as piping an object to Get-Member. The differences are as follows:

-- When you pipe a collection of objects to Get-Member, Get-Member gets the members of the individual objects in the collection, such as the properties of each string in an array of strings.

-- When you use InputObject to submit a collection of objects, Get-Member gets the members of the collection, such as the properties of the array in an array of strings.

Required?	false
Position?	named
Default value	
Accept pipeline input?	true (ByValue)
Accept wildcard characters?	false

You can see in the preceding output that in the description it says Accept pipeline input? true (ByValue). This means that the Get-Member -InputObject parameter accepts input from the pipeline.

The ByValue parameter binding means that PowerShell binds the entire input object to the parameter.

In the following figure, you will see that the pipeline binds the output of the Get-Member cmdlet to the –InputObject parameter of the Get-Member cmdlet:

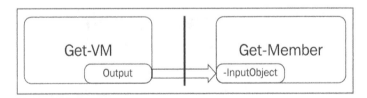

Using the ByPropertyName parameter binding

If PowerShell can't find a parameter that accepts pipeline input using `ByValue`, it tries to find parameters that accept pipeline input using `ByPropertyName`. When a parameter accepts pipeline input using `ByPropertyName`, it means that the value of a property of the input object is bound to a cmdlet parameter with the same name as the property.

An example of a PowerShell cmdlet that accepts input from the pipeline using the `ByPropertyName` parameter binding is the `Get-Date` cmdlet, which returns a `System.DateTime` object. The `-Date` parameter of this cmdlet accepts pipeline input using both `ByValue` and `ByPropertyName`. The PowerCLI `Get-VIEvent` cmdlet retrieves information about the events on a vCenter Server system, for example:

```
PowerCLI C:\> Get-VIEvent | Select-Object -First 1
```

```
ScheduledTask        : VMware.Vim.ScheduledTaskEventArgument
Entity               : VMware.Vim.ManagedEntityEventArgument
Key                  : 64835
ChainId              : 64835
CreatedTime          : 12/28/2013 9:04:01 PM
UserName             :
Datacenter           :
ComputeResource      :
Host                 :
Vm                   :
Ds                   :
Net                  :
Dvs                  :
FullFormattedMessage : Running task VMware vCenter Update Manager
                       Check Notification on Datacenters in
                       datacenter
ChangeTag            :
DynamicType          :
DynamicProperty      :
```

The output has a property `CreatedTime`. The value of the `CreatedTime` property has a `DateTime` object type.

Let's try to pipe the output of the preceding command into the `Get-Date` cmdlet:

```
VMware vSphere PowerCLI 5.5 Release 1                    — □ ×
PowerCLI C:\> Get-VIEvent | Select-Object -First 1 | Get-Date

Get-Date : The input object cannot be bound to any
parameters for the command either because the command does
not take pipeline input or the input and its properties do
not match any of the parameters that take pipeline input.
At line:1 char:40
+ Get-VIEvent | Select-Object -First 1 | Get-Date
                                         ~~~~~~~~
+ CategoryInfo          : InvalidArgument: (VMware.Vim.
UserLogoutSessionEvent:PSObject) [Get-Date], ParameterB
indingException
+ FullyQualifiedErrorId : InputObjectNotBound,Microsoft
.PowerShell.Commands.GetDateCommand
```

This gives an error message because the output of the `Get-VIEvent` cmdlet does not have a `Date` property that matches the `-Date` parameter of the `Get-Date` cmdlet. We will now use a calculated property to rename the `CreatedTime` property in `Date`:

```
PowerCLI C:\> Get-VIEvent | Select-Object -First 1 |
>> Select-Object @{Name="Date";Expression={$_.CreatedTime}} |
>> Get-Date
>>


Saturday, December 28, 2013 9:04:01 PM
```

Because the output of the `Select-Object` cmdlet has a `Date` property, and this property matches the `Get-Date` parameter `-Date` using the `ByPropertyName` parameter binding, the pipeline now works.

The following figure shows that the pipeline binds the value of the `Date` property in the output of the `Select-Object` cmdlet to the `-Date` property of the `Get-Date` cmdlet:

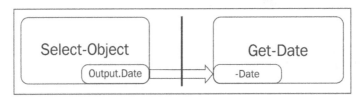

Most PowerCLI cmdlets will accept input from the pipeline using the `ByValue` parameter binding. However, only a few PowerCLI cmdlets will accept input from the pipeline using the `ByPropertyName` parameter binding. You can find these cmdlets with the following PowerShell code:

```
PowerCLI C:\> Get-VICommand |
>> Where-Object {$_.ParameterSets.Parameters |
>> Where-Object {
>> $_.ValueFromPipeline -and $_.ValueFromPipelineByPropertyName}}
>>
```

This is the output of the preceding command:

CommandType	Name	ModuleName
Cmdlet	Add-EsxSoftwareDepot	VMware.ImageBuilder
Cmdlet	Add-EsxSoftwarePackage	VMware.ImageBuilder
Cmdlet	Compare-EsxImageProfile	VMware.ImageBuilder
Cmdlet	Export-EsxImageProfile	VMware.ImageBuilder
Cmdlet	New-EsxImageProfile	VMware.ImageBuilder
Cmdlet	Remove-EsxImageProfile	VMware.ImageBuilder
Cmdlet	Remove-EsxSoftwareDepot	VMware.ImageBuilder
Cmdlet	Remove-EsxSoftwarePackage	VMware.ImageBuilder
Cmdlet	Set-EsxImageProfile	VMware.ImageBuilder

The script uses the `Get-VICommand` cmdlet to get all of the PowerCLI cmdlets. It then filters only those cmdlets that have parameters that accept pipeline input using `ByPropertyName`. As you see in the preceding output, when writing this book, only cmdlets from the PowerCLI `VMware.ImageBuilder` module accept pipeline input using `ByPropertyName`.

Using the PowerShell object cmdlets

PowerShell has some cmdlets that are designed to work with all kinds of objects. You can easily recognize them because they all have `-Noun Object`. You can use the `Get-Command` cmdlet's `-Noun` parameter to find them:

```
PowerCLI C:\> Get-Command -Noun Object
```

The output of the preceding command is as follows:

```
CommandType  Name             ModuleName
-----------  ----             ----------
Cmdlet       Compare-Object   Microsoft.PowerShell.Utility
Cmdlet       ForEach-Object   Microsoft.PowerShell.Core
Cmdlet       Group-Object     Microsoft.PowerShell.Utility
Cmdlet       Measure-Object   Microsoft.PowerShell.Utility
Cmdlet       New-Object       Microsoft.PowerShell.Utility
Cmdlet       Select-Object    Microsoft.PowerShell.Utility
Cmdlet       Sort-Object      Microsoft.PowerShell.Utility
Cmdlet       Tee-Object       Microsoft.PowerShell.Utility
Cmdlet       Where-Object     Microsoft.PowerShell.Core
```

In the following section, we will discuss the Object cmdlets.

Using the Select-Object cmdlet

If you want to retrieve a subset of the properties of an object, select unique objects, select a specific number of objects, or select specific objects from an array, you can use the Select-Object cmdlet. You can also use the Select-Object cmdlet to add properties to an object using calculated properties as you have seen in *Chapter 2, Learning Basic PowerCLI Concepts*.

The Select-Object cmdlet has the following syntax:

```
Select-Object [[-Property] <Object[]>] [-ExcludeProperty <String[]>]
[-ExpandProperty <String>] [-First <Int32>] [-InputObject <PSObject>]
[-Last <Int32>] [-Skip <Int32>] [-Unique [<SwitchParameter>]] [-Wait
[<SwitchParameter>]] [<CommonParameters>]


Select-Object [-Index <Int32[]>] [-InputObject <PSObject>] [-Unique
[<SwitchParameter>]] [-Wait [<SwitchParameter>]] [<CommonParameters>]
```

As you can see, the Select-Object cmdlet has two parameter sets: one parameter set contains the -Index parameter and the other doesn't. You can use Select as an alias for the Select-Object cmdlet.

The Get-VM cmdlet returns the Name, PowerState, NumCpu, and MemoryGB properties of the virtual machines by default. But what if you want to return the Name, VMHost, and Cluster properties instead? If you look at the properties of a virtual machine object, you will see the VMhost property, but you will not see a Cluster property. However, if you look at a VMHostImpl object, you will find a Parent property. The Parent property of a VMhostImpl object contains the cluster that the host is a member of.

You can use this information to create a PowerCLI one-liner to get the host and cluster of all of the virtual machines:

```
PowerCLI C:\> Get-VM | Select-Object -Property Name,VMHost,@
{Name="Cluster";Expression={$_.VMHost.Parent}}


Name VMHost          Cluster
---- ------          -------
DC1  192.168.0.133 Cluster01
```

The preceding command uses the Select-Object cmdlet to select the Name and VMHost properties of the virtual machine objects; it creates a calculated property named Cluster that retrieves the cluster via the VMHost.Parent property.

 You can create a one-liner from all of your PowerShell scripts by using the semicolon as a separator between the commands. Use this only on the command line. It makes your scripts hard to read.

You can use the Select-Object -First parameter to specify the number of objects to select from the beginning of an array of input objects. For example, to retrieve the first three hosts, type the following command:

```
PowerCLI C:\> Get-VMHost | Select-Object -First 3
```

If you are typing commands at the pipeline, you can also use their aliases. For Select-Object, the alias is Select. Therefore, the next example will give the same result as the previous one:

```
PowerCLI C:\> Get-VMHost | Select -First 3
```

To select a number of objects starting from the end of an array of objects, use the Select-Object -Last parameter. The following command retrieves the last cluster:

```
PowerCLI C:\> Get-Cluster | Select-Object -Last 1
```

You can also skip objects from the beginning or the end of an array using the Select-Object -Skip parameter. The following command returns all of the folder objects except the first two:

```
PowerCLI C:\> Get-Folder | Select-Object -Skip 2
```

A very interesting parameter of the `Select-Object` cmdlet is the `-ExpandProperty` parameter. If the property contains an object, you can use this parameter to expand the object. For example, if you want to get the `VMHostImpl` object of the virtual machine named `dc1`, you can execute the following command:

```
PowerCLI C:\> Get-VM -Name dc1 | Select-Object -ExpandProperty VMHost
```

Using the Where-Object cmdlet

If you only want a subset of all of the objects that a command returns, you can use the `Where-Object` cmdlet to filter the output of a command and only return the objects that match the criteria of the filter.

The `Where-Object` cmdlet syntax definition is so long that it would take up too much space in this book. You can easily get the `Where-Object` cmdlet syntax with the following command:

```
PowerCLI C:\> Get-Help Where-Object
```

PowerShell v3 introduced a new, easier syntax for the `Where-Object` cmdlet. I will show you both the v2 and the v3 syntaxes. First, let's see the new PowerShell v3 syntax.

Let's try to find all virtual machines that have only one virtual CPU. You can do this by searching for virtual machines that have a `NumCPU` property with a value of 1:

```
PowerCLI C:\> Get-VM | Where-Object NumCpu -eq 1
```

Name	PowerState	Num CPUs	MemoryGB
DC1	PoweredOff	1	0.250

If you use the alias `Where`, the command looks more like a natural language:

```
PowerCLI C:\> Get-VM | Where NumCpu -eq 1
```

You can also use the alias `?` if you want to type less on the command line:

```
PowerCLI C:\> Get-VM | ? NumCpu -eq 1
```

The PowerShell v2 syntax is a bit more obscure. You have to use a script block as the value of the `Where-Object -FilterScript` parameter:

```
PowerCLI C:\> Get-VM | Where-Object -FilterScript {$_.NumCpu -eq 1}
```

Because the `-FilterScript` parameter is the first positional parameter of the `Where-Object` cmdlet, nobody uses the parameter name, and you will always see one of the following command lines being used:

```
PowerCLI C:\> Get-VM | Where-Object {$_.NumCpu -eq 1}
PowerCLI C:\> Get-VM | where {$_.NumCpu -eq 1}
```

The advantage of the PowerShell v2 syntax over the v3 syntax is that you can create complex filtering scripts, for example:

```
PowerCLI C:\> Get-VM |
>> Where-Object {$_.NumCpu -gt 2 -and $_.MemoryGB -lt 16}
>>
```

The preceding command will show you all of the virtual machines with more than two virtual CPUs and less than 16 GB of memory. If you want to create the same filter using the PowerShell v3 syntax, you have to use two filters: one for the number of CPUs and one for the memory. Here is an example command:

```
PowerCLI C:\> Get-VM | Where NumCpu -gt 2 | Where MemoryGB -lt 16
```

Using the ForEach-Object cmdlet

Some cmdlets don't accept properties from the pipeline. On the other hand, you might like to use a cmdlet in the pipeline but the property you want to use in the pipeline doesn't accept pipeline input. This is where the PowerShell `ForEach-Object` cmdlet will help you.

The `ForEach-Object` cmdlet has the following syntax:

```
ForEach-Object [-Process] <ScriptBlock[]> [-Begin <ScriptBlock>] [-
End <ScriptBlock>] [-InputObject <PSObject>] [-RemainingScripts
<ScriptBlock[]>] [-Confirm [<SwitchParameter>]] [-WhatIf
[<SwitchParameter>]] [<CommonParameters>]

ForEach-Object [-MemberName] <String> [-ArgumentList <Object[]>] [-
InputObject <PSObject>] [-Confirm [<SwitchParameter>]] [-WhatIf
[<SwitchParameter>]] [<CommonParameters>]
```

The names of the parameter sets are `ScriptBlockSet` and `PropertyAndMethodSet`. The `-Process` parameter is required for the `ScriptBlockSet` parameter set. The `-MemberName` parameter is required for the `PropertyAndMethodSet` parameter set. The `PropertyAndMethodSet` parameter set was introduced in PowerShell v3.

The default first parameter is -Process; it is generally omitted when using the cmdlet. The -Process parameter has a scriptblock as its parameter value and this scriptblock will run for every object that passes the pipeline. The following command will retrieve the names of all of your virtual machines:

```
PowerCLI C:\> Get-VM | ForEach-Object {$_.Name}
```

In the scriptblock, the special variable $_ is used. The $_ variable is the current object that passes through the pipeline. Thus, $_.Name will return the value of the name property of the current object.

You can also use the alias foreach:

```
PowerCLI C:\> Get-VM | foreach {$_.Name}
```

In PowerShell v3, the command is even simpler:

```
PowerCLI C:\> Get-VM | foreach Name
```

If you want the ForEach-Object cmdlet to execute code before the objects start to pass through the pipeline — say to initialize a variable — you can create a scriptblock and use it as an argument value for the -Begin parameter. If you want the ForEach-Object cmdlet to execute code after the objects finish passing through the pipeline — for example, to return the result of a calculation you did on all of the objects in the pipeline — you can create a scriptblock and use it as an argument value for the -End parameter. For example use the following command:

```
PowerCLI C:\> 1,2,3,4 |
>> ForEach-Object -Begin {"Start of the Script"; $Sum = 0} `
>> -Process {$Sum += $_} -End {"Sum of the elements: $Sum"}
>>
Start of the Script
Sum of the elements: 10
```

The preceding example was just to demonstrate the ForEach-Object cmdlet. If you want to take the sum of the objects in the pipeline, it is better to use the Measure-Object cmdlet that will be discussed in one of the following sections.

> In the example, you can see that the semicolon character is used to separate PowerShell commands. The **backtick** character (`) used as the last character of a line is used to escape the newline character and treat the newline character as a space. This enables you to break long lines of code and continue them on the next line.

To specify 1, 2, 3, and 4 you can also use the PowerShell range operator (. .) as follows:

```
1..4
```

The preceding operator is equivalent to the following:

```
1, 2, 3, 4
```

The `ForEach-Object -Process` scriptblock is run at least once even if the input object is $null, as you can see in the following example:

```
PowerCLI C:\> $null | ForEach-Object -Process {"Hello world."}
Hello world.
```

You probably don't want to return anything if the input object is $null. You can solve this problem by testing with `if ($_)` to check whether the input object exists inside the scriptblock:

```
PowerCLI C:\> $null | ForEach-Object -Process {if ($_) {"Hello."}}
```

Using the Sort-Object cmdlet

PowerCLI returns objects in random order. If you want the objects to be sorted, you can use the `Sort-Object` cmdlet to sort them.

The `Sort-Object` cmdlet has the following syntax:

```
Sort-Object [[-Property] <Object[]>] [-CaseSensitive
[<SwitchParameter>]] [-Culture <String>] [-Descending
[<SwitchParameter>]] [-InputObject <PSObject>] [-Unique
[<SwitchParameter>]] [<CommonParameters>]
```

The `Sort-Object` cmdlet sorts objects in ascending or descending order based on the values of the properties of the object.

You can specify a single property or multiple properties (for a multi-key sort), and you can select a case-sensitive or case-insensitive sort. You can also direct `Sort-Object` to display only the objects with a unique value for a particular property.

The following example will give a list of all of your virtual machines and their hosts sorted in ascending order on the host name and the virtual machine name.

```
PowerCLI C:\> Get-VM | Select-Object -Property VMHost,Name |
>> Sort-Object -Property VMHost,Name
>>
```

Using the aliases `select` for `Select-Object` and `sort` for `Sort-Object`, and also using positional parameters, the preceding example can be shortened into this:

```
PowerCLI C:\> Get-VM | select VMHost,Name | sort VMHost,Name
```

Using the Measure-Object cmdlet

If you want to count objects or calculate the minimum, maximum, sum, and average of the numeric values of properties, you can use the `Measure-Object` cmdlet. For text objects, it can count and calculate the number of lines, words, and characters.

The `Measure-Object` cmdlet has the following syntax:

```
Measure-Object [[-Property] <String[]>] [-Average
[<SwitchParameter>]] [-InputObject <PSObject>] [-Maximum
[<SwitchParameter>]] [-Minimum [<SwitchParameter>]] [-Sum
[<SwitchParameter>]] [<CommonParameters>]

Measure-Object [[-Property] <String[]>] [-Character
[<SwitchParameter>]] [-IgnoreWhiteSpace [<SwitchParameter>]] [-
InputObject <PSObject>] [-Line [<SwitchParameter>]] [-Word
[<SwitchParameter>]] [<CommonParameters>]
```

The names of the parameter sets are `GenericMeasure` and `TextMeasure`. There are no required parameters.

Let's get back to our example from the `ForEach-Object` cmdlet, where we counted the sum of the numbers 1, 2, 3, and 4. You can do this more easily using the `Measure-Object` cmdlet with the following command:

```
PowerCLI C:\> (1..4 | Measure-Object -Sum).Sum
10
```

The only output property that the `Measure-Object` cmdlet fills by default is the `Count` property. To count the number of virtual machines in your environment, type the following command:

```
PowerCLI C:\> Get-VM | Measure-Object
```

The output of the preceding command will be as follows:

```
Count    : 12
Average  :
Sum      :
Maximum  :
```

```
Minimum   :

Property :
```

If you just want the count value, you can specify the Count property:

```
PowerCLI C:\> (Get-VM | Measure-Object).Count
12
```

Alternatively, you can use the Select-Object -ExpandProperty parameter:

```
PowerCLI C:\> Get-VM | Measure-Object |
>> Select-Object -ExpandProperty Count
>>
12
```

You can also use the alias measure for Measure-Object:

```
PowerCLI C:\> (Get-VM | measure).Count
12
```

To get the average, sum, maximum, and minimum values of a property, you have to specify the property name and the parameters for the values that you want to retrieve. The following command will retrieve the average, sum, maximum, and minimum values of the ProvisionedSpaceGB property for all of your virtual machines:

```
PowerCLI C:\> Get-VM | Measure-Object -Property ProvisionedSpaceGB
-Average -Sum -Maximum -Minimum


Count     : 12
Average   : 60.590376389601
Sum       : 727.084516675211
Maximum   : 221.090891393833
Minimum   : 2.58988594077528
Property : ProvisionedSpaceGB
```

To count the number of characters, words, and lines in a string, you can use the -Line, -Word, and -Character parameters:

```
PowerCLI C:\> "Learning PowerCLI" |
>> Measure-Object -Line -Word -Character
>>
```

```
         Lines              Words          Characters Property
         -----              -----          ---------- --------
           1                  2                17
```

You can also use the `Measure-Object` cmdlet to count the number of lines, words, and characters in the here-string:

```
PowerCLI C:\> @"
>> Every vSphere admin should
>> Learn PowerCLI!
>> "@ | Measure-Object -Line -Word -Character
>>
```

```
         Lines              Words          Characters Property
         -----              -----          ---------- --------
           2                  6                42
```

Rounding a value

If you don't want a value to have several fractional digits, you can use the .NET `Math.Round` method to round a value to the nearest integer or to the specified number of fractional digits. The first parameter of the `Math.Round` method is the value that you want to round. The optional second parameter is the number of fractional digits that you want the value to round to. If you don't specify the second parameter, the value will be rounded to the nearest integer. For example, use the following command:

```
PowerCLI C:\> [math]::Round(60.590376389601,2)
60.59
```

You can use the `Math.Round` method in a calculated property. For example:

```
PowerCLI C:\> Get-VM | Measure-Object -Property ProvisionedSpaceGB
-Average -Sum -Maximum -Minimum |
>> Select-Object -Property Count,
>> @{Name="Average";Expression={[math]::Round($_.Average,2)}}
>>
```

```
Count           Average
-----           -------
   12             60.59
```

Using the Group-Object cmdlet

The `Group-Object` cmdlet groups objects that contain the same value for the specified properties. Using the `Group-Object` cmdlet can be very useful, for example, when you want to count the number of instances of a specific value of a property.

The `Group-Object` cmdlet has the following syntax:

```
Group-Object [[-Property] <Object[]>] [-AsHashTable
[<SwitchParameter>]] [-AsString [<SwitchParameter>]] [-CaseSensitive
[<SwitchParameter>]] [-Culture <String>] [-InputObject <PSObject>] [-
NoElement [<SwitchParameter>]] [<CommonParameters>]
```

Let's create a PowerCLI command to count the number of instances of each operating system installed on a virtual machine. In a traditional scripting language, you would have to loop through all of your virtual machines and increment counters for each operating system. In PowerCLI, you can achieve this much easier using the `Group-Object` cmdlet. The name of the guest operating system is in a virtual machine's `Guest.OSFullName` property. You can use the `Group-Object` cmdlet to group the objects on the `Guest.OSFullName` property using a calculated property. The `Group-Object` cmdlet will return the `Count`, `Name`, and `Group` properties by default. Using the `-NoElement` parameter will remove the `Group` property from the output. The following example groups the virtual machines on the `Guest.OSFullname` property and returns the `Count` and `Name` properties for each `Guest.OSFullName` property.

```
PowerCLI C:\> Get-VM |
>> Group-Object -Property @{Expression={$_.Guest.OSFullName}} -NoElement
|
>> Format-Table -AutoSize
>>


Count Name
----- ----
    1 Microsoft Windows Server 2012 (64-bit)
    1 SUSE Linux Enterprise 11 (32-bit)
    3 SUSE Linux Enterprise 11 (64-bit)
    1
    2 Microsoft Windows Server 2008 R2 (64-bit)
    1 CentOS 4/5/6 (32-bit)
```

```
2 Other (64-bit)
1 CentOS 4/5/6 (64-bit)
1 CentOS 4/5/6 (64-bit)
```

 The one virtual machine that does not have a guest operating system name is powered off for a long time. The guest operating system is determined using the VMware Tools. **VMware vSphere** can't find the guest operating system for this virtual machine while it is powered off.

The `Format-Table -AutoSize` command formats the output, so you will get the full operating system name.

Using the Compare-Object cmdlet

If you want to compare two objects or sets of objects, you have to use the `Compare-Object` cmdlet.

The `Compare-Object` cmdlet has the following syntax:

```
Compare-Object [-ReferenceObject] <PSObject[]> [-DifferenceObject]
<PSObject[]> [-CaseSensitive [<SwitchParameter>]] [-Culture <String>]
[-ExcludeDifferent [<SwitchParameter>]] [-IncludeEqual
[<SwitchParameter>]] [-PassThru [<SwitchParameter>]] [-Property
<Object[]>] [-SyncWindow <Int32>] [<CommonParameters>]
```

From the sets of objects that the `Compare-Object` cmdlet compares, one set of objects is called the **reference set** and the other is called the **difference set**.

Let's compare two strings:

```
PowerCLI C:\> $string1 = "Learning PowerCLI"
PowerCLI C:\> $string2 = "Learning PowerCLI!"
PowerCLI C:\> Compare-Object -ReferenceObject $string1 `
>> -DifferenceObject $string2
>>


InputObject                      SideIndicator
-----------                      -------------
Learning PowerCLI!               =>
Learning PowerCLI                <=
```

The output shows that the strings are not the same. The `<=` symbol indicates objects from the reference set. The `=>` symbol indicates objects from the difference set. If you use the `-IncludeEqual` parameter, the `Compare-Object` cmdlet will also show objects that are equal in both sets. These objects are indicated by the `==` symbol.

Using the Tee-Object cmdlet

The `Tee-Object` cmdlet saves the command output in a file or variable and also sends it down the pipeline. It sends the output of a command in two directions, as in the letter "T". If `Tee-Object` is the last command in the pipeline, the command output is displayed at the prompt.

The `Tee-Object` cmdlet has the following syntax:

```
Tee-Object [-FilePath] <String> [-Append [<SwitchParameter>]] [-
InputObject <PSObject>] [<CommonParameters>]


Tee-Object [-InputObject <PSObject>] -LiteralPath <String>
[<CommonParameters>]


Tee-Object [-InputObject <PSObject>] -Variable <String>
[<CommonParameters>]
```

The following example retrieves all of your virtual machines and saves the virtual machine objects in a variable named `VMs`. It also sends the objects down the pipeline and displays the `Name` and `PowerState` properties of the virtual machines.

```
PowerCLI C:\> Get-VM | Tee-Object -Variable VMs |
>> Select-Object -Property Name,PowerState
>>
```

The following figure shows that the `Tee-Object` cmdlet writes its output to the variable $VMs and pipes its output to the next command in the pipeline:

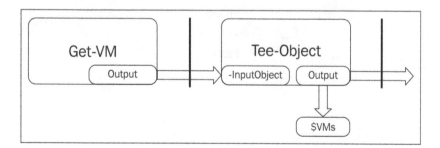

Creating your own objects

There are several ways to create new objects in PowerCLI. In fact, you have already been creating new objects by using the `Select-Object -Property` command. In this section, you will learn more ways to create new objects.

Using the New-Object cmdlet

PowerShell has its own cmdlet for creating objects: `New-Object`. You can use this cmdlet to create a Microsoft .NET Framework or COM object.

The `New-Object` cmdlet has the following syntax:

```
New-Object [-TypeName] <String> [[-ArgumentList] <Object[]>] [-
Property <IDictionary>] [<CommonParameters>]


New-Object [-ComObject] <String> [-Property <IDictionary>] [-Strict
[<SwitchParameter>]] [<CommonParameters>]
```

Using a hash table to create an object

The easiest way to create a Microsoft .NET Framework object as the output of your PowerCLI scripts is to create a `PSObject` type object using a hash table. The following example creates an object with two members of member type `NoteProperty`—`Name` and `VMHost`:

```
PowerCLI C:\> $Object = New-Object -TypeName PSObject -Property @{
>> Name = "VM1"
>> VMHost = "ESX1"
>> }
>>
PowerCLI C:\> $Object


Name                           VMHost
----                           ------
VM1                            ESX1
```

If you look at the object with `Get-Member`, you will see four standard methods and the `NoteProperty` member types named `Name` and `VMHost`:

```
PowerCLI C:\> $Object | Get-Member


    TypeName: System.Management.Automation.PSCustomObject

Name         MemberType   Definition
----         ----------   ----------
Equals       Method       bool Equals(System.Object obj)
GetHashCode  Method       int GetHashCode()
GetType      Method       type GetType()
ToString     Method       string ToString()
Name         NoteProperty System.String Name=VM1
VMHost       NoteProperty System.String VMHost=ESX1
```

The four methods `Equals`, `GetHashCode`, `GetType`, and `ToString` are methods that every PowerShell object has.

This technique is fast and is easy to use. It has the disadvantage that PowerShell might output the properties in a different order than you added them. You can solve this problem by piping the object to `Select-Object` and specifying the properties there in the right order as follows:

```
PowerCLI C:\> $Object | Select-Object -Property Name,VMHost

Name                          VMHost
----                          ------
VM1                           ESX1
```

Creating objects using the Select-Object cmdlet

If you use the `Select-Object` cmdlet to select only specific properties of an object, you are creating a new object type. For example, the objects returned by the `Get-VM` cmdlet are of type `VMware.VimAutomation.ViCore.Impl.V1.Inventory.VirtualMachineImpl`. However, if you pipe the output of the `Get-VM` cmdlet to `Select-Object`, you will get the following output:

```
PowerCLI C:\> Get-VM | Select-Object -Property Name | Get-Member
```

```
    TypeName: Selected.VMware.VimAutomation.ViCore.Impl.V1.Inventory
.VirtualMachineImpl
```

In the `TypeName` output, you can see that the original type name is prefixed by `Selected`. You can create a new object from scratch if you pipe an empty string to `Select-Object`, as in the following example:

```
PowerCLI C:\> $Report = "" | Select-Object -Property VM,VMHost
PowerCLI C:\> $Report.VM = "VM1"
PowerCLI C:\> $Report.VMHost = "ESX1"
PowerCLI C:\> $Report
```

```
VM                          VMHost
--                          ------
VM1                         ESX1
```

In the first line, you have created a new object `$Report` that has two blank properties: `VM` and `VMHost`. In the second and third lines, values are assigned to these properties. In the last line, the `$Report` object is returned.

This technique was used a lot in PowerShell v1 and you still see it used often. In PowerShell v2 and above, I prefer using a hash table.

Adding properties to an object with Add-Member

If you want to add one or more properties to an existing object, you can use the `Add-Member` cmdlet.

The `Add-Member` cmdlet has the following syntax:

```
Add-Member [-PassThru [<SwitchParameter>]] -InputObject <PSObject> -
TypeName <String> [<CommonParameters>]
```

```
Add-Member [-MemberType] <PSMemberTypes> [-Name] <String> [[-Value]
<Object>] [[-SecondValue] <Object>] [-Force [<SwitchParameter>]] [-
PassThru [<SwitchParameter>]] [-TypeName <String>] -InputObject
<PSObject> [<CommonParameters>]
```

```
Add-Member [-NotePropertyName] <String> [-NotePropertyValue] <Object>
[-Force [<SwitchParameter>]] [-PassThru [<SwitchParameter>]] [-
TypeName <String>] -InputObject <PSObject> [<CommonParameters>]
```

```
Add-Member [-NotePropertyMembers] <IDictionary> [-Force
[<SwitchParameter>]] [-PassThru [<SwitchParameter>]] [-TypeName
<String>] -InputObject <PSObject> [<CommonParameters>]
```

You can create a new object with the `New-Object` cmdlet and then use the `Add-Member` cmdlet to add properties, as follows:

```
PowerCLI C:\> $Object = New-Object -TypeName PSObject
PowerCLI C:\> $Object | Add-member NoteProperty VM "VM1"
PowerCLI C:\> $Object | Add-member NoteProperty VMHost "ESX1"
PowerCLI C:\> $Object


VM                                    VMHost
--                                    ------
VM1                                   ESX1
```

This technique was also common in PowerShell v1. Because it is the slowest option, it is rarely used anymore.

The `Add-Member` cmdlet adds properties to the input object and does not generate output unless you specify the `-PassThru` parameter. If you want to use more than one `Add-Member` command in a pipeline, don't forget to use the `-PassThru` parameter.

Using type declarations

PowerShell v3 introduced a new way to create an object using a type declaration of a `pscustomobject` object. The advantage over the technique using a hash table is that the properties come out in the same order in which you added them. If you use PowerShell v3, this becomes a very clean and fast technique to use.

```
PowerCLI C:\> $Object = [pscustomobject]@{
>> VM = "VM1"
>> VMHost = "ESX1"
>> }
>> $Object
>>


VM                                    VMHost
--                                    ------
VM1                                   ESX1
```

Using COM objects

You can also use the `New-Object` cmdlet to create an instance of a COM object. COM objects were used a lot in VBScript. In PowerShell, you can still use them to do things that you cannot do in native PowerShell. The following example will use the `SAPI.SpVoice` COM object to output a text as voice. It will say "The script is finished." Append this piece of code at the end of your PowerCLI script and you will hear your computer say that the script is finished. This way, you don't have to keep watching your computer screen. Isn't this cool?

```
PowerCLI C:\> $Voice = New-Object -ComObject SAPI.SpVoice
PowerCLI C:\> $Voice.Speak("The script is finished.") | Out-Null
```

You can get a list of all of the COM objects on your computer with the following PowerShell code:

```
Get-ChildItem -Path HKLM:\Software\Classes -ErrorAction `
SilentlyContinue |
Where-Object {$_.PSChildName -match '^\w+\.\w+$' -and `
  (Get-Itemproperty "$($_.PSPath)\CLSID" -ErrorAction `
SilentlyContinue)} |
Format-Table -Property PSChildName
```

The script lists all of the subkeys in the `HKEY_LOCAL_MACHINE\Software\Classes` registry key. It then uses a regular expression to select only the subkeys with a `PSChildName` property that contains two words separated by a dot. The subkeys must themselves have a subkey, named `CLSID`. Finally, the value of the `PSChildName` property is shown in table format.

The script uses the backtick or "grave accent" (`` ` ``), the Windows PowerShell continuation character, to continue commands on the next line.

You cannot use all of the COM objects in a PowerShell script. Some COM objects are not compatible with PowerShell.

Summary

In this chapter, you learned how to use PowerShell objects, their properties, and methods. You saw variable and subexpression expansion in strings and here-strings. You learned about the PowerShell pipeline and parameter binding using the `ByValue` or `ByPropertyName` parameter binding types. You learned how to use the PowerShell object cmdlets: `Select-Object`, `Where-Object`, `ForEach-Object`, `Sort-Object`, `Measure-Object`, `Group-Object`, `Compare-Object`, `Tee-Object`, and `New-Object`. We looked at different methods to create new objects. Finally, you saw an example of how to use COM objects.

In the next chapter, you will learn how to manage VMware vSphere hosts with PowerCLI.

4
Managing vSphere Hosts with PowerCLI

In a VMware vSphere environment, the hosts are the work horses; they provide the power on which the virtual machines run. So before you can deploy your virtual machines, you first have to deploy your hosts.

In this chapter, you will learn how to manage your hosts using PowerCLI. We will focus on:

- Adding a host to a VMware vCenter Server
- Enabling and disabling maintenance mode
- Working with host profiles
- Working with host services
- Configuring the host firewall
- Configuring vSphere Image Builder and Auto Deploy
- Using esxcli from PowerCLI
- Using the vSphere CLI commands from PowerCLI
- Removing a host from the VMware vCenter Server

Adding a host to a VMware vCenter Server

The VMware vCenter Server provides a centralized platform to manage your VMware vSphere environments. In this section, you will learn how to add a host to a VMware vCenter Server.

Creating a datacenter

After deploying a new vCenter Server, you cannot add a host to a vCenter Server until you have created a datacenter. So we will start with creating a datacenter. To create a datacenter, you have to use the `New-Datacenter` cmdlet. This cmdlet has the following syntax:

```
New-Datacenter [-Location] <VIContainer> [-Name] <String> [-Server
<VIServer[]>] [-WhatIf] [-Confirm] [<CommonParameters>]
```

The `-Location` and `-Name` parameters are required.

When you create a datacenter, you have to specify a value for the location parameter. This location has to be a folder. You can create the datacenter in the root of your vCenter Server environment. This root is actually a folder called `Datacenters`. You can also create a subfolder in the `Datacenters` folder and create the datacenter in this subfolder. It is not possible to create a datacenter in a folder inside another datacenter. You can use the next command to find all of the folders that can be used to create datacenters in:

```
PowerCLI C:\> Get-Folder -Type Datacenter

Name                            Type
----                            ----
Datacenters                     Datacenter
```

The next screenshot shows how you can create a datacenter in the vSphere Web Client. This is different from PowerCLI because you can specify the vCenter Server as the location in the vSphere Web Client.

In the following example, we will create a datacenter called New York in the Datacenters folder. First we use the Get-Folder cmdlet to get the Datacenters folder. Then we use the pipeline to pass the Datacenters folder to the -Location parameter of the New-Datacenter cmdlet. The -Location parameter accepts the pipeline input ByValue.

```
PowerCLI C:\> $Datacenter = Get-Folder -Name Datacenters |
>> New-Datacenter -Name "New York"
>>
PowerCLI C:\> $Datacenter


Name

----

New York
```

Creating a cluster

You probably want to create a cluster in which you place your hosts so you can take advantage of **High Availability (HA)** and **Dynamic Resource Scheduling (DRS)**. In *Chapter 8, Managing High Availability and Clustering with PowerCLI*, you will learn all about clusters. However, we will show you how to create a default cluster here, so you can make your hosts a member of the cluster.

The next screenshot shows how you can create a cluster in the vSphere Web Client.

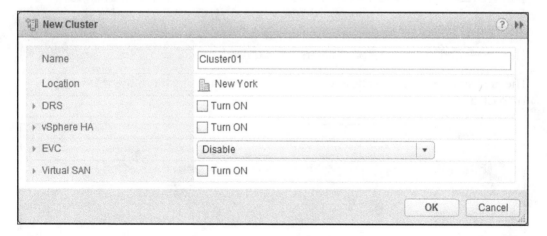

You have to use the `New-Cluster` cmdlet to create a cluster. The `New-Cluster` cmdlet has the following syntax:

```
New-Cluster [-HARestartPriority <HARestartPriority>]
[-HAIsolationResponse <HAIsolationResponse>] [-VMSwapfilePolicy
<VMSwapfilePolicy>] [-Name] <String> -Location <VIContainer> [-HAEnabled]
[-HAAdmissionControlEnabled] [-HAFailoverLevel <Int32>] [-DrsEnabled]
[-DrsMode <DrsMode>] [-DrsAutomationLevel <DrsAutomationLevel>]
[-VsanDiskClaimMode <VsanDiskClaimMode>] [-VsanEnabled [<Boolean>]]
[-Server <VIServer[]>] [-WhatIf] [-Confirm] [<CommonParameters>]
```

To create a default cluster, you only have to specify the name and location. The `-Name` and `-Location` parameters are required.

```
PowerCLI C:\> $Cluster = New-Cluster -Name Cluster01 -Location
$Datacenter
PowerCLI C:\> $Cluster
```

Name	HAEnabled	HAFailoverLevel	DrsEnabled	DrsAutomationLevel
Cluster01	False	1	False	FullyAutomated

Adding a host

To add a host to a VMware vCenter Server, you need to use the `Add-VMHost` cmdlet. This cmdlet has the following syntax:

```
Add-VMHost [-Name] <String> [-Port <Int32>] [-Location] <VIContainer>
[-Credential <PSCredential>] [-User <String>] [-Password <String>]
[-Force] [-RunAsync] [-Server <VIServer[]>] [-WhatIf] [-Confirm]
[<CommonParameters>]
```

The `-Name` and `-Location` parameters are required.

The next screenshot shows how you can add a host to a cluster in the vSphere Web Client:

While adding a host to a vCenter Server, you have to supply the username and the password for the user you want to use, to authenticate with the host. You can specify the username and password as a string or you can use the `-Credential` parameter and pass a PSCredential object created with the `Get-Credential` cmdlet. You also have to specify the DNS name or IP address of the host and the location where you want to add the host. Let's try to add the host to the cluster we created in the previous section.

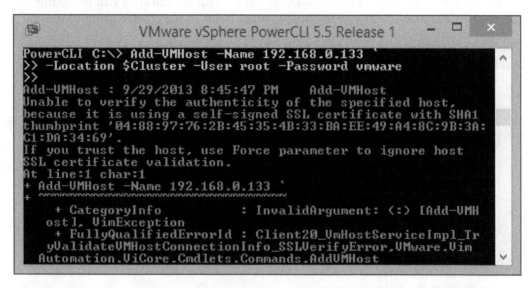

As you can see from the error message, the command failed because the host is using a self-signed SSL certificate. You have to give the host a trusted certificate or you can use the `-Force` parameter to skip the certificate check.

```
PowerCLI C:\> Add-VMHost -Name 192.168.0.133 -Location $Cluster `
>> -User root -Password vmware -Force
>>

Name                ConnectionState PowerState NumCpu CpuUsageMhz
----                --------------- ---------- ------ -----------
192.168.0.133       Connected       PoweredOn       2           0
```

The host is now added to the cluster. You can check this with:

```
PowerCLI C:\> $Cluster | Get-VMHost

Name                ConnectionState PowerState NumCpu CpuUsageMhz
----                --------------- ---------- ------ -----------
192.168.0.133       Connected       PoweredOn       2          49
```

Enabling and disabling maintenance mode

If you want to shut down, patch, upgrade, or reconfigure a host, you do not want any virtual machines running on the host. If you put a host in **maintenance mode**, you are sure that no virtual machines will be moved to or started on the host. If the host is running on a fully automated DRS-enabled cluster, the DRS will move the running virtual machines from the host to other hosts in the cluster using vMotion.

The next screenshot of the vSphere Web Client shows the different DRS automation levels that a cluster can have:

To put a host in maintenance mode, you have to use the Set-VMHost cmdlet.

This cmdlet has the following syntax:

```
Set-VMHost [-VMHost] <VMHost[]> [[-State] <VMHostState>]
[-VMSwapfilePolicy <VMSwapfilePolicy>] [-VMSwapfileDatastore <Datastore>]
[-Profile <VMHostProfile>] [-Evacuate] [-TimeZone <VMHostTimeZone>]
[-LicenseKey <String>] [-Server <VIServer[]>] [-RunAsync] [-WhatIf]
[-Confirm] [<CommonParameters>]
```

The -VMHost parameter is required.

To put a host in maintenance mode, you have to set the state to Maintenance. To disable maintenance mode, you have to set the state to Connected. The Set-VMHost -State parameter has a third possible value, which is Disconnected. You can use Disconnected to disconnect a host from the vCenter Server.

So let's put the host in maintenance mode first:

```
PowerCLI C:\> $VMHost = Get-VMHost -Name 192.168.0.133
PowerCLI C:\> $VMHost | Set-VMHost -State Maintenance
Name            ConnectionState PowerState NumCpu CpuUsageMhz
----            --------------- ---------- ------ -----------
192.168.0.133 Maintenance       PoweredOn        2          47
```

To disable maintenance mode, you have to use:

```
PowerCLI C:\> $VMHost | Set-VMHost -State Connected

Name            ConnectionState PowerState NumCpu CpuUsageMhz
----            --------------- ---------- ------ -----------
192.168.0.133 Connected         PoweredOn        2         139
```

Working with host profiles

A host profile is a collection of all of the configuration settings for an ESXi host, such as storage and networking configurations and security settings. You can create a host profile from a reference host or import an existing host profile. After attaching a host profile to a host, the host can be checked for compliance with the host profile. If the host is compliant, you know the settings of the host are the same as the settings of the host profile. If the host is not compliant, the host profile can be applied to the host to make the host compliant.

The next screenshot of the vSphere Web Client shows you some of the settings that you can configure in a host profile:

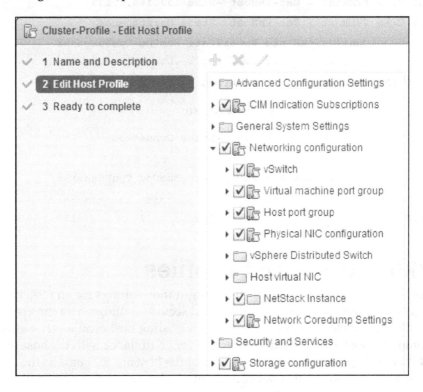

Common Information Model (CIM) Indication Subscriptions are subscriptions to the notifications for hardware-related events, such as problems with the cooling, battery, processor, memory, or power of an ESXi server.

Creating a host profile

To get started, you first need to configure a reference host. You have to configure general system settings, such as date and time configuration; network configuration, such as switches, portgroups and NICs; security and services; and storage and advanced configuration settings such as DirectPath I/O configuration. Once you are happy with the configuration of the reference host, you create a new host profile using the configuration of the reference host as a base. You need to use New-VMHostProfile to create the host profile.

The New-VMHostProfile cmdlet has the following syntax:

```
New-VMHostProfile [-Name] <String> [-ReferenceHost] <VMHost>
[-Description <String>] [-CompatibilityMode] [-Server <VIServer[]>]
[-WhatIf] [-Confirm] [<CommonParameters>]
```

Let's create a host profile called Cluster-Profile using host 192.168.0.133 as a reference host.

The next screenshot shows how you can create a host profile in the vSphere Web Client:

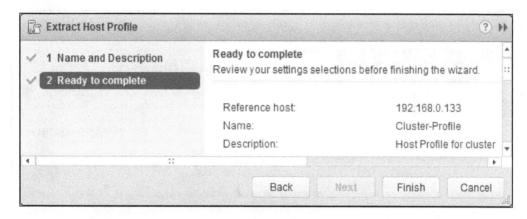

```
PowerCLI C:\> New-VMHostProfile -Name Cluster-Profile -ReferenceHost
192.168.0.133 -Description "Host Profile for cluster"
```

Name	Description
Cluster-Profile	Host Profile for cluster

Attaching the host profile to a cluster or a host

After creating the host profile, you have to attach the host profile to a cluster or a host. You can attach a profile using the PowerCLI Apply-VMHostProfile -AssociateOnly command.

The `Apply-VMHostProfile` cmdlet has the following syntax:

```
Apply-VMHostProfile [-Entity] <InventoryItem[]> [-Profile
<VMHostProfile>] [-Variable <Hashtable>] [-AssociateOnly]
[-ApplyOnly] [-RunAsync] [-Server <VIServer[]>] [-WhatIf] [-Confirm]
[<CommonParameters>]
```

The `-Entity` parameter is required and accepts pipeline input.

The next screenshot shows you how to attach a host profile in the vSphere Web Client.

Let's attach the host profile to cluster `Cluster01` we created earlier in this chapter.

```
PowerCLI C:> Get-Cluster -Name Cluster01 |
>> Apply-VMHostProfile -Profile Cluster-Profile -AssociateOnly
-Confirm:$false>>
>>

Name        HAEnabled HAFailoverLevel DrsEnabled DrsAutomationLevel
----        --------- --------------- ---------- ------------------
Cluster01 False       1               False      FullyAutomated
```

The `-Confirm:$false` parameter suppresses the prompt for confirmation before executing the command.

Testing the host profile for compliance

After attaching a host profile to a cluster or a host, you can use the `Test-VMHostProfileCompliance` cmdlet for compliance with the profile.

The `Test-VMHostProfileCompliance` cmdlet has the following syntax:

```
Test-VMHostProfileCompliance [-VMHost] <VMHost[]> [-UseCache] [[-Server]
<VIServer[]>] [<CommonParameters>]
```

```
Test-VMHostProfileCompliance [-Profile] <VMHostProfile[]> [-UseCache]
[[-Server] <VIServer[]>] [<CommonParameters>]
```

The `-VMHost` or `-Profile` parameter is required. The cmdlet has two parameter sets named `VMHostCompliance` and `ProfileCompliance`. You can use the first parameter set to specify a host to test for compliance with the attached profile. The second parameter set can be used to specify a host profile. All of the clusters and hosts attached to the profile will be tested for compliance against the host profile. There is no parameter set in which you can specify a cluster to check for compliance. If you want to check a cluster for compliance against a host profile, you either have to specify the host profile or all of the hosts in the cluster.

Let's test the `Cluster-Profile` host profile for compliance against all attached clusters and hosts:

```
PowerCLI C:\> Test-VMHostProfileCompliance -Profile Cluster-Profile
```

If the command returns nothing, it means that the host profile is compliant against all attached clusters and hosts. In this case, you could expect that the `Cluster-Profile` host profile is compliant because we used the host `192.168.0.133` as a reference host and this host is the only host in the cluster.

Let's add a second host to the cluster and test it for compliance:

```
PowerCLI C:\> Add-VMHost -Name 192.168.0.134 -Location $Cluster `
>> -User root -Password vmware -Force
>>
```

Name	ConnectionState	PowerState	NumCpu	CpuUsageMhz
192.168.0.134	Maintenance	PoweredOn	2	0

I made some changes to the configuration of the new host, so let's check if the `Test-VMHostProfileCompliance` cmdlet finds them:

```
PowerCLI C:\> Test-VMHostProfileCompliance -Profile Cluster-Profile |
>> Select-Object -ExpandProperty IncomplianceElementList
>>

PropertyName      Description
------------      -----------
network.ipRo...   Number of IPv4 routes did not match
network-vswi...   Additional vSwitch(es) vSwitch1 found
network-port...   Additional portgroup(s) vMotion found
```

As you can see, the command found three things that are not compliant with the host profile.

Applying a host profile to a host or cluster

You can apply a host profile to a host or cluster so that the configuration of this host or cluster becomes compliant with the host profile. To apply a host profile, you have to use the `Apply-VMHostProfile` cmdlet that we have used before to attach a host profile to a cluster or a host. The host or cluster must be in maintenance mode before you can apply a host profile to it.

We will set the host in maintenance mode first and then apply the host profile that is attached to the cluster:

```
PowerCLI C:\> $VMHost = Get-VMHost -Name 192.168.0.134
PowerCLI C:\> $VMHost | Set-VMHost -State Maintenance

Name            ConnectionState PowerState NumCpu CpuUsageMhz
----            --------------- ---------- ------ -----------
192.168.0.134   Maintenance     PoweredOn       2          45


PowerCLI C:\> $VMHost | Apply-VMHostProfile -Confirm:$false

Name            ConnectionState PowerState NumCpu CpuUsageMhz
----            --------------- ---------- ------ -----------
192.168.0.134   Maintenance     PoweredOn       2         420
```

You can now test the host for compliance with the host profile:

```
PowerCLI C:\> Test-VMHostProfileCompliance -VMHost $VMHost
```

If the command returns nothing, the host is compliant.

Using host profile answer files

If you apply a host profile and the host profile requires additional information, because settings are configured as `Prompt the user ...`, the `Apply-VMHostProfile` cmdlet will return a hash table with the settings that need to be answered. For example:

```
PowerCLI C:\> $VMHost = Get-VMHost -Name 192.168.0.134
PowerCLI C:\> $VMHost | Apply-VMHostProfile -Confirm:$false
```

```
Name                          Value
----                          -----
network.hostPortGroup["key-... 00:0c:29:4a:aa:55 network.
hostPortGroup["key-...
network.hostPortGroup["key-...
network.dnsConfig.HostNameP...
```

You can save the hash table in a `$HashTable` variable:

```
PowerCLI C:\> $HashTable = $VMHost |
>> Apply-VMHostProfile -Confirm:$false
>>
```

You can get the full key names of the hash table elements with:

```
PowerCLI C:\> $HashTable.Keys
network.hostPortGroup["key-vim-profile-host-HostPortgroupProfile-Ma
nagementNetwork"].MacAddressPolicy.mac
network.hostPortGroup["key-vim-profile-host-HostPortgroupProfile-Ma
nagementNetwork"].ipConfig.IpAddressPolicy.address
network.hostPortGroup["key-vim-profile-host-HostPortgroupProfile-Ma
nagementNetwork"].ipConfig.IpAddressPolicy.subnetmask
network.dnsConfig.HostNamePolicy.hostName
```

For every empty value in the hash table, you have to specify a value:

```
PowerCLI C:\> $HashTable['network.hostPortGroup["key-vim-profile-hos
t-HostPortgroupProfile-ManagementNetwork"].ipConfig.IpAddressPolicy.
address'] = '192.168.0.134'
PowerCLI C:\> $HashTable['network.hostPortGroup["key-vim-profile-hos
t-HostPortgroupProfile-ManagementNetwork"].ipConfig.IpAddressPolicy.
subnetmask'] = '255.255.255.0'
PowerCLI C:\> $HashTable['network.dnsConfig.HostNamePolicy.hostName'
] = 'Esx001'
```

You are now ready to apply the host profile to the host with the answers you provided in the hash table using the `$HashTable` variable as the value of the `-Variable` parameter:

```
PowerCLI C:\> $HashTable = $VMHost |
>> Apply-VMHostProfile -Variable $HashTable -Confirm:$false
>>
```

Exporting a host profile

You can use the `Export-VMHostProfile` cmdlet to export a host profile to a file that is in the VMware profile format (`.vpf`). This can be useful if you want to transfer a host profile to another vCenter Server. Just export the host profile on the first vCenter Server and then import the host profile on the second vCenter Server.

When exporting, a host profile administrator and user profile passwords are not exported for security reasons. When a host profile is imported and applied to a host, you will be prompted to enter values for the passwords.

The syntax of the `Export-VMHostProfile` cmdlet is:

```
Export-VMHostProfile [-FilePath] <String> [-Profile] <VMHostProfile>
[-Force] [-Server <VIServer>] [<CommonParameters>]
```

Let's export the `Cluster-Profile` host profile to a `.vpf` file:

```
PowerCLI C:\> Get-VMHostProfile -Name Cluster-Profile |
>> Export-VMHostProfile -FilePath ~\Cluster-Profile.vpf
>>
```

```
Mode              LastWriteTime         Length Name
----              -------------         ------ ----
-a---             12/29/2013  11:35 AM  911587 Cluster-Profile.vpf
```

The ~ character in the file path is a PowerShell way to specify the default directory of the current user account.

The `Cluster-Profile.vpf` file is an XML file that contains the configuration of the reference host that was used to create the host profile. This is a huge file. If you are wondering what is in this file, take a look at the content with Notepad or another editor.

Importing a host profile

You can use the `Import-VMHostProfile` cmdlet to import a host profile from a file.

The `Import-VMHostProfile` cmdlet has the following syntax:

```
Import-VMHostProfile [-FilePath] <String> [-Name] <String>
[[-ReferenceHost] <VMHost>] [-Description <String>] [-Server
<VIServer[]>] [-WhatIf] [-Confirm] [<CommonParameters>]
```

Let's import the `Cluster-Profile.vpf` file that we just created to create a new host profile called `New-Profile`:

```
PowerCLI C:\> Import-VMHostProfile -Name New-Profile `
>> -FilePath C:\Users\Robert\Cluster-Profile.vpf `
>> -ReferenceHost 192.168.0.133 -Description "New profile"
>>
```

```
Name                          Description
----                          -----------
New-Profile                   New profile
```

You can now attach `New-Profile` to a cluster or to a host.

> When writing this book, the Import-VMHostProfile cmdlet did not understand the ~ character in the value of the -FilePath parameter. This is why I used the full path for the Cluster-Profile.vpf file.

Working with host services

PowerCLI has a number of cmdlets to work with host services. You can easily find these cmdlets using the Get-Command cmdlet:

```
PowerCLI C:\> Get-Command -Noun VMHostService
```

```
CommandType  Name                    ModuleName
-----------  ----                    ----------
Cmdlet       Get-VMHostService       VMware.VimAutomation.Core
Cmdlet       Restart-VMHostService   VMware.VimAutomation.Core
Cmdlet       Set-VMHostService       VMware.VimAutomation.Core
Cmdlet       Start-VMHostService     VMware.VimAutomation.Core
Cmdlet       Stop-VMHostService      VMware.VimAutomation.Core
```

Retrieving information about host services

You can use the Get-VMHostService cmdlet to retrieve information about the services running on a host.

The syntax of the Get-VMHostService cmdlet is:

```
Get-VMHostService [-VMHost] <VMHost[]> [-Refresh] [-Server <VIServer[]>]
[<CommonParameters>]
```

Let's retrieve a list of all the services of one of the hosts:

```
PowerCLI C:\> Get-VMHostService -VMHost 192.168.0.133
```

Key	Label	Policy	Running
DCUI	Direct Console UI	on	True
TSM	ESXi Shell	off	False
TSM-SSH	SSH	off	False
lbtd	lbtd	on	True

lsassd	Local Security Authenticati...	off	False
lwiod	I/O Redirector (Active Dire...	off	False
netlogond	Network Login Server (Activ...	off	False
ntpd	NTP Daemon	off	False
sfcbd-watchdog	CIM Server	on	True
snmpd	snmpd	on	False
vmware-fdm	vSphere High Availability A...	off	False
vprobed	vprobed	off	False
vpxa	vpxa	on	True
xorg	xorg	on	False

 The default output of the Get-VMHostService cmdlet also shows the values of the Required property. I removed the Required column to fit the output to the page width of this book.

Starting a host service

Starting a host service can be useful to temporarily enable a service. For example, if you want to enable the ESXi shell to login into an ESXi server, you need to start the TSM service. The Start-VMHostService cmdlet will start a host service. The syntax of this cmdlet is:

```
Start-VMHostService [-HostService] <HostService[]> [-WhatIf] [-Confirm]
[<CommonParameters>]
```

The –HostService parameter is required.

For example, to start the TSM service, you can use:

```
PowerCLI C:\> Get-VMHost -Name 192.168.0.133 | Get-VMHostService |
>> Where-Object {$_.Key -eq "TSM"} | Start-VMHostService
>>
```

Key	Label	Policy	Running
---	-----	------	-------
TSM	ESXi Shell	off	True

Stopping a host service

After you have temporarily enabled a service, you should stop the service if you don't plan to use it anymore. Some services, such as the SSH service, produce a warning if you keep them running. To stop a service, you need to use the Stop-VMHostService cmdlet. The syntax is similar to the Start-VMHostService cmdlet's syntax:

```
Stop-VMHostService [-HostService] <HostService[]> [-WhatIf] [-Confirm]
[<CommonParameters>]
```

To stop the TSM service we started in the previous section, use the following command line:

```
PowerCLI C:\> Get-VMHost -Name 192.168.0.133 | Get-VMHostService |
>> Where-Object {$_.Key -eq 'TSM'} |
>> Stop-VMHostService -Confirm:$false
>>
```

Key	Label	Policy	Running
TSM	ESXi Shell	off	False

Restarting a host service

If you want to restart a host service because it is not running well or you modified the settings of the service, you can use the Restart-VMHostService cmdlet.

The syntax of this cmdlet is:

```
Restart-VMHostService [-HostService] <HostService[]> [-WhatIf] [-Confirm]
[<CommonParameters>]
```

In the next example, we will restart the TSM service. I modified this example, in comparison with the previous start and stop host services examples, to show you that in PowerCLI there are different ways you can use to perform a task.

```
PowerCLI C:\> $HostService = Get-VMHost -Name 192.168.0.133 |
>> Get-VMHostService | Where-Object {$_.Key -eq 'TSM'}
>> Restart-VMHostService -HostService $HostService -Confirm:$false
>>
```

Key	Label	Policy	Running	Required
TSM	ESXi Shell	off	True	False

Modifying the startup policy of a host service

You can use the Set-VMHostService cmdlet to modify the startup policy of a host service.

The next screenshot shows you how to edit the startup policy of a host service in the vSphere Web Client:

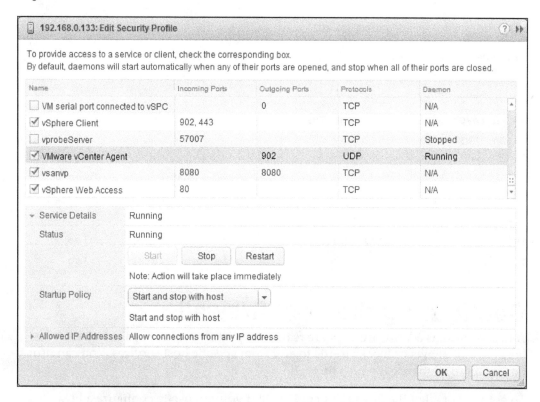

The syntax of the Set-VMHostService cmdlet is:

```
Set-VMHostService [-HostService] <HostService[]> [-Policy]
<HostServicePolicy> [-WhatIf] [-Confirm] [<CommonParameters>]
```

Possible values for the -Policy parameter are: automatic, on, and off. These values correspond with the following values in the VMware vSphere Client:

VMware vSphere Client service startup policy	Set-VMHostService –Policy value
Start and stop with port usage	automatic
Start and stop with host	on
Start and stop manually	off

Let's modify the startup policy of the TSM service and set it to on. We will use the $HostService variable from the previous example:

```
PowerCLI C:\> Set-VMHostService -HostService $HostService -Policy on
```

Key	Label	Policy	Running	Required
TSM	ESXi Shell	on	True	False

In the next example, the startup policy of the TSM service for all of your hosts will be set to off:

```
PowerCLI C:\> Get-VMHost | Get-VMHostService |
>> Where-Object {$_.Key -eq 'TSM'} |
>> Set-VMHostService -Policy Off
>>
```

Key	Label	Policy	Running	Required
TSM	ESXi Shell	off	True	False
TSM	ESXi Shell	off	False	False

Configuring the host firewall

A host firewall is a VMware vSphere feature to protect the host against attacks. The host firewall allows or blocks traffic to and from specific host services. You can use PowerCLI to configure the host firewall.

To get a list of all of the PowerCLI cmdlets that you can use to configure a host firewall, type:

```
PowerCLI C:\> Get-Command -Noun VMHostFirewall*
```

CommandType	Name
Cmdlet	Get-VMHostFirewallDefaultPolicy
Cmdlet	Get-VMHostFirewallException
Cmdlet	Set-VMHostFirewallDefaultPolicy
Cmdlet	Set-VMHostFirewallException

Getting the host firewall default policy

To get the host firewall default policy of a host, you have to use the `Get-VMHostFirewallDefaultPolicy` cmdlet.

The syntax of the `Get-VMHostFirewallDefaultPolicy` cmdlet is:

```
Get-VMHostFirewallDefaultPolicy [-VMHost] <VMHost[]> [[-Server]
<VIServer[]>] [<CommonParameters>]
```

Let's first get the host firewall default policy for a host:

```
PowerCLI C:\> $VMHost = Get-VMHost -Name 192.168.0.133
PowerCLI C:\> Get-VMHostFirewallDefaultPolicy -VMHost $VMHost


IncomingEnabled OutgoingEnabled
--------------- ---------------
False           False
```

In the given example, the default policy is that the incoming and outgoing traffic is disabled. This is, of course, the most secure policy and it is recommended to keep this policy unless you have a very good reason to change it.

Modifying the host firewall default policy

You can change the host firewall default policy using the `Set-VMHostFirewallDefaultPolicy` cmdlet.

The `Set-VMHostFirewallDefaultPolicy` cmdlet has the following syntax:

```
Set-VMHostFirewallDefaultPolicy [[-AllowIncoming] [<Boolean>]]
[[-AllowOutgoing] [<Boolean>]] [-Policy] <VMHostFirewallDefaultPolicy[]>
[-WhatIf] [-Confirm] [<CommonParameters>]
```

If your host firewall default policy enables incoming or outgoing traffic, you can set it to be disabled for both with:

```
PowerCLI C:\> $VMHost = Get-VMHost -Name 192.168.0.133
PowerCLI C:\> $Policy = $VMHost | Get-VMHostFirewallDefaultPolicy
PowerCLI C:\> $Policy | Set-VMHostFirewallDefaultPolicy `
>> -AllowIncoming $false -AllowOutgoing $false
>>


IncomingEnabled OutgoingEnabled
--------------- ---------------
False           False
```

Getting the host firewall exceptions

You can specify exceptions from the host firewall default policy. To get a list of all of the exceptions for a specific host, you have to use the Get-VMHostFirewallException cmdlet.

This cmdlet has the following syntax:

```
Get-VMHostFirewallException [[-Name] <String[]>] [-VMHost] <VMHost[]>
[-Port <Int32[]>] [-Enabled [<Boolean>]] [-Server <VIServer[]>]
[<CommonParameters>]
```

To get a list of all of the exceptions, you can use:

```
PowerCLI C:\> $VMHost | Get-VMHostFirewallException
```

Name	Enabled	IncomingPorts	OutgoingPorts	Protocols
CIM Server	True	5988		TCP
CIM Secure Server	True	5989		TCP
CIM SLP	True	427	427	UDP, TCP
DHCPv6	True	546	547	TCP, UDP
DVFilter	False	2222		TCP
DVSSync	False	8301, 8302	8302, 8301	UDP
HBR	True		31031, 44046	TCP
IKED	False	500	500	UDP
NFC	True	902	902	TCP
WOL	True		9	UDP
Active Directory All	False		88, 123, 13...	UDP, TCP
DHCP Client	True	68	68	UDP
DNS Client	True	53	53	UDP, TCP
Fault Tolerance	True	8100, 8200,...	80, 8100, 8...	TCP, UDP
vSphere High Avai...	False	8182	8182	TCP, UDP
FTP Client	False	20	21	TCP
gdbserver	False	1000-9999, ...		TCP
httpClient	False		80, 443	TCP
Software iSCSI Cl...	False		3260	TCP
NFS Client	False		0-65535	TCP
NTP Client	False		123	UDP
VM serial port co...	False	23, 1024-65535	0-65535	TCP

SNMP Server	True	161		UDP
SSH Client	False		22	TCP
SSH Server	True	22		TCP
syslog	False		514, 1514	UDP, TCP
vCenter Update Ma...	False		80, 9000-9100	TCP
vMotion	True	8000	8000	TCP
VM serial port co...	False		0-65535	TCP
vSphere Client	True	902, 443		TCP
vprobeServer	False	57007		TCP
VMware vCenter Agent	True		902	UDP
vSphere Web Access	True	80		TCP

You can use the -Name or -Port parameters to filter for a specific exception. For example, to get all of the exceptions for port number 22, use:

```
PowerCLI C:\> $VMHost | Get-VMHostFirewallException -Port 22
```

Name	Enabled	IncomingPorts	OutgoingPorts	Protocols
----	-------	-------------	-------------	---------
NFS Client	False		0-65535	TCP
VM serial port co...	False	23, 1024-65535	0-65535	TCP
SSH Client	False		22	TCP
SSH Server	True	22		TCP
VM serial port co...	False		0-65535	TCP

Modifying a host firewall exception

Sometimes it is necessary to make changes to the host firewall exceptions, for example, when you want to configure an external syslog server. In this section, I will show you how to do this.

To modify the host firewall exceptions, you have to use the Set-VMHostFirewallException cmdlet. This cmdlet has the following syntax:

```
Set-VMHostFirewallException [-Enabled] [<Boolean>] [-Exception]
<VMHostFirewallException[]> [-WhatIf] [-Confirm] [<CommonParameters>]
```

Let's assume that we have configured a syslog server on a vCenter Server 192.168.0.132. To configure the syslog server on the host, you can use the Set-VMHostSysLogServer cmdlet. The syntax of this cmdlet is:

```
Set-VMHostSysLogServer [[-SysLogServer] <NamedIPEndPoint>] [-VMHost]
<VMHost[]> [-SysLogServerPort <Int32>] [-Server <VIServer[]>] [-WhatIf]
[-Confirm] [<CommonParameters>]
```

First you need to set the remote syslog server:

```
PowerCLI C:\> $VMHost | Set-VMHostSysLogServer `
>> -SysLogServer 192.168.0.132 -SysLogServerPort 514
>>

Host                              Port
----                              ----
192.168.0.132                     514
```

After this, you have to enable the host firewall exception for the syslog server:

```
PowerCLI C:\> $VMHost | Get-VMHostFirewallException -Name syslog | `
>> Set-VMHostFirewallException -Enabled $true
>>

Name          Enabled IncomingPorts  OutgoingPorts  Protocols
----          ------- -------------  -------------  ---------
syslog        True                   514, 1514      UDP, TCP
```

Configuring vSphere Image Builder and Auto Deploy

VMware vSphere Auto Deploy is a cool feature introduced in VMware vSphere 5.0 that enables you to provide physical hosts with the ESXi software via the PXE boot instead of installing an ESXi server from a CD-ROM. Auto Deploy can be useful if you need to deploy many ESXi servers. If you only have a few ESXi servers, Auto Deploy is probably not the best solution for you because of the amount of work you have to do to set up Auto Deploy. To enable Auto Deploy, you need a vCenter Server, an Auto Deploy server, a DNS server, a DHCP server, a TFTP server, and PowerCLI. Yes, you have seen it right. PowerCLI is a core component of Auto Deploy. All the information you need to enable and configure Auto Deploy can be found in the VMware document, "vSphere Installation and Setup Guide". You can download this document from the VMware vSphere documentation page: https://www.vmware.com/support/pubs/vsphere-esxi-vcenter-server-pubs.html

Because this is a PowerCLI book, we will focus on the PowerCLI cmdlets that you can use to create and deploy a host image.

Configuring Image Builder

Before you can deploy an image using Auto Deploy, you first have to create the image using Image Builder. In PowerCLI, the Image Builder cmdlets are in a separate module called `VMware.ImageBuilder`. This module is loaded by default if you start PowerCLI. Let's get a list of all of the Image Builder cmdlets:

```
PowerCLI C:\> Get-Command -Module VMware.ImageBuilder
```

```
CommandType  Name                        ModuleName
-----------  ----                        ----------
Cmdlet       Add-EsxSoftwareDepot        VMware.ImageBuilder
Cmdlet       Add-EsxSoftwarePackage      VMware.ImageBuilder
Cmdlet       Compare-EsxImageProfile     VMware.ImageBuilder
Cmdlet       Export-EsxImageProfile      VMware.ImageBuilder
Cmdlet       Get-EsxImageProfile         VMware.ImageBuilder
Cmdlet       Get-EsxSoftwareDepot        VMware.ImageBuilder
Cmdlet       Get-EsxSoftwarePackage      VMware.ImageBuilder
Cmdlet       New-EsxImageProfile         VMware.ImageBuilder
Cmdlet       Remove-EsxImageProfile      VMware.ImageBuilder
Cmdlet       Remove-EsxSoftwareDepot     VMware.ImageBuilder
Cmdlet       Remove-EsxSoftwarePackage   VMware.ImageBuilder
Cmdlet       Set-EsxImageProfile         VMware.ImageBuilder
```

First, you have to add an ESXi software depot to your PowerCLI session. An ESXi software depot contains image profiles and **vSphere Installation Bundle (VIB)** files. An image profile is a list of VIBs. If you want to know what is in a VIB, you can find out at http://blogs.vmware.com/vsphere/2011/09/whats-in-a-vib.html.

Use the `Add-EsxSoftwareDepot` cmdlet to add an ESXi software depot to your PowerCLI session. You can use an ESXi software depot provided on the VMware website or you can download the ESXi installable from the VMware website in the `depot.zip` format. For example, for ESXi 5.5, this file is called `VMware-ESXi-5.5.0-1331820-depot.zip`.

The `Add-EsxSoftwareDepot` cmdlet has the following syntax:

```
Add-EsxSoftwareDepot [-DepotUrl] <String[]> [-WarningAction
<ActionPreference>] [-WarningVariable <String>] [<CommonParameters>]
```

To add the official VMware software depot to your PowerCLI session, use:

```
PowerCLI C:\> Add-EsxSoftwareDepot -DepotUrl https://hostupdate.vmwa
re.com/software/VUM/PRODUCTION/main/vmw-depot-index.xml


Depot Url
---------

https://hostupdate.vmware.com/software/VUM/PRODUCTION/main/vmw-d...
```

If you want to deploy HA modules for your ESXi servers, you also have to connect to the HA depot on your vCenter Server. For example:

```
PowerCLI C:\> Add-EsxSoftwareDepot `
>> -DepotUrl http://192.168.0.132/vSphere-HA-depot/index.xml
>>


Depot Url
---------

http://192.168.0.132/vSphere-HA-depot/index.xml
```

To add the software depot from a depot.zip file that you downloaded from the VMware website, use:

```
PowerCLI C:\> Add-EsxSoftwareDepot -DepotUrl 'C:\users\robert\Downlo
ads\VMware vSphere 5.5\VMware-ESXi-5.5.0-1331820-depot.zip'


Depot Url
---------

zip:C:\users\robert\Downloads\VMware vSphere 5.5\VMware-ESXi-5.5...
```

After adding an ESXi software depot to your PowerCLI session, you can use the Get-EsxImageProfile cmdlet to see the contents of the ESXi software depot.

The Get-EsxImageProfile cmdlet has the following syntax:

```
Get-EsxImageProfile [[-Name] <String[]>] [[-Vendor] <String[]>]
[[-AcceptanceLevel] <AcceptanceLevels[]>] [-WarningAction
<ActionPreference>] [-WarningVariable <String>] [-WhatIf] [-Confirm]
[<CommonParameters>]
```

For example:

```
PowerCLI C:\> Get-EsxImageProfile
```

```
Name                         Vendor       Last Modified        Accepta
                                                                nce Lev

----                         ------       -------------        -------
ESXi-5.5.0-1331820-standard VMware, Inc. 9/19/2013 6:07:00 AM Partner
ESXi-5.5.0-1331820-no-tools VMware, Inc. 9/19/2013 6:07:00 AM Partner
```

Configuring Auto Deploy

The Auto Deploy cmdlets are in the PowerCLI module VMware.DeployAutomation.
You can use the Get-Command cmdlet to list all the Auto Deploy cmdlets:

```
PowerCLI C:\> Get-Command -Module VMware.DeployAutomation
```

```
CommandType Name                            ModuleName

----------- ----                            ----------
Cmdlet      Add-DeployRule                  VMware.DeployAutomation
Cmdlet      Apply-ESXImageProfile           VMware.DeployAutomation
Cmdlet      Copy-DeployRule                 VMware.DeployAutomation
Cmdlet      Get-DeployOption                VMware.DeployAutomation
Cmdlet      Get-DeployRule                  VMware.DeployAutomation
Cmdlet      Get-DeployRuleSet               VMware.DeployAutomation
Cmdlet      Get-VMHostAttributes            VMware.DeployAutomation
Cmdlet      Get-VMHostImageProfile          VMware.DeployAutomation
Cmdlet      Get-VMHostMatchingRules         VMware.DeployAutomation
Cmdlet      New-DeployRule                  VMware.DeployAutomation
Cmdlet      Remove-DeployRule               VMware.DeployAutomation
Cmdlet      Repair-DeployImageCache         VMware.DeployAutomation
Cmdlet      Repair-DeployRuleSetCompliance VMware.DeployAutomation
Cmdlet      Set-DeployOption                VMware.DeployAutomation
Cmdlet      Set-DeployRule                  VMware.DeployAutomation
Cmdlet      Set-DeployRuleSet               VMware.DeployAutomation
Cmdlet      Switch-ActiveDeployRuleSet      VMware.DeployAutomation
Cmdlet      Test-DeployRuleSetCompliance    VMware.DeployAutomation
```

Now that we have the image profiles created with Image Builder, we need to create deploy rules to specify the image to be deployed to the hosts. You can create a deploy rule using the `New-DeployRule` cmdlet that has the following syntax:

```
New-DeployRule [-Name] <String> -Pattern <String[]> -Item
<VIObjectCore[]> [<CommonParameters>]
```

```
New-DeployRule [-Name] <String> -AllHosts -Item <VIObjectCore[]>
[<CommonParameters>]
```

Let's create a deploy rule that will deploy the `ESXi-5.5.0-1331820-standard` image to all hosts:

```
PowerCLI C:\> New-DeployRule -Name ImageRule `
>> -Item ESXi-5.5.0-1331820-standard -AllHosts
>>
```

The preceding command generates too much output to show in this book.

You also need to create a deploy rule that specifies the location for the hosts. Let's locate the hosts in the datacenter `New York`:

```
PowerCLI C:\> New-DeployRule -Name LocationRule -Item "New York" `
>> -AllHosts
>>


Name        : LocationRule
PatternList :
ItemList    : {New York}
```

Now, we have to add the newly created rules to the working ruleset using the `Add-DeployRule` cmdlet. The `Add-DeployRule` cmdlet has the following syntax:

```
Add-DeployRule [-DeployRule] <DeployRule[]> [[-At] <UInt32>]
[-NoActivate] [<CommonParameters>]
```

To add both rules to the working ruleset, use:

```
PowerCLI C:\> Add-DeployRule -DeployRule ImageRule

Name        : ImageRule
PatternList :
ItemList    : {ESXi-5.5.0-1331820-standard}


PowerCLI C:\> Add-DeployRule -DeployRule LocationRule

Name        : ImageRule
PatternList :
ItemList    : {ESXi-5.5.0-1331820-standard}


Name        : LocationRule
PatternList :
ItemList    : {New York}
```

To check which rulesets are active, you can use the Get-DeployRuleSet cmdlet. This cmdlet has the following syntax:

```
Get-DeployRuleSet [-Active] [-Working] [<CommonParameters>]
```

The cmdlet has two parameters –Active and –Working. The –Active parameter will retrieve the active ruleset. The active ruleset shows how new hosts are to be deployed. The –Working parameter will retrieve the working ruleset. This ruleset can be used to test changes before making them active.

Let's retrieve the active deploy ruleset:

```
PowerCLI C:\> Get-DeployRuleSet -Active

Name        : ImageRule
PatternList :
ItemList    : {ESXi-5.5.0-1331820-standard}


Name        : LocationRule
PatternList :
ItemList    : {New York}
```

Now, you are almost ready to deploy hosts using Auto Deploy. The hosts only need configuration, which will be done using host profiles. You have to connect the host profiles to Auto Deploy using deploy rules. Let's assume you have a host profile called `Cluster-Profile`. You can connect this host profile to Auto Deploy using the `New-DeployRule` and `Add-DeployRule` cmdlets that you have seen before. Let's create a deploy rule named `HostProfileRule`, which connects the host profile `Cluster-Profile` to all hosts:

```
PowerCLI C:\> New-DeployRule -Name HostProfileRule `
>> -Item Cluster-Profile -AllHosts
>>


Name        : HostProfileRule
PatternList :
ItemList    : {Cluster-Profile}


PowerCLI C:\> Add-DeployRule -DeployRule HostProfileRule



Name        : ImageRule
PatternList :
ItemList    : {ESXi-5.5.0-1331820-standard}

Name        : LocationRule
PatternList :
ItemList    : {New York}

Name        : HostProfileRule
PatternList :
ItemList    : {Cluster-Profile}
```

To configure the host name and IP addresses, the preferred way is to use static DHCP entries. An alternative is to use static IP addresses in the host profile and use answer files for each host.

Using esxcli from PowerCLI

VMware offers more command-line interfaces for vSphere than PowerCLI. One of them is the **vSphere Command-Line Interface (vSphere CLI)**. The vSphere CLI has a command called `esxcli`. PowerCLI has built-in support for this `esxcli` command in the `Get-EsxCli` cmdlet.

> There are no `New-EsxCli`, `Set-EsxCli`, and `Remove EsxCli` cmdlets. The `Get-EsxCli` cmdlet exposes the `esxcli` functionality for a host. You cannot create a new one, modify, or remove it.

The syntax of the `Get-EsxCli` cmdlet is:

```
Get-EsxCli -VMHost <VMHost[]> [[-Server] <VIServer[]>]
[<CommonParameters>]
```

Use the `Get-EsxCli` cmdlet to connect to the `esxcli` functionality of a host and save the connection in a variable `$esxcli`:

```
PowerCLI C:\> $esxcli = Get-EsxCli -VMHost 192.168.0.133
```

In the vSphere CLI, the command to get information about the CPUs in your host is:

```
C:\>esxcli --server=192.168.0.133 hardware cpu list
Enter username: root
Enter password:
```

In PowerCLI, the command becomes a little different. The `Get-EsxCLI` cmdlet returns a PowerShell object and you have to use the properties and methods of this object to create the commands. This is why you have to put dots between all of the words in the command. And if the last word is a method, you have to specify parentheses for a parameter list even if there are no parameters. The command from the preceding example becomes the following in PowerCLI:

```
PowerCLI C:\> $esxcli.hardware.cpu.list()
```

You can, of course, use the vSphere documentation to find the available `esxcli` commands. But you can also use PowerCLI for help. If you type in a partial command, you will get a list of elements and methods that are possible for this command. Let's start with `$esxcli` itself:

```
PowerCLI C:\> $esxcli

=====================
EsxCli: 192.168.0.133
```

```
Elements:
---------
device
esxcli
fcoe
graphics
hardware
iscsi
network
sched
software
storage
system
vm
vsan
```

You see that one of the elements is `hardware`. Let's try `hardware` as the next command:

```
PowerCLI C:\> $esxcli.hardware
```

```
========================
EsxCliElement: hardware

    Elements:
    ---------
    bootdevice
    clock
    cpu
    ipmi
    memory
    pci
    platform
    trustedboot
```

You now have all the command elements you can use after `hardware`. Let's try `cpu`:

```
PowerCLI C:\> $esxcli.hardware.cpu

==================
EsxCliElement: cpu

    Elements:
    ---------
    cpuid
    global


    Methods:
    --------
    Cpu[] list()
```

And now you have obtained the `list()` method that we used in the previous example.

A lot of the `esxcli` commands also provide a `help()` method that gives information about the command. To get help about the `$esxcli.hardware.cpu` command, type:

```
PowerCLI C:\> $esxcli.hardware.cpu.help()

=====================================================================
vim.EsxCLI.hardware.cpu
---------------------------------------------------------------------
CPU information.


ChildElement
---------------------------------------------------------------------
- hardware.cpu.cpuid | Information from the CPUID instruction on ea
                     | ch CPU.
- hardware.cpu.globa | Information and configuration global to all
  l                  | CPUs.


Method
---------------------------------------------------------------------
- list               | List all of the CPUs on this host.
```

If you want to know what the parameters for an esxcli method are, you can use the vSphere documentation or you can use the Get-Member cmdlet:

```
PowerCLI C:\> $esxcli.hardware.cpu | Get-Member
```

```
    TypeName:
VMware.VimAutomation.ViCore.Impl.V1.EsxCli.EsxCliElementImpl
```

Name	MemberType	Definition
list	CodeMethod	vim.EsxCLI.hardware.cpu.list.Cpu[]...
cpuid	CodeProperty	VMware.VimAutomation.Sdk.Util10Ps....
global	CodeProperty	VMware.VimAutomation.Sdk.Util10Ps....
ConvertToVersion	Method	T VersionedObjectInterop.ConvertTo...
Equals	Method	bool Equals(System.Object obj)
GetHashCode	Method	int GetHashCode()
GetType	Method	type GetType()
help	Method	VMware.VimAutomation.ViCore.Types....
IsConvertableTo	Method	bool VersionedObjectInterop.IsConv...
ToString	Method	string ToString()
Client	Property	VMware.VimAutomation.ViCore.Intero...
FullName	Property	string FullName {get;}
Id	Property	string Id {get;}
Name	Property	string Name {get;}
Uid	Property	string Uid {get;}

The relevant information in the Definition column is abbreviated because of the limited width of a book page. You will get more information if you run this command in a PowerCLI session with a larger window width.

Listing all of the available esxcli commands

You can use PowerCLI to list all of the available esxcli commands for a host using the Get-ESXCliCommand function. If you save the function in a file called Get-EsxCliCommand.ps1, you can load the function into your PowerCLI session by dot-sourcing the file:

```
PowerCLI C:\> . .\Get-EsxCliCommand.ps1
```

Dot-sourcing is the PowerShell way to load the functions of a PowerShell script into your PowerShell session. You have to specify a dot and a space in front of the path to a PowerShell script file. If you just run the PowerShell script without dot-sourcing, after the script is finished the functions defined in the script will not be available in your PowerShell session.

Now that you have loaded the `Get-ESXCliCommand` function into your PowerCLI session, you can call the function with the `$esxcli` variable as the `-EsxCli` parameter value to list all the available `esxcli` commands:

```
PowerCLI C:\> Get-EsxCliCommand -EsxCli $esxcli
```

Showing the output of the preceding command is beyond the scope of this book. If you want to see the output and all of the possible `esxcli` commands, take a look at my blogpost at `http://rvdnieuwendijk.com/2012/08/19/how-to-list-all-the-powercli-esxcli-commands/` where you can also download the `Get-EsxCliCommand` function.

```
function Get-EsxCliCommand {
```

The `Get-EsxCliCommand` function starts with the comment-based function `help`. This makes it possible that, after defining the function in your PowerCLI session, you can use the `Get-Help` cmdlet to get help about the function:

```
<#
 .SYNOPSIS
   Lists all the possible PowerCLI ESXCLI commands.

 .DESCRIPTION
   Lists all the possible PowerCLI ESXCLI commands.

 .PARAMETER EsxCli
   The VMware.VimAutomation.ViCore.Impl.V1.EsxCli.EsxCliImpl or
   VMware.VimAutomation.ViCore.Impl.V1.EsxCli.EsxCliElementImpl
   object for which all the possible PowerCLI ESXCLI command
   must be returned.

 .PARAMETER Name
   The top level name of the listed commands. The default is
   '$esxcli'.

 .EXAMPLE
   PS C:\> $esxcli = Get-EsxCli -VMhost ESX1.yourdomain.com
   PS C:\> Get-EsxCliCommand -EsxCli $esxcli
```

```
                Lists all the PowerCLI ESXCLI commands for server
                ESX1.yourdomain.com.

            .EXAMPLE
                PS C:\> $esxcli = Get-EsxCli -VMhost ESX1.yourdomain.com
                PS C:\> Get-EsxCliCommand -EsxCli $esxcli.network `
                        -Name '$esxcli.network'

                Lists all the PowerCLI ESXCLI network commands for server
                ESX1.yourdomain.com.

            .INPUTS
                VMware.VimAutomation.ViCore.Impl.V1.EsxCli.EsxCliImpl
                VMware.VimAutomation.ViCore.Impl.V1.EsxCli.EsxCliElementImpl
                System.String

            .OUTPUTS
                System.String

            .NOTES
                Author: Robert van den Nieuwendijk
                Version: 1.0
                Date: 19-8-2012

            .LINK
                http://rvdnieuwendijk.com/

    #>
```

The next part of the function defines the output of the function as a string, the
-EsxCli parameter as a mandatory parameter, and -Name as a parameter consisting
of an array of strings. The -Name parameter is used in recursive calls to the function
to specify the name of the current position in the tree:

```
    [CmdletBinding()]
    [OutputType([string])]
    param(
        [parameter(Mandatory=$true,Position=0)]$EsxCli,
        [parameter(Position=1)][String[]]$Name='$esxcli'
    )
```

The next part writes the current `esxcli` command to the output:

```
# Write the current command to the output stream
[string]::Join('.',$Name)
```

The next part uses recursion to list all of the properties of the current `esxcli` command. Recursion means that a function calls itself. The `Get-Member` cmdlet is used to select only the properties:

```
# List all the properties recursive
$EsxCli |
  Get-Member -MemberType CodeProperty |
  ForEach-Object {
    if ($_)
    {
      # Call this function recursive for a sublevel
      $SubLevel = $_.Name
      Get-EsxCliCommand -EsxCli $EsxCli.$SubLevel -Name `
        ($Name + $SubLevel)
    }
  }
```

The next part uses recursion to list all of the methods of the current `esxcli` command. The `Get-Member` cmdlet is used to select only the methods:

```
# List all the methods
$EsxCli |
  Get-Member -MemberType CodeMethod |
  ForEach-Object {
    if ($_)
    {
      # Write the method to the output stream
      $SubLevel = $_.Name
      [string]::Join('.',$Name) + '.' + $SubLevel + `
        '(' + $_.Definition.Split('(')[1]
    }
  }
}
```

Using the vSphere CLI commands from PowerCLI

If you installed both VMware vSphere PowerCLI and VMware vSphere CLI on the same computer, you can use the vSphere CLI Perl commands from PowerCLI. Using the VMware vSphere CLI commands, you can perform tasks that you cannot do with PowerCLI natively, such as configuring IPsec on your ESXi host with the `vicfg-ipsec` command.

The `Add-vCLIfunction` function creates a function string for each Perl script in the vSphere CLI bin directory. The function strings are executed using the PowerShell `Invoke-Expression` cmdlet. This creates a PowerShell function for each vSphere CLI Perl script.

```
function Add-vCLIfunction {
  <#
  .SYNOPSIS
    Adds the VMware vSphere Command-Line Interface Perl scripts
    as PowerCLI functions.

  .DESCRIPTION
    Adds all the VMware vSphere Command-Line Interface Perl
    scripts as PowerCLI functions.
    VMware vSphere Command-Line Interface has to be installed on
    the system where you run this function.
    You can download the VMware vSphere Command-Line Interface
    from:

http://communities.vmware.com/community/vmtn/server/vsphere/
automationtools/vsphere_cli?view=overview

  .EXAMPLE
    Add-vCLIfunction
    Adds all the VMware vSphere Command-Line Interface Perl
    scripts as PowerCLI functions to your PowerCLI session.

  .COMPONENT
    VMware vSphere PowerCLI
```

```
.NOTES
  Author:   Robert van den Nieuwendijk
  Date:     12/29/2013
  Version:  1.1

.LINK
  http://rvdnieuwendijk.com/

#>


# Test if VMware vSphere Command-Line Interface is installed
if (${env:ProgramFiles(x86)})
{
  $ProgramFiles = ${env:ProgramFiles(x86)}
}
else
{
  $ProgramFiles = $env:ProgramFiles
}
$vCLIBinDirectory = "$ProgramFiles\VMware\VMware vSphere CLI\Bin\"
If (-not (Test-Path -Path $vCLIBinDirectory)) {
  Write-Error "VMware vSphere CLI should be installed before running
this function."
  }
  else {
    # Add all the VMware vSphere CLI perl scripts as PowerCLI
    # functions
    Get-ChildItem -Path "$vCLIBinDirectory\*.pl" |
    ForEach-Object {
      $Function = "function global:$($_.Name.Split('.')[0]) { perl
'$vCLIBinDirectory\$($_.Name)'"
      $Function += ' $args }'
      Invoke-Expression $Function
    }
  }
}
```

After you have run the `Add-vCLIfunction` function, you can use the vSphere CLI Perl scripts from your PowerCLI session. The next example uses the vSphere CLI `vicfg-nics -1` command to retrieve all of the NICs from all of the hosts. Although I know that you can do this in PowerCLI as well, using the `Get-VMHostNetworkAdapter` cmdlet, I use this example to show the power of the combination of PowerCLI and vSphere CLI.

To prevent you from having to enter the username and password for every vSphere CLI command that you run, you can store them in the environment variables VI_USERNAME and VI_PASSWORD:

```
# Example how you can use PowerCLI to run VMware vSphere CLI
# Perl scripts
Add-vCLIfunction
$env:VI_USERNAME="root"
$env:VI_PASSWORD="TopSecret"
Get-VMHost | ForEach-Object {
  vicfg-nics -l --server $_.Name
}
```

You can use the method shown in the Add-vCLIfunction function to extend PowerShell with custom functions from third-party binaries.

Removing a host from the VMware vCenter Server

To remove a host from your vCenter Server inventory, you have to use the Remove-VMHost cmdlet. The Remove-VMHost cmdlet has the following syntax:

```
Remove-VMHost [-VMHost] <VMHost[]> [-Server <VIServer[]>] [-WhatIf]
[-Confirm] [<CommonParameters>]
```

Let's try to remove a host as seen in the following screenshot:

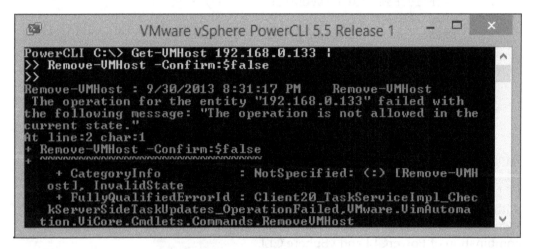

The operation failed because the host should have been in maintenance mode or a disconnected state before you could remove it.

So let's put the host in maintenance mode first and then try to remove it:

```
PowerCLI C:\> $VMHost = Get-VMHost -Name 192.168.0.133
PowerCLI C:\> $VMHost | Set-VMHost -State Maintenance


Name                ConnectionState PowerState NumCpu CpuUsageMhz
----                --------------- ---------- ------ -----------
192.168.0.133       Maintenance     PoweredOn     2           41


PowerCLI C:\> $VMHost | Remove-VMHost -Confirm:$false
```

The preceding command sets the host in maintenance mode and will remove it from the vCenter Server inventory and cluster.

Summary

In this chapter, we covered working with ESXi hosts using PowerCLI. You saw how to add and remove hosts to and from your vSphere vCenter Server inventory. We looked at putting a host in maintenance mode and how to exit maintenance mode. We have seen how PowerCLI commands work with host profiles and host services. You learned to use the PowerCLI commands for Image Builder and Auto Deploy and finally the use of the esxcli command and the vSphere CLI commands from PowerCLI was discussed.

The next chapter will be about managing virtual machines with PowerCLI.

5

Managing Virtual Machines with PowerCLI

As a VMware vSphere administrator, you probably spend a lot of your time creating, modifying, or removing virtual machines. In this chapter, you will learn how to do this with PowerCLI.

The topics that will be covered in this chapter are:

- Creating a virtual machine
- Registering a virtual machine
- Using OS customization specifications
- Starting and stopping a virtual machine
- Modifying the settings of a virtual machine
- Converting a virtual machine into a template
- Moving a virtual machine to another folder, host, cluster, resource pool, or datastore
- Updating VMware Tools
- Upgrading the virtual machine compatibility
- Using snapshots
- Running commands in the guest OS
- Configuring Fault Tolerance
- Opening the console of a virtual machine
- Removing a virtual machine

Creating a virtual machine

There are several ways in which you can create a new virtual machine, such as:

- Deploying a virtual machine from a template

- Cloning another virtual machine

- Using VMware vCenter Converter to convert a physical computer to a virtual machine (P2V)

- Building a new virtual machine from scratch using traditional methods such as an installation CD-ROM or ISO file to install the operating system

To create a new virtual machine using PowerCLI, you have to use the New-VM cmdlet. The New-VM cmdlet has the following syntax containing four parameter sets.

The default parameter set is shown in the following command line:

```
New-VM [-AdvancedOption <AdvancedOption[]>] [[-VMHost] <VMHost>]
[-Version <VMVersion>] -Name <String> [-ResourcePool <VIContainer>]
[-VApp <VApp>] [-Location <Folder>] [-Datastore <StorageResource>]
[-DiskMB <Int64[]>] [-DiskGB <Decimal[]>] [-DiskPath <String[]>]
[-DiskStorageFormat <VirtualDiskStorageFormat>] [-MemoryMB <Int64>]
[-MemoryGB <Decimal>] [-NumCpu <Int32>] [-Floppy] [-CD] [-GuestId
<String>] [-AlternateGuestName <String>] [-NetworkName <String[]>]
[-Portgroup <VirtualPortGroupBase[]>] [-HARestartPriority
<HARestartPriority>] [-HAIsolationResponse <HAIsolationResponse>]
[-DrsAutomationLevel <DrsAutomationLevel>] [-VMSwapfilePolicy
<VMSwapfilePolicy>] [-Server <VIServer[]>] [-RunAsync] [-Notes
<String>] [-WhatIf] [-Confirm] [<CommonParameters>]
```

The parameter set for creating a virtual machine from a template is as follows:

```
New-VM [-AdvancedOption <AdvancedOption[]>] [[-VMHost] <VMHost>]
-Name <String> [-ResourcePool <VIContainer>] [-VApp <VApp>]
[-Location <Folder>] [-Datastore <StorageResource>] [-Template]
<Template> [-DiskStorageFormat <VirtualDiskStorageFormat>]
[-OSCustomizationSpec <OSCustomizationSpec>] [-HARestartPriority
<HARestartPriority>] [-HAIsolationResponse <HAIsolationResponse>]
[-DrsAutomationLevel <DrsAutomationLevel>] [-Server <VIServer[]>]
[-RunAsync] [-Notes <String>] [-WhatIf] [-Confirm] [<CommonParameters>]
```

The parameter set for cloning a virtual machine is as follows:

```
New-VM [-AdvancedOption <AdvancedOption[]>] [[-VMHost] <VMHost>]
[-Name <String>] [-ResourcePool <VIContainer>] [-VApp <VApp>]
[-Location <Folder>] [-Datastore <StorageResource>]
[-DiskStorageFormat <VirtualDiskStorageFormat>] [-OSCustomizationSpec
<OSCustomizationSpec>] [-HARestartPriority <HARestartPriority>]
[-HAIsolationResponse <HAIsolationResponse>] [-DrsAutomationLevel
<DrsAutomationLevel>] [-LinkedClone] [-ReferenceSnapshot <Snapshot>]
[-Server <VIServer[]>] [-RunAsync] [-Notes <String>] -VM
<VirtualMachine[]> [-WhatIf] [-Confirm] [<CommonParameters>]
```

The parameter set for registering a virtual machine is as follows:

```
New-VM [[-VMHost] <VMHost>] [-Name <String>] [-ResourcePool
<VIContainer>] [-VApp <VApp>] [-Location <Folder>]
[-HARestartPriority <HARestartPriority>] [-HAIsolationResponse
<HAIsolationResponse>] [-DrsAutomationLevel <DrsAutomationLevel>]
-VMFilePath <String> [-Server <VIServer[]>] [-RunAsync] [-Notes
<String>] [-WhatIf] [-Confirm] [<CommonParameters>]
```

The `-Name`, `-Template`, `-VM`, and `-VMFilePath` parameters are required for creating a virtual machine.

Remember that, if you use parameters, they will all have to come from the same set. How would you find the names of the parameter sets? You can find these names using the `Get-Command` cmdlet, as shown in the following command:

```
PowerCLI C:\> (Get-Command New-VM).ParameterSets.Name
```

The output of the previous command is as follows:

```
DefaultParameterSet
Template
CloneVm
RegisterVm
```

The preceding command is in PowerShell v3 syntax. In PowerShell v2, the command is as follows:

```
PowerCLI C:\> (Get-Command New-VM).ParameterSets |
>> Select-Object -ExpandProperty Name
>>
```

You can see that the PowerShell v3 syntax is shorter and more elegant. If you are still using PowerShell v2, I encourage you to upgrade to v3.

> You can find the PowerShell version of your session with the following command:
>
> `PowerCLI C:\> $PSVersionTable.PSVersion`
>
> As you can see from the following output, I am using PowerShell v3:
>
> | Major | Minor | Build | Revision |
> | ----- | ----- | ----- | -------- |
> | 3 | 0 | -1 | -1 |

As you can see in the preceding command, Get-Command shows you the names of the four parameter sets, in this case, DefaultParameterSet, Template, CloneVm, and RegisterVm. You can see that there are different parameter sets for creating a virtual machine from a template, cloning a virtual machine, and registering a virtual machine. Registering a virtual machine is not really creating a new virtual machine. It is adding an existing virtual machine to a vSphere inventory. I will show you examples from all of these parameter sets in the following sections: *Creating a virtual machine from scratch, Creating a virtual machine from a template, Cloning a virtual machine*, and *Registering a virtual machine*.

Creating a virtual machine from scratch

In this section, we'll start with creating a virtual machine from scratch. For this purpose, you'll need to use the DefaultParameterSet parameter set. You'll need to specify values for the -Name parameter, which is required, and one of these parameters: -ResourcePool, -VMHost, or -VApp. The -ResourcePool parameter accepts VMHost, Cluster, ResourcePool, and VApp objects. All of these objects individually act as a resource pool. We will create a virtual machine named VM1 and add it to the cluster Cluster01 with the following command lines:

```
PowerCLI C:\> $Cluster = Get-Cluster -Name Cluster01
PowerCLI C:\> New-VM -Name VM1 -ResourcePool $Cluster
```

The output of the preceding command is as follows:

Name	PowerState	Num CPUs	MemoryGB
VM1	PoweredOff	1	0.250

You have now created your first virtual machine with PowerCLI. This virtual machine has the default settings because you only specified the minimum required parameters. For example, the virtual machine has only 256 MB of memory and a 4 GB disk. You probably want to change these figures. To do this, you can use other parameters, such as -Datastore, -DiskGB, -DiskStorageFormat, -MemoryGB, -NumCpu, and -NetworkName, to create a virtual machine that fulfills your needs. After creating a virtual machine, you can modify it using the Set-VM cmdlet, which will be discussed later in this chapter. However, some settings, such as the disk size, you are better off knowing right from the start. This is because increasing the disk size also requires changes to the filesystem. Shrinking the disk size is only possible by making a backup of the disk, removing the disk, creating a smaller disk, and then restoring the backup.

Let's create a more advanced virtual machine named VM2 with the help of the following command:

```
PowerCLI C:\> $DataStoreCluster = Get-DatastoreCluster -Name `
>> DatastoreCluster1
>>
PowerCLI C:\> New-VM -Name VM2 -ResourcePool $Cluster -Datastore `
>> $DataStoreCluster -DiskGB 20 -DiskStorageFormat Thin `
>> -MemoryGB 4 -NumCPU 2 -NetworkName "VM Network"
>>
```

The output of the preceding command is as follows:

```
Name                    PowerState Num CPUs MemoryGB
----                    ---------- -------- --------
VM2                     PoweredOff 2         4.000
```

While creating VM2, we specified a datastore cluster so that Storage DRS could provide the best datastore in the datastore cluster for initial placement of the virtual machine. We also specified Thin as the storage format , to **thin provision** the disk, and the memory size in GB, the number of virtual CPUs, and the name of the virtual machine's network.

The virtual machines VM1 and VM2 have no operating system installed. To install an operating system, you can start the virtual machine and connect a CD-ROM or an ISO file containing an operating system installation disk; alternatively, you can use methods such as a PXE boot.

Creating a virtual machine from a template

Deploying a virtual machine from a template is much easier than installing one from scratch. When you deploy a virtual machine from a template, you create a new virtual machine that is a copy of the template.

To create the template, you first have to create a virtual machine. Install the operating system with all of the software and patches to be included for each virtual machine deployed. When the virtual machine is ready, you have to convert it into a template. You will learn how to do this with PowerCLI later in this chapter.

If you have different operating systems that you need to deploy, you can create a template for each one, for example, Microsoft Windows Server 2012, Red Hat Enterprise Linux 6 (64-bit), and so on. After creating the template, you can deploy a virtual machine from this template using the New-VM -Template parameter.

VM1 is a template. We will use this template to deploy virtual machine VM3 with the following command lines:

```
PowerCLI C:\> $Cluster = Get-Cluster -Name Cluster01
PowerCLI C:\> New-VM -Name VM3 -Template VM1 -ResourcePool $Cluster
```

The preceding command lines will give the following output:

```
Name                   PowerState Num CPUs MemoryGB
----                   ---------- -------- --------
VM3                    PoweredOff 1        0.250
```

 You can also specify other parameters to change settings.

Cloning a virtual machine

If you clone a virtual machine, you will create a duplicate of the virtual machine with the same configuration and installed software as those on the original virtual machine. This can be done while the source virtual machine is powered on. You have to specify the source virtual machine in the value of the -VM parameter.

Let's clone the VM3 virtual machine into a new virtual machine called VM4:

```
PowerCLI C:\> $Cluster = Get-Cluster -Name Cluster01
PowerCLI C:\> New-VM -Name VM4 -VM VM3 -ResourcePool $Cluster
```

The output will be as follows:

```
Name                    PowerState Num CPUs MemoryGB
----                    ---------- -------- --------
VM4                     PoweredOff 1           0.250
```

Registering a virtual machine

To register an existing virtual machine to your vCenter inventory, you have to specify the path to a .vmx file. A .vmx file contains the configuration for an existing virtual machine. Here are a few lines from a .vmx file:

```
.encoding = "UTF-8"
config.version = "8"
virtualHW.version = "10"
vmci0.present = "TRUE"
displayName = "vm4"
extendedConfigFile = "vm4.vmxf"
floppy0.present = "FALSE"
memSize = "256"
```

You typically don't modify a .vmx file with an editor, because you might break the connection to the virtual machine. The VMware **Knowledge Base** article (available at http://kb.vmware.com/kb/1714) gives tips for editing a .vmx file.

The following example will register a virtual machine named VM4:

```
PowerCLI C:\> $Cluster = Get-Cluster -Name Cluster01
PowerCLI C:\> New-VM -Name VM4 -ResourcePool $Cluster `
>> -VMFilePath "[Datastore2] VM4/VM4.vmx"
>>
```

The output of the preceding command is as follows:

```
Name                    PowerState Num CPUs MemoryGB
----                    ---------- -------- --------
VM4                     PoweredOff 1           0.250
```

In the following screenshot of the vSphere Web Client, you will see all of the files of a virtual machine in its datastore folder:

Name	Size	Modified	Type
VM4.vmdk	4,194,304.00 KB	2/6/2013 4:37 PM	Virtual Disk
VM4.vmx	2.07 KB	2/9/2013 2:09 PM	Virtual Machine
VM4.vmxf	0.25 KB	2/9/2013 7:49 AM	File
VM4.vmsd	0.00 KB	2/6/2013 4:37 PM	File
VM4.flp	1,440.00 KB	2/8/2013 12:32 ...	Floppy Image
VM4.nvram	8.48 KB	2/9/2013 2:09 PM	Non-volatile Memory File
vmware-1.log	91.34 KB	2/9/2013 1:48 PM	VM Log File
vmware-2.log	91.88 KB	2/9/2013 1:51 PM	VM Log File
vmware-3.log	91.79 KB	2/9/2013 1:52 PM	VM Log File
vmware-4.log	91.78 KB	2/9/2013 1:54 PM	VM Log File
vmware-5.log	91.88 KB	2/9/2013 1:56 PM	VM Log File
vmware-6.log	91.79 KB	2/9/2013 1:59 PM	VM Log File
VM4-057c0801.vmss	263,218.33 KB	2/9/2013 2:09 PM	File
vmware.log	94.79 KB	2/9/2013 2:09 PM	VM Log File

Using OS customization specifications

OS customization specifications are XML files that contain guest operating system settings—such as the computer name, network settings, and license settings—for virtual machines.

Let's get a list of all the OS customization specifications cmdlets:

```
PowerCLI C:\> Get-Command -Noun OSCustomization* |
>> Select-Object -Property Name
>>
```

The output of the preceding command is as follows:

```
Name
----
Get-OSCustomizationNicMapping
Get-OSCustomizationSpec
New-OSCustomizationNicMapping
New-OSCustomizationSpec
Remove-OSCustomizationNicMapping
```

```
Remove-OSCustomizationSpec
Set-OSCustomizationNicMapping
Set-OSCustomizationSpec
```

To create an OS customization specification or to clone an existing one, you have to use the New-OSCustomizationSpec cmdlet. This cmdlet has the following syntaxes:

```
New-OSCustomizationSpec [-OSType <String>] [-Server <VIServer[]>]
[-Name <String>] [-Type <OSCustomizationSpecType>] [-DnsServer
<String[]>] [-DnsSuffix <String[]>] [-Domain <String>] [-NamingScheme
<String>] [-NamingPrefix <String>] [-Description <String>] [-WhatIf]
[-Confirm] [<CommonParameters>]

New-OSCustomizationSpec -OSCustomizationSpec <OSCustomizationSpec>
[-Server <VIServer[]>] [-Name <String>] [-Type
<OSCustomizationSpecType>] [-WhatIf] [-Confirm] [<CommonParameters>]

New-OSCustomizationSpec -FullName <String> -OrgName <String> [-OSType
<String>] [-ChangeSid] [-DeleteAccounts] [-Server <VIServer[]>]
[-Name <String>] [-Type <OSCustomizationSpecType>] [-DnsServer
<String[]>] [-DnsSuffix <String[]>] [-GuiRunOnce <String[]>]
[-AdminPassword <String>] [-TimeZone <String>] [-AutoLogonCount
<Int32>] [-Domain <String>] [-Workgroup <String>] [-DomainCredentials
<PSCredential>] [-DomainUsername <String>] [-DomainPassword <String>]
[-ProductKey <String>] [-NamingScheme <String>] [-NamingPrefix
<String>] [-Description <String>] [-LicenseMode <LicenseMode>]
[-LicenseMaxConnections <Int32>] [-WhatIf] [-Confirm]
[<CommonParameters>]
```

The -OSCustomizationSpec, -FullName, and -OrgName parameters are required to create or clone OS customization specifications.

The cmdlet has three parameter sets: the first one is for Linux operating systems, the second for cloning OS customization specifications, and the third for Windows guest operating systems.

To use the New-OSCustomizationSpec cmdlet, you have to be connected to a vCenter Server and you have to use PowerCLI in 32-bit mode. If you are using a 32-bit computer, PowerCLI will always be 32-bit. However, if you are using a 64-bit computer, you will have both 64-bit and 32-bit versions of PowerCLI installed. To start the 32-bit version of PowerCLI, click on **VMware vSphere PowerCLI (32-Bit)**.

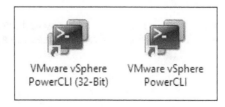

VMware vSphere   VMware vSphere
PowerCLI (32-Bit)   PowerCLI

Let's start with creating a Linux OS customization specification called `LinuxOSSpec` that specifies `Linux` as the type of operating system, and `blackmilktea.com` as the domain name using the following command:

```
PowerCLI C:\> New-OSCustomizationSpec -Name LinuxOSSpec `
>> -OSType Linux -Domain blackmilktea.com -Description "Linux spec"
>>
```

The preceding command will give the following output:

```
Name                                Description Type
----                                ----------- ----
LinuxOSSpec                         Linux spec Persistent
```

Now, we can clone this OS customization specification with the following command:

```
PowerCLI C:\ > New-OSCustomizationSpec -Name LinuxOSSpec2 `
>> -OSCustomizationSpec LinuxOSSpec
>>
```

The output to the preceding command is as follows:

```
Name                                Description Type
----                                ----------- ----
LinuxOSSpec2                        Linux spec Persistent
```

Creating a Windows OS customization specification requires some more parameters.

```
PowerCLI C:\> New-OSCustomizationSpec -Name WindowsOSSpec `
>> -OSType Windows `
>> -Domain blackmilktea.com -DomainUsername DomainAdmin `
>> -DomainPassword TopSecret -FullName "Domain administrator" `
>> -OrgName "Black Milk Tea Inc." -Description "Windows Spec"
>>
```

The output to the preceding command is as follows:

```
Name                                Description Type
----                                ----------- ----
WindowsOSSpec                       Windows Spec Persistent
```

You can now use an OS customization specification if you create a virtual machine from a template or when you clone a virtual machine. For example, you can use the following command:

```
PowerCLI C:\> New-VM -Name VM5 -Template Windows2012Template `
>> -OSCustomizationSpec WindowsOSSpec -VMHost 192.168.0.133
>>
```

The output to the preceding command is as follows:

```
Name                    PowerState Num CPUs MemoryGB
----                    ---------- -------- --------
VM5                     PoweredOff 1           4.000
```

Starting and stopping a virtual machine

You have created your virtual machine but it is still powered off. In this section, you will learn how to start, suspend, and stop a virtual machine using PowerCLI.

Starting a virtual machine

To start a virtual machine, you can use the Start-VM cmdlet. This cmdlet has the following syntax:

```
Start-VM [-RunAsync] [-VM] <VirtualMachine[]> [-Server <VIServer[]>]
[-WhatIf] [-Confirm] [<CommonParameters>]
```

The -VM parameter is required to start a virtual machine.

In the first example, we will start the virtual machine VM2 using the following command:

```
PowerCLI C:\> Start-VM -VM VM2
```

The output to the preceding command is as follows:

```
Name                    PowerState Num CPUs MemoryGB
----                    ---------- -------- --------
VM2                     PoweredOn  1           1.000
```

To start all of your virtual machines that are powered off, you can pipe the output of the Get-VM cmdlet with a where filter to select only those virtual machines that are powered off. Pipe the result to the Start-VM cmdlet using the following command and all of your virtual machines that are powered off will be started:

```
PowerCLI C:\> Get-VM |
>> Where-Object {$_.PowerState -eq 'PoweredOff'} | Start-VM
>>
```

The output to the preceding command is as follows:

```
Name                 PowerState Num CPUs MemoryGB
----                 ---------- -------- --------
VM4                  PoweredOn  1        0.250
VM2                  PoweredOn  1        1.000
VM1                  PoweredOn  1        0.250
VM3                  PoweredOn  1        0.250
```

Suspending a virtual machine

If you want to put a virtual machine on hold without powering it down, you can suspend it using the Suspend-VM cmdlet. This cmdlet has the following syntax:

```
Suspend-VM [-RunAsync] [-VM] <VirtualMachine[]> [-Server
<VIServer[]>] [-WhatIf] [-Confirm] [<CommonParameters>]
```

The -VM parameter is required.

In the following example, we will suspend the VM4 virtual machine:

```
PowerCLI C:\> Get-VM -Name VM4 | Suspend-VM -Confirm:$false
```

The output to the preceding command is as follows:

```
Name                 PowerState Num CPUs MemoryGB
----                 ---------- -------- --------
VM4                  Suspended  1        0.250
```

If you want to restart a virtual machine, you have to use the Start-VM cmdlet.

Shutting down a virtual machine's guest operating system

If you want to shut down the operating system of a virtual machine, you should use the Shutdown-VMGuest cmdlet. This cmdlet uses VMware Tools to ask the guest operating system to perform a graceful shutdown. If the VMware Tools are not running in the virtual machine, the Shutdown-VMGuest cmdlet will not work and generate an error message. The cmdlet returns immediately and does not wait until the guest operating system has been shut down.

The `Shutdown-VMGuest` cmdlet has the following syntax:

```
Shutdown-VMGuest [[-VM] <VirtualMachine[]>] [[-Server] <VIServer[]>]
[-WhatIf] [-Confirm] [<CommonParameters>]

Shutdown-VMGuest [[-Guest] <VMGuest[]>] [-WhatIf] [-Confirm]
[<CommonParameters>]
```

You must specify either the `-Guest` or `-VM` parameter.

In the following example, we will shut down the guest operating system of the VM4 virtual machine:

```
PowerCLI C:\> Shutdown-VMGuest -VM VM4 -Confirm:$false
```

The output to the preceding command is as follows:

State	IPAddress	OSFullName
Running	{192.168.0.145, f...	Microsoft Windows Server 2012 (64-bit)

Stopping a virtual machine

If shutting down a virtual machine is not possible, because VMware Tools is not installed on the guest operating system, you can use the `Stop-VM` cmdlet to stop a virtual machine. The `Stop-VM` cmdlet works like the power switch on a physical computer. This will force the virtual machine to power off without gracefully shutting down the guest operating system. The syntax of the `Stop-VM` cmdlet is as follows:

```
Stop-VM [-Kill] [-RunAsync] [-VM] <VirtualMachine[]> [-Server
<VIServer[]>] [-WhatIf] [-Confirm] [<CommonParameters>]
```

The `-VM` parameter is required.

In the following example, we will stop the VM3 virtual machine:

```
PowerCLI C:\> Stop-VM -VM VM3 -Confirm:$False
```

The output to the preceding command is as follows:

Name	PowerState	Num CPUs	MemoryGB
VM3	PoweredOff	1	0.250

Modifying the settings of a virtual machine

To modify the settings of a virtual machine, you can use the Set-VM cmdlet. This cmdlet has the following syntax:

```
Set-VM [-VM] <VirtualMachine[]> [-Name <String>] [-Version
<VMVersion>] [-MemoryMB <Int64>] [-MemoryGB <Decimal>] [-NumCpu
<Int32>] [-GuestId <String>] [-AlternateGuestName <String>] [-
OSCustomizationSpec <OSCustomizationSpec>] [-HARestartPriority
<HARestartPriority>] [-HAIsolationResponse <HAIsolationResponse>] [-
DrsAutomationLevel <DrsAutomationLevel>] [-Server <VIServer[]>] [-
RunAsync] [-VMSwapFilePolicy <VMSwapfilePolicy>] [-Notes <String>] [-
WhatIf] [-Confirm] [<CommonParameters>]

Set-VM [-VM] <VirtualMachine[]> [-Name <String>] [-Snapshot
<Snapshot>] [-OSCustomizationSpec <OSCustomizationSpec>] [-
HARestartPriority <HARestartPriority>] [-HAIsolationResponse
<HAIsolationResponse>] [-DrsAutomationLevel <DrsAutomationLevel>] [-
Server <VIServer[]>] [-RunAsync] [-VMSwapFilePolicy
<VMSwapfilePolicy>] [-WhatIf] [-Confirm] [<CommonParameters>]

Set-VM [-VM] <VirtualMachine[]> [-Name <String>] [-Server
<VIServer[]>] [-RunAsync] [-ToTemplate] [-WhatIf] [-Confirm]
[<CommonParameters>]
```

The -VM parameter is required.

The first parameter set is the default. The second parameter set is for reverting a virtual machine to a snapshot. The third parameter set converts a virtual machine into a template.

Using the preceding parameter sets, you can modify the name, hardware version, amount of memory, number of virtual CPUs, guest operating system, high availability settings, DRS settings, swap file policy, and the description of the virtual machine. You can also use the Set-VM cmdlet to apply an OS customization specification to a virtual machine.

In this example, we will rename the virtual machine VM7 to DNS1 and give the virtual machine two CPUs and 8 GB of memory. If CPU hot plug and memory hot plug are not enabled, you have to power off the virtual machine before executing the next command or the command will fail and generate the following message:

```
"CPU hot plug is not supported for this virtual machine."
```

To perform the renaming and memory allocation, use the following command:

```
PowerCLI C:\> Set-VM -VM VM7 -Name DNS1 -NumCpu 2 -MemoryGB 8 -
Confirm:$false
```

The output to the preceding command is as follows:

```
Name                     PowerState Num CPUs MemoryGB

----                     ---------- -------- --------

DNS1                     PoweredOff 2        8.000
```

In the following screenshot of the vSphere Web Client, you will see the **Virtual Hardware** tab in the **Edit Settings** window for the virtual machine DNS1 after running the preceding PowerCLI command:

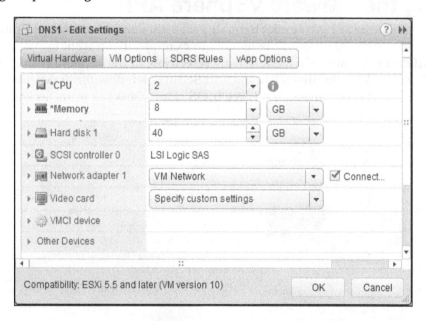

In this next example, we will configure the DNS1 virtual machine as a Microsoft Windows Server 2012 (64-bit) server using the -GuestId parameter. We will also modify the description of the virtual machine to "DNS Server".

```
PowerCLI C:\> Set-VM -VM DNS1 -GuestID windows8Server64Guest `
>> -Notes "DNS Server" -Confirm:$false
>>
```

The output to the preceding command is as follows:

```
Name                    PowerState Num CPUs MemoryGB
----                    ---------- -------- --------
DNS1                    PoweredOff 2        8.000
```

 Go to the following website and click on vSphere API Reference: `http://www.vmware.com/support/developer/vc-sdk/` You will find a list of valid `GuestId` values for specific ESXi versions in the description of the `VirtualMachineGuestOsIdentifier` enumeration type.

Using the VMware vSphere API

You cannot use the `Set-VM` cmdlet to modify all virtual machine settings. Sometimes, you have to use the VMware vSphere API, for example, if you want to enable the **Force BIOS setup** feature. In the following screenshot of the vSphere Web Client, you will see the **VM Options** tab in the **Edit Settings** window for the virtual machine **VM2**. As you can see, the **Force BIOS setup** checkbox is unchecked:

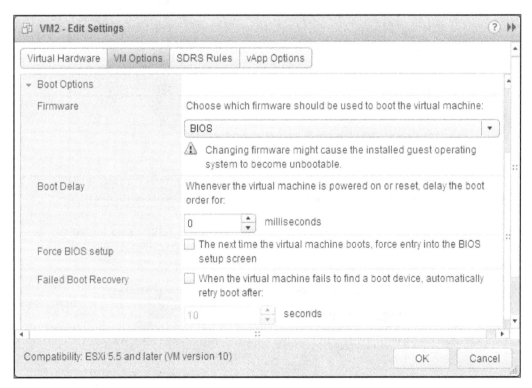

In the following example, I will show you how to enable **Force BIOS setup** for the virtual machine VM2:

```
$spec = New-Object Vmware.Vim.VirtualMachineConfigSpec
$spec.bootOptions = New-Object `
Vmware.Vim.VirtualMachineBootOptions
$spec.bootOptions.enterBIOSSetup = $true
$vm = Get-VM -Name VM2
$vm.ExtensionData.ReconfigVM_Task($spec)
```

In the preceding example, we first created a Vmware.Vim. VirtualMachineConfigSpec object. Then, we created a Vmware.Vim. VirtualMachineBootOptions object and added it to the bootOptions property to the VirtualMachineConfigSpec object. The bootOptions.enterBIOSSetup property is set to $true. Finally, the ReconfigVM_Task method is run for the virtual machine to reconfigure the virtual machine asynchronously.

> If you are unsure of how to write VMware vSphere API code, take a look at the VMware Onyx Fling. Onyx is a code generator. It can generate PowerCLI code for tasks that you perform in the VMware vSphere client. You can download Onyx and other VMware Flings at http://labs.vmware.com/flings. Unfortunately, Onyx does not support the vSphere Web Client.

Adding devices to a virtual machine

There are several cmdlets that you can use to add devices to your virtual machines:

- New-HardDisk
- New-NetworkAdapter
- New-FloppyDrive
- New-ScsiController
- New-CDDrive

We will discuss these cmdlets in this section.

> While writing this book, there are no PowerCLI cmdlets to add serial ports, parallel ports, USB controllers, USB devices, or PCI devices to a virtual machine or to remove them. If you want to perform any of these tasks, you have to use the VMware vSphere API.

Adding a hard disk

The `New-HardDisk` cmdlet has the following syntax:

```
New-HardDisk [-AdvancedOption <AdvancedOption[]>] [[-Persistence]
<String>] [-Controller <ScsiController>] [[-DiskType] <DiskType>]
[-CapacityKB <Int64>] [-CapacityGB <Decimal>] [-Split]
[-ThinProvisioned] [-StorageFormat <VirtualDiskStorageFormat>]
[-DeviceName <String>] [-Datastore <StorageResource>] [-VM]
<VirtualMachine[]> [-Server <VIServer[]>] [-WhatIf] [-Confirm]
[<CommonParameters>]

New-HardDisk [[-Persistence] <String>] [-Controller <ScsiController>]
-DiskPath <String> [-VM] <VirtualMachine[]> [-Server <VIServer[]>]
[-WhatIf] [-Confirm] [<CommonParameters>]
```

The first parameter set is to create a new hard disk, and the second parameter set is to use an existing hard disk. The `-VM` and `-DiskPath` parameters are required.

Some of the parameters are obsolete and scheduled for removal in a future PowerCLI version. These parameters are: `-CapacityKB`, `-Split`, and `-ThinProvisioned`. You should avoid using these parameters in your scripts if you want your scripts to be compatible with future PowerCLI versions.

Let's add a 20 GB, thin-provisioned hard disk drive to the VM2 virtual machine:

```
PowerCLI C:\> Get-VM -Name VM2 |
>> New-HardDisk -CapacityGB 20 -StorageFormat Thin
>>
```

The output to the preceding command is as follows:

CapacityGB	Persistence	Filename
20.000	Persistent	[Datastore1] VM2/VM2_1.vmdk

You don't have to power off a virtual machine to add a hard disk. This can be done while the virtual machine is running.

The hard disk will be created on the same datastore as the virtual machine because the `-Datastore` parameter is not specified.

Adding a SCSI controller

To add a new SCSI controller to a virtual machine, you can use the `New-ScsiController` cmdlet. The syntax of this cmdlet is as follows:

```
New-ScsiController [-HardDisk] <HardDisk[]> [[-Type]
<ScsiControllerType>] [[-BusSharingMode] <ScsiBusSharingMode>]
[-WhatIf] [-Confirm] [<CommonParameters>]
```

The `-HardDisk` parameter is required. The valid values for the `-Type` parameter are: `ParaVirtual`, `VirtualBusLogic`, `VirtualLsiLogic`, and `VirtualLsiLogicSAS`. The valid values for the `-BusSharingMode` parameter are: `NoSharing`, `Physical`, and `Virtual`.

Did you notice that the `New-ScsiController` cmdlet doesn't have a `-VM` parameter? You have to specify a new or existing hard disk for which you want to add a new SCSI controller. Because the hard disk is connected to a virtual machine, you automatically connect the new SCSI controller to this virtual machine through the hard disk.

A virtual machine must be powered off before you add a SCSI controller to it. For example, you can use the following command:

```
PowerCLI C:\> Get-VM -Name VM3 |
>> New-HardDisk -CapacityGB 10 -StorageFormat Thin |
>> New-ScsiController -Type ParaVirtual
>>
```

The output to the preceding command is as follows:

Type	BusSharingMode	UnitNumber
ParaVirtual	NoSharing	5

In the preceding example, we added a new SCSI controller for a new, 10 GB, thin-provisioned hard disk to the VM3 virtual machine.

Adding a network adapter

The syntax of the `New-NetworkAdapter` cmdlet is as follows:

```
New-NetworkAdapter [-MacAddress <String>] -NetworkName <String> [-
StartConnected] [-WakeOnLan] [-Type <VirtualNetworkAdapterType>] [-
VM] <VirtualMachine[]> [-Server <VIServer[]>] [-WhatIf] [-Confirm]
[<CommonParameters>]

New-NetworkAdapter [-MacAddress <String>] [-StartConnected] [-
WakeOnLan] [-Type <VirtualNetworkAdapterType>] -PortId <String> -
DistributedSwitch <DistributedSwitch> [-VM] <VirtualMachine[]> [-
Server <VIServer[]>] [-WhatIf] [-Confirm] [<CommonParameters>]

New-NetworkAdapter [-MacAddress <String>] [-StartConnected] [-
WakeOnLan] [-Type <VirtualNetworkAdapterType>] -Portgroup
<VirtualPortGroupBase> [-VM] <VirtualMachine[]> [-Server
<VIServer[]>] [-WhatIf] [-Confirm] [<CommonParameters>]
```

The first parameter set is the default one, the second parameter set is the advanced one, and the third parameter set is for connecting to a port group.

The `-VM`, `-NetworkName`, `-PortId`, `-DistributedSwitch`, and `-Portgroup` parameters are required. The valid virtual network adapter types for the `-Type` parameter are `e1000`, `Flexible`, `Vmxnet`, `EnhancedVmxnet`, `Vmxnet3`, and `Unknown`. If no value is given to the `-Type` parameter, the new network adapter will be of the type recommended by VMware for the given guest OS.

The following example will add a network adapter of type `Vmxnet3` to the `VM2` virtual machine. The network adapter will be connected to `"VM network"` when the virtual machine is started.

```
PowerCLI C:\> Get-VM -Name VM2 |
>> New-NetworkAdapter -NetworkName "VM Network" `
>> -StartConnected -Type Vmxnet3
>>
```

The output to the preceding command is as follows:

Name	Type	NetworkName	MacAddress	WakeOnLanEnabled
Network adapter 2	Vmxnet3	VM Network	00:50:56:a4:c1:40	False

In the following screenshot of the vSphere Web Client, you see the **Virtual Hardware** tab in the **Edit Settings** window for the virtual machine VM2. It shows the new network adapter that has just been added to the virtual machine.

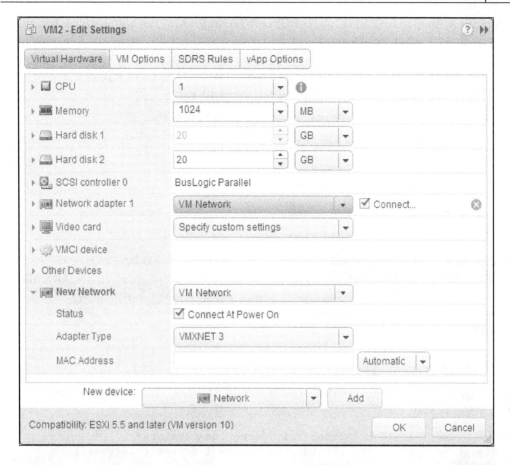

Adding a floppy drive

You can use the New-FloppyDrive cmdlet to connect a virtual machine to a floppy disk drive in an ESXi server or to connect a virtual machine to a floppy image file. Modern server hardware doesn't include floppy disk drives anymore. This is why I will show you only how to connect to a floppy image.

The New-FloppyDrive cmdlet has the following syntax:

```
New-FloppyDrive [-FloppyImagePath <String>] [-NewFloppyImagePath
<String>] [-HostDevice <String>] [-StartConnected] [-VM]
<VirtualMachine[]> [-Server <VIServer[]>] [-WhatIf] [-Confirm]
[<CommonParameters>]
```

The -VM parameter is required.

The following example adds a floppy image file to the VM3 virtual machine and the floppy drive starts connected when the virtual machine is powered on. You can only add a floppy drive to a virtual machine while the virtual machine is powered off. The value of the –NewFloppyImagePath parameter has to be a path to a file on a datastore. Let's do it with the following command:

```
PowerCLI C:\> New-FloppyDrive –VM VM3 –StartConnected `
>> -NewFloppyImagePath '[Datastore2] VM3/VM3.flp'
>>
```

The output to the preceding command is as follows:

```
FloppyImage           HostDevice              RemoteDevice
-----------           ----------              ------------
```

The command returns property names with no values. This is because the default output of the New-FloppyDrive cmdlet shows the FloppyImage, HostDevice, and RemoteDevice properties, which are empty when you add a floppy image file to a virtual machine. These properties are only used when you connect a floppy drive to a floppy disk drive in an ESXi server.

Adding a CD drive

The New-CDDrive cmdlet creates a new virtual CD drive. This cmdlet has the following syntax:

```
New-CDDrive [-IsoPath <String>] [-HostDevice <String>]
[-StartConnected] [-VM] <VirtualMachine[]> [-Server <VIServer[]>]
[-WhatIf] [-Confirm] [<CommonParameters>]
```

The –VM parameter is required.

This cmdlet looks a lot like the New-FloppyDrive cmdlet. You can connect to the CD drive on the virtual machine's host or you can connect to an ISO file on a datastore.

In the following example, we will connect a new CD drive to the VM4 virtual machine. The CD drive will start connected when the virtual machine is powered on and will be connected to a Windows Server 2012 ISO file located in the ISOs folder in Datastore2:

```
PowerCLI C:\> New-CDDrive –VM VM4 –StartConnected `
>> -IsoPath '[Datastore2] ISOs\WindowsServer2012.iso'
>>
```

The output to the preceding command is as follows:

```
IsoPath                    HostDevice                    RemoteDevice

-------                    ----------                    ------------

[Datastore2] ISOs...
```

You can use the vSphere PowerCLI Datastore Provider to search for files in datastores. Datastore Provider was introduced in *Chapter 2, Learning Basic PowerCLI Concepts*.

Modifying devices added to a virtual machine

After having added devices to your virtual machines, you might want to change the settings for these devices. The reason may be a hard disk that needs to grow or a network adapter that must move to another virtual network. To modify a device, you can use the Set-* cmdlets: Set-HardDisk, Set-ScsiController, Set-NetworkAdapter, Set-FloppyDrive, and Set-CDDrive.

Modifying a hard disk

To modify a hard disk, you can use the Set-HardDisk cmdlet. This cmdlet has four parameter sets. They are as follows:

```
Set-HardDisk [-HardDisk] <HardDisk[]> [[-CapacityKB] <Int64>]
[-CapacityGB <Decimal>] [[-Persistence] <String>] [[-Datastore]
<Datastore>] [-StorageFormat <VirtualDiskStorageFormat>] [-Controller
<ScsiController>] [-Server <VIServer[]>] [-WhatIf] [-Confirm]
[<CommonParameters>]

Set-HardDisk [-HardDisk] <HardDisk[]> [[-CapacityKB] <Int64>]
[-CapacityGB <Decimal>] [[-Persistence] <String>] [[-Datastore]
<Datastore>] [-StorageFormat <VirtualDiskStorageFormat>] [-Controller
<ScsiController>] [-Server <VIServer[]>] [-HostCredential
<PSCredential>] [-HostUser <String>] [-HostPassword <SecureString>]
[-GuestCredential <PSCredential>] [-GuestUser <String>]
[-GuestPassword <SecureString>] [-ToolsWaitSecs <Int32>] [-HelperVM
<VirtualMachine>] [-Partition <String>] [-ResizeGuestPartition]
[-WhatIf] [-Confirm] [<CommonParameters>]

Set-HardDisk [-HardDisk] <HardDisk[]> [-Inflate] [-WhatIf] [-Confirm]
[<CommonParameters>]

Set-HardDisk [-HardDisk] <HardDisk[]> [-ZeroOut] [-WhatIf] [-Confirm]
[<CommonParameters>]
```

The -HardDisk parameter is required.

The first parameter set is for changing the capacity, persistence, datastore, storage format, or SCSI controller of a hard disk. The second parameter set is for resizing a guest partition of a hard disk. The third parameter set is for inflating a hard disk. Lastly, the fourth parameter set is for filling a hard disk with zeroes.

In the following example, we will increase the size of the hard disk for virtual machine VM6 ('Hard Disk 1') to 8 GB:

```
PowerCLI C:\> Get-VM -Name VM6 | Get-HardDisk |
>> Where-Object {$_.Name -eq 'Hard Disk 1'} |
>> Set-HardDisk -CapacityGB 8 -Confirm:$false
>>
```

The output to the preceding command is as follows:

CapacityGB	Persistence	Filename
8.000	Persistent	[Datastore2] vm6/vm6.vmdk

It is not possible to shrink a hard disk using the Set-HardDisk cmdlet. This prevents you from corrupting a guest operating filesystem after making a disk too small.

In the following example, we will modify the persistence of the hard disk for virtual machine VM6 ("Hard Disk 1") to IndependentPersistent to prevent the disk from participating in virtual machine snapshots:

```
PowerCLI C:\> Get-VM -Name VM6 | Get-HardDisk |
>> Where-Object {$_.Name -eq "Hard Disk 1"} |
>> Set-HardDisk -Persistence IndependentPersistent -Confirm:$false
>>
```

The output to the preceding command is as follows:

CapacityGB	Persistence	Filename
8.000	IndependentPersis...	[Datastore2] vm6/vm6.vmdk

Moving a hard disk to another datastore

You can use the `Move-HardDisk` cmdlet to move a hard disk to another datastore and modify the storage format of the hard disk. This is useful if a datastore is running out of space or if a datastore has a high I/O load and you want to move a hard disk to another datastore to balance the load. If you want to move all of the disks of a virtual machine to the same datastore, it is better to use the `Move-VM` cmdlet; it will be discussed later in this chapter. The `Move-HardDisk` cmdlet has the following syntax:

```
Move-HardDisk [-HardDisk] <HardDisk[]> [-Datastore] <Datastore>
[-StorageFormat <VirtualDiskStorageFormat>] [-Server <VIServer[]>]
[-RunAsync] [-WhatIf] [-Confirm] [<CommonParameters>]
```

Let's move `Hard Disk 2` from the `VM2` virtual machine to `Datastore1` and change the storage format to `Thick` with the following command:

```
PowerCLI C:\> Get-VM -Name VM2 | Get-HardDisk |
>> Where-Object {$_.Name -eq "Hard Disk 2"} |
>> Move-HardDisk -Datastore Datastore1 -StorageFormat Thick -
Confirm:$false
>>
```

The output to the preceding command is as follows:

CapacityGB	Persistence	Filename
20.000	Persistent	[Datastore1] VM2/VM2_1.vmdk

Modifying a SCSI controller

To modify a SCSI controller, you can use the `Set-ScsiController` cmdlet. This cmdlet has the following syntax:

```
Set-ScsiController [-ScsiController] <ScsiController[]>
[-BusSharingMode <ScsiBusSharingMode>] [-Type <ScsiControllerType>]
[-WhatIf] [-Confirm] [<CommonParameters>]
```

You cannot use the `-Type` and `-BusSharing` parameters at the same time. First, you have to run the `Set-ScsiController` cmdlet to set the type and then run the cmdlet again to configure the bus sharing mode. The valid values for the `-Type` and `-BusSharing` parameters are the same as the parameters for the `New-ScsiController` cmdlet. To modify a SCSI controller, the virtual machine needs to be powered off.

First, we will modify the type of SCSI controller for the VM4 virtual machine to type `ParaVirtual`. Make sure that you have the VMware Tools installed on your virtual machine because the VMware Tools contain the drivers for the **paravirtual** devices.

```
PowerCLI C:\> Get-ScsiController -VM VM4 |
>> Set-ScsiController -Type ParaVirtual -Confirm:$false
>>
```

The output to the preceding command is as follows:

Type	BusSharingMode	UnitNumber
ParaVirtual	NoSharing	3

After this, we modify the SCSI controller's `BusSharingMode` parameter to `Virtual`. This enables virtual disks to be shared by virtual machines on the same host. If you set `BusSharingMode` to `Physical`, the virtual disks on this SCSI controller can be shared by virtual machines on any vSphere host:

```
PowerCLI C:\> Get-ScsiController -VM VM4 |
>> Set-ScsiController -BusSharingMode Virtual -Confirm:$false
>>
```

The output to the preceding command is as follows:

Type	BusSharingMode	UnitNumber
ParaVirtual	Virtual	3

Modifying a network adapter

The `Set-NetworkAdapter` cmdlet modifies the configuration of a virtual network adapter. You can change the MAC address, adapter type, and the network name, and configure the `Connected`, `StartConnected`, and `WakeOnLan` properties of the adapter.

The `Set-NetworkAdapter` cmdlet has the following syntax:

```
Set-NetworkAdapter [-NetworkAdapter] <NetworkAdapter[]> [-MacAddress
<String>] [-NetworkName <String>] [-StartConnected [<Boolean>]]
[-Connected [<Boolean>]] [-WakeOnLan [<Boolean>]] [-Type
<VirtualNetworkAdapterType>] [-RunAsync] [-Server <VIServer[]>]
[-WhatIf] [-Confirm] [<CommonParameters>]
```

```
Set-NetworkAdapter [-NetworkAdapter] <NetworkAdapter[]> [-MacAddress
<String>] [-StartConnected [<Boolean>]] [-Connected [<Boolean>]]
[-WakeOnLan [<Boolean>]] [-Type <VirtualNetworkAdapterType-]
-PortId <String> -DistributedSwitch <DistributedSwitch> [-RunAsync]
[-Server <VIServer[]>] [-WhatIf] [-Confirm] [<CommonParameters>]

Set-NetworkAdapter [-NetworkAdapter] <NetworkAdapter[]> -Portgroup
<VirtualPortGroupBase> [-RunAsync] [-Server <VIServer[]>] [-WhatIf]
[-Confirm] [<CommonParameters>]
```

The first parameter set is the default one. The second parameter set is for connecting to a port by key. The third parameter set is for connecting to a port group. The required parameters are –NetworkAdapter, -PortId, -DistributedSwitch, and –Portgroup.

If you want to give a network adapter a fixed MAC address, this address has to be in the range 00:50:56:00:00:00 to 00:50:56:3F:FF:FF. In the following example, we'll give the network adapter of the VM4 virtual machine a fixed MAC address of 00:50:56:00:00:01:

```
PowerCLI C:\> Get-VM -Name VM4 | Get-NetworkAdapter |
>> Set-NetworkAdapter -MacAddress 00:50:56:00:00:01 -Confirm:$false
>>
```

The output to the preceding command is as follows:

```
Name                 Type      NetworkName MacAddress          WakeOnLanEnabled
----                 ----      ----------- ----------          ----------
Network adapter 1 Flexible VM Network  00:50:56:00:00:01 False
```

We will now modify the adapter type to e1000, the network name to Vlan 7, and enable StartConnected and WakeOnLan for the same network adapter:

```
PowerCLI C:\> Get-VM -Name VM4 | Get-NetworkAdapter |
>> Set-NetworkAdapter -NetworkName "Vlan 7" -Type e1000 `
>> -StartConnected:$true –WakeOnLan:$true -Confirm:$false
>>
```

The output to the preceding command is as follows:

```
Name                 Type  NetworkName MacAddress          WakeOnLanEnabled
----                 ----  ----------- ----------          -------------
Network adapter 1 e1000 Vlan 7      00:50:56:00:00:01 True
```

Modifying a floppy drive

You can use the Set-FloppyDrive cmdlet to modify a floppy drive. The syntax of this cmdlet is:

```
Set-FloppyDrive [-Floppy] <FloppyDrive[]> [-FloppyImagePath <String>]
[-HostDevice <String>] [-NoMedia] [-StartConnected [<Boolean>]]
[-Connected [<Boolean>]] [-WhatIf] [-Confirm] [<CommonParameters>]
```

The -Floppy parameter is required.

To modify the floppy drive of the VM4 virtual machine to StartConnected, you can use the following command:

```
PowerCLI C:\> Get-VM -Name VM3 | Get-FloppyDrive |
>> Set-FloppyDrive -StartConnected:$true -Confirm:$false
>>
```

The output to the preceding command is as follows:

```
FloppyImage            HostDevice              RemoteDevice
-----------            ----------              ------------
```

Modifying a CD drive

To modify a virtual CD drive, use the Set-CDDrive cmdlet, which has the following syntax:

```
Set-CDDrive [-CD] <CDDrive[]> [-IsoPath <String>] [-HostDevice
<String>] [-NoMedia] [-StartConnected [<Boolean>]] [-Connected
[<Boolean>]] [-WhatIf] [-Confirm] [<CommonParameters>]
```

The -CD parameter is required to modify a CD drive.

You can use the -IsoPath parameter to point the CD to an ISO image. You can enable or disable the StartConnected and Connected flags. If the -NoMedia parameter is set to $true, it removes the CD drive's media backing and disconnects it.

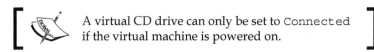

A virtual CD drive can only be set to Connected if the virtual machine is powered on.

In the following example, we will mount an ISO image from a datastore to the CD drive of the VM4 virtual machine:

```
PowerCLI C:\> Get-VM -Name VM4 | Get-CDDrive |
>> Set-CDDrive -IsoPath '[Cluster01_Vmfs01] ISOs\CentOS-6.5-x86_64-
LiveCD.iso' -Confirm:$false
>>
```

The output to the preceding command is as follows:

```
IsoPath               HostDevice                    RemoteDevice
-------               ----------                    ------------
[Cluster01_Vmfs01...
```

In the following example, we will remove the VM4 virtual machine's CD drive's media backing, disconnect it, and disable the StartConnected flag:

```
PowerCLI C:\> Get-VM -Name VM4 | Get-CDDrive |
>> Set-CDDrive -NoMedia:$true -StartConnected:$false -Confirm:$false
>>
```

The output to the preceding command is as follows:

```
IsoPath               HostDevice                    RemoteDevice
-------               ----------                    ------------
```

Removing devices from a virtual machine

To remove devices from a virtual machine, you can use these Remove-* cmdlets: Remove-HardDisk, Remove-NetworkAdapter, Remove-FloppyDrive, and Remove-CDDrive. However, there is no Remove-ScsiController cmdlet. When you remove the last hard disk from a SCSI controller, the SCSI controller is also removed.

Removing a hard disk

You can use the Remove-HardDisk cmdlet to remove a hard disk from a virtual machine. The Remove-HardDisk cmdlet has the following syntax:

```
Remove-HardDisk [-HardDisk] <HardDisk[]> [-DeletePermanently]
[-WhatIf] [-Confirm] [<CommonParameters>]
```

The -HardDisk parameter is required. To remove the hard disk not only from the inventory but also from the datastore, you have to use the -DeletePermanently parameter. You can remove a hard disk while the virtual machine is powered on.

The following example removes Hard Disk 3 from the VM2 virtual machine and also deletes the hard disk from the datastore:

```
PowerCLI C:\> Get-VM -Name VM2 | Get-HardDisk |
>> Where-Object {$_.Name -eq "Hard Disk 3"} |
>> Remove-HardDisk -DeletePermanently -Confirm:$false
>>
```

Removing a network adapter

To remove a network adapter from a virtual machine, you can use the Remove-NetworkAdapter cmdlet. This cmdlet has the following syntax:

```
Remove-NetworkAdapter [-NetworkAdapter] <NetworkAdapter[]> [-WhatIf]
 [-Confirm] [<CommonParameters>]
```

The -NetworkAdapter parameter is required. You can only remove a network adapter while the virtual machine is powered off.

Let's remove Network Adapter 2 from the VM4 virtual machine using the following command:

```
PowerCLI C:\> Get-VM -Name VM4 | Get-NetworkAdapter |
>> Where-Object {$_.Name -eq "Network adapter 2"} |
>> Remove-NetworkAdapter -Confirm:$false
>>
```

Removing a floppy drive

You can use the Remove-FloppyDrive cmdlet to remove a floppy drive from a virtual machine. The Remove-FloppyDrive cmdlet's syntax is similar to other Remove-* cmdlet syntaxes:

```
Remove-FloppyDrive [-Floppy] <FloppyDrive[]> [-WhatIf] [-Confirm]
[<CommonParameters>]
```

The -Floppy parameter is required. You can only remove a floppy drive while the virtual machine is powered off.

The following example removes all of the floppy drives from the VM4 virtual machine:

```
PowerCLI C:\> Get-VM -Name VM4 | Get-FloppyDrive |
>> Remove-FloppyDrive -Confirm:$false
>>
```

Removing a CD drive

Removing a CD drive can be done with the `Remove-CDDrive` cmdlet, which has the following syntax:

```
Remove-CDDrive [-CD] <CDDrive[]> [-WhatIf] [-Confirm]
[<CommonParameters>]
```

The `-CD` parameter is required. You can only remove a CD drive while the virtual machine is powered off.

The following command will remove `'CD/DVD drive 2'` from the `VM4` virtual machine:

```
PowerCLI C:\> Get-VM -Name VM4 | Get-CDDrive |
>> Where-Object {$_.Name -eq 'CD/DVD drive 2'} |
>> Remove-CDDrive -Confirm:$false
>>
```

Converting a virtual machine into a template

You have already learned how to deploy a virtual machine from a template. You now need to know how to create a template. You begin with creating a virtual machine and installing the operating system and application software and patches that you need for all of the virtual machines that you want to deploy. After you are finished creating your new virtual machine, you have to convert it into a template using the `Set-VM` cmdlet, which you have already seen in the previous section. Let's convert the `VM1` virtual machine into a template:

```
PowerCLI C:\> Get-VM -Name VM1 | Set-VM -ToTemplate -Confirm:$false
```

The output to the preceding command is as follows:

```
Name

----

VM1
```

To confirm that `VM1` is now a template, you can use the `Get-Template` cmdlet to view all of the templates:

```
PowerCLI C:\> Get-Template
```

The output to the preceding command is as follows:

```
Name

----

VM1
```

The `Get-Template` cmdlet has the following syntax:

```
Get-Template [-Location <VIContainer[]>] [-Datastore
<StorageResource[]>] [[-Name] <String[]>] [-NoRecursion]
[-Server <VIServer[]>] [<CommonParameters>]

Get-Template -Id <String[]> [-Server <VIServer[]>]
[<CommonParameters>]
```

The parameters of the `Get-Template` cmdlet are filters to retrieve only templates from a certain location or datastore or with a specific ID. The first parameter set is the default one. The second parameter set is for retrieving templates by ID.

Converting a template into a virtual machine

Now that you have this template, you have to keep it updated with the latest software versions and patches. However, you cannot start a template to modify the installed operating system. You have to convert it into a virtual machine first, then start the virtual machine, install the latest software versions and patches, and finally shut the virtual machine down and convert it back into a template.

To convert a template to a virtual machine, you have to use the `Set-Template` cmdlet's `-ToVM` parameter. The `Set-Template` cmdlet has the following syntax:

```
Set-Template [-Template] <Template[]> [-Name <String>] [-ToVM]
[-Server <VIServer[]>] [-RunAsync] [-WhatIf] [-Confirm]
[<CommonParameters>]
```

Here is an example to convert a template into a virtual machine:

```
PowerCLI C:\> Set-Template -Template VM1 –ToVM
```

The output to the preceding command is as follows:

```
Name                PowerState Num CPUs MemoryGB

----                ---------- -------- --------

VM1                 PoweredOff 1        0.250
```

Modifying the name of a template

You can also use the `Set-Template` cmdlet to give your template a more meaningful name. You have to use the `-Name` parameter to specify the new name:

```
PowerCLI C:\> Set-Template -Template VM1 -Name Windows2012Template
```

The output to the preceding command is as follows:

```
Name
----
Windows2012Template
```

Removing a template

To remove a template, you can use the `Remove-Template` cmdlet. This cmdlet has the following syntax:

```
Remove-Template [-Template] <Template[]> [-DeletePermanently]
[-RunAsync] [-Server <VIServer[]>] [-WhatIf] [-Confirm]
[<CommonParameters>]
```

To remove the template `Windows2012Template` from the vCenter Server inventory and also from the datastore, you can use the following command:

```
PowerCLI C:\> Remove-Template -Template Windows2012Template `
>> -DeletePermanently -Confirm:$false
>>
```

Moving a virtual machine to another folder, host, cluster, resource pool, or datastore

To move a virtual machine to another folder, host, cluster, resource pool, or datastore, you can use the `Move-VM` cmdlet. This cmdlet has the following syntax:

```
Move-VM [-AdvancedOption <AdvancedOption[]>] [[-Destination]
<VIContainer>] [-Datastore <StorageResource>] [-DiskStorageFormat
<VirtualDiskStorageFormat>] [-RunAsync] [-VM] <VirtualMachine[]>
[-Server <VIServer[]>] [-WhatIf] [-Confirm] [<CommonParameters>]
```

In the first example, we will move the VM2 virtual machine to host 192.168.0.133:

```
PowerCLI C:\> Get-VM -Name VM2 | Move-VM -Destination 192.168.0.133
```

The output to the preceding command is as follows:

Name	PowerState	Num CPUs	MemoryGB
VM2	PoweredOn	1	1.000

In the second example, we will move virtual machine DNS1 to folder Infrastructure:

```
PowerCLI C:\> $Folder = Get-Folder -Name Infrastructure
PowerCLI C:\> Get-VM -Name DNS1 | Move-VM -Destination $Folder
```

The output to the preceding command is as follows:

Name	PowerState	Num CPUs	MemoryGB
DNS1	PoweredOff	2	8.000

In the final example, we will move virtual machine DNS1 to datastore Datastore2:

```
PowerCLI C:\> Move-VM -VM DNS1 -Datastore Datastore2
```

The output to the preceding command is as follows:

Name	PowerState	Num CPUs	MemoryGB
DNS1	PoweredOff	2	8.000

Updating the VMware Tools

When there is a new version of the vSphere ESXi software, it normally comes with a new version of the VMware Tools. There are two methods of updating the VMware Tools in a guest operating system:

- Use the Update-Tools cmdlet
- Enable the **Check and upgrade VMware Tools before each power on** checkbox and reboot the virtual machine

In this section, we will discuss both options.

In the following screenshot of the vSphere Web Client, you will see the **VM Options** tab in the **Edit Settings** window for the **VM2** virtual machine. The **Check and upgrade VMware Tools before each power on** checkbox is enabled.

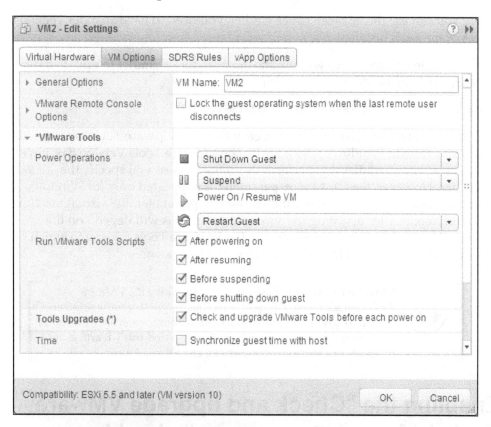

Using the Update-Tools cmdlet

The Update-Tools cmdlet will update the VMware Tools in a guest operating system. The syntax of this cmdlet is:

```
Update-Tools [-NoReboot] [-RunAsync] [[-Guest] <VMGuest[]>]
[<CommonParameters>]

Update-Tools [-NoReboot] [-RunAsync] [[-VM] <VirtualMachine[]>]
[[-Server] <VIServer[]>] [<CommonParameters>]
```

You can use the first parameter set to specify virtual machines by the VMGuest object. The second parameter set is for specifying virtual machines by the VirtualMachine object or name.

Before you can use the Update-Tools cmdlet, you need to have an older version of the VMware Tools installed.

In the following example, we will use the Update-Tools cmdlet to update the VMware Tools in the VM2 virtual machine:

```
PowerCLI C:\> Get-VM -Name VM2 | Update-Tools
```

Linux virtual machines require a reboot each time the VMware Tools are upgraded. This is also true for Windows systems with the VMware Tools Version 8 or lower. The Update-Tools cmdlet will perform this reboot unless you specify the -NoReboot parameter. However, the -NoReboot parameter is supported only for Windows operating systems. Even if you use the –NoReboot parameter, the virtual machine might still reboot after updating the VMware Tools. This will depend on the currently installed VMware Tools version, the VMware Tools version to which you want to upgrade, and the vCenter Server/ESXi versions.

VMware Knowledge Base article, *Determining if a VMware Tools upgrade requires a reboot of a Windows guest operating system (2015163)*, gives you more information about when a VMware Tools upgrade requires a reboot. You can find this KB article at http://kb.vmware.com/kb/2015163.

Enabling the "Check and upgrade VMware Tools before each power on" checkbox

In the next example, we will enable the **Check and upgrade VMware Tools before each power on** checkbox for all of the virtual machines in the inventory. Because there is no PowerCLI cmdlet to do this, we have to go back to the VMware vSphere API.

In the first line, we will create a VirtualMachineConfigSpec object. In the second line, we will create a ToolsConfigInfo object and add this object to the tools property of the VirtualMachineConfigSpec object. In the third line, we will set the ToolsUpgradePolicy object to "UpgradeAtPowerCycle". In the last line, we loop through all of our virtual machines and run the ReconfigVM_Task method with the just-created VirtualMachineConfigSpec object as a parameter to reconfigure the virtual machine and enable the **Check and upgrade VMware Tools before each power on** checkbox.

```
$Spec = New-Object VMware.Vim.VirtualMachineConfigSpec
$Spec.Tools = New-Object VMware.Vim.ToolsConfigInfo
$Spec.Tools.ToolsUpgradePolicy = "UpgradeAtPowerCycle"
Get-VM | ForEach-Object {$_.ExtensionData.ReconfigVM_Task($Spec)}
```

To really upgrade the VMware Tools after enabling the **Check and upgrade VMware Tools before each power on** checkbox, you need to restart all of the virtual machines with the following command:

```
PowerCLI C:\> Get-VM | Restart-VMGuest
```

 Don't try the preceding command in your production environment. It will restart all of your virtual machines!

Upgrading virtual machine compatibility

To upgrade virtual machine compatibility, you can use the Set-VM cmdlet that you have seen before. You have to use the -Version parameter and specify the new compatibility version as a parameter value. At the time of writing this book, the only valid versions are v4, v7, v8, v9, and v10. Virtual machines compatible with Version 10 can no longer be edited with the vSphere C# Client. You will have to use the vSphere Web Client or PowerCLI to edit the configuration for these virtual machines.

The following example will upgrade the VM7 virtual machine to compatibility Version 10:

```
PowerCLI C:\> Get-VM -Name VM7 | `
>>  Set-VM -Version V10 -Confirm:$false
>>
```

The output to the preceding command is as follows:

```
Name                 PowerState Num CPUs MemoryGB
----                 ---------- -------- --------
VM7                  PoweredOn  1        0.250
```

The virtual machine has to be powered off, or you will get the following error message:

The attempted operation cannot be performed in the current state (Powered on).

It is not possible to downgrade to an earlier compatibility version. If you specify a version lower or equal to the version the virtual machine already has, you will get the following error message:

Virtual machine compatibility is already up-to-date.

The version numbers correspond to the following virtual machine compatibilities:

Virtual machine version	Virtual machines compatible with
v4	ESX/ESXi 3.5 and later
v7	ESX/ESXi 4.0 and later
v8	ESXi 5.0 and later
v9	ESXi 5.1 and later
v10	ESXi 5.5 and later

In the following screenshot of the vSphere Web Client, you will see the **VM Hardware** window containing the status of a virtual machine with **Compatibility** showing **ESXi 5.5 and later (VM version 10)**:

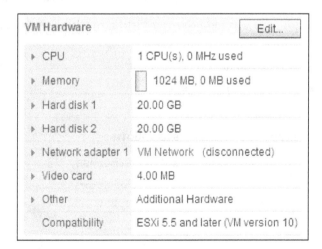

Using snapshots

Snapshots are a point-in-time to which you can revert a virtual machine when changes made to the virtual machine after creating the snapshot should be discarded. For example, snapshots are useful when you are installing or upgrading software in a virtual machine. If the installation or upgrade goes wrong, you can easily restore to the time the last snapshot was taken, in order to get back to the state before you started the installation or upgrade. If you have verified that the installation or upgrade was successful, you should remove the snapshot, because snapshots use valuable space on your datastores and decrease the performance of your virtual machine.

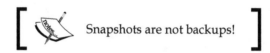 Snapshots are not backups!

In this section, we will discuss the PowerCLI commands to work with snapshots.

Creating snapshots

To create a new snapshot of a virtual machine, you have to use the New-Snapshot cmdlet. This cmdlet has the following syntax:

```
New-Snapshot [-VM] <VirtualMachine[]> [-Name] <String> [-Description
<String>] [-Memory] [-Quiesce] [-Server <VIServer[]>] [-RunAsync]
[-WhatIf] [-Confirm] [<CommonParameters>]
```

The -VM, and -Name parameters are required.

In the following example, we will create a snapshot of the VM2 virtual machine before upgrading it. If something goes wrong during the upgrade, we can revert to the snapshot and will have our original virtual machine back.

```
PowerCLI C:\> New-Snapshot -VM VM2 -Name "Before Upgrade" `
>> -Description "Made before upgrading the virtual machine"
>>
```

The output to the preceding command is as follows:

```
Name                    Description                     PowerState

----                    -----------                     ----------

Before Upgrade          Made before upgrading the v... PoweredOff
```

In the following screenshot of the vSphere Web Client, you will see the **Manage VM Snapshots for VM2** window showing the snapshot created in the previous PowerCLI command:

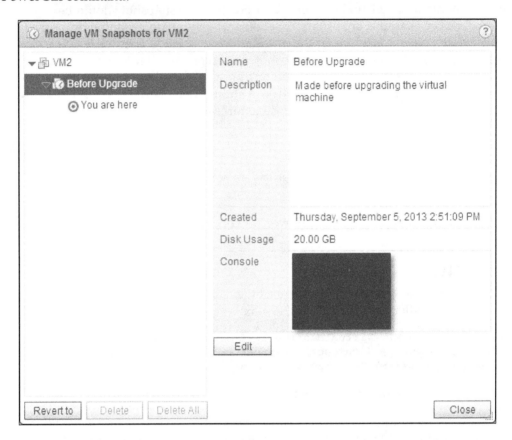

If the virtual machine is powered on, you can use the -Memory parameter to preserve the virtual machine's memory state with the snapshot. In the powered on state, you can also use the -Quiesce parameter to quiesce the filesystem of the virtual machine using the VMware Tools. Quiescing ensures that a snapshot represents a consistent state of the guest filesystems.

In the following example, we will create a new snapshot of the VM2 virtual machine that includes the virtual machine's memory, and we will quiesce the virtual machine's filesystem before creating the snapshot:

```
PowerCLI C:\> New-Snapshot -VM VM2 -Name "Before patching" `
>> -Memory -Quiesce
>>
```

The output to the preceding command is as follows:

```
Name                     Description                     PowerState
----                     -----------                     ----------
Before patching                                          PoweredOn
```

The value of the snapshot's `PowerState` property, `PoweredOn`, indicates that the virtual machine's memory is included in the snapshot.

Retrieving snapshots

To get a list of all of the snapshots that a virtual machine has or to retrieve a specific snapshot, you can use the `Get-Snapshot` cmdlet. The syntax of this cmdlet is as follows:

```
Get-Snapshot [[-Name] <String[]>] [-Id <String[]>] [-VM]
<VirtualMachine[]> [-Server <VIServer[]>] [<CommonParameters>]
```

The `-VM` parameter is required.

Let's get a list of all of the snapshots of the `VM2` virtual machine using the following command:

```
PowerCLI C:\> Get-VM -Name VM2 | Get-Snapshot
```

The output to the preceding command is as follows:

```
Name                     Description                     PowerState
----                     -----------                     ----------
Before Upgrade           Made before upgrading the v... PoweredOff
Before patching                                          PoweredOn
```

To retrieve the snapshot named `Before Upgrade`, you can use the following command:

```
PowerCLI C:\> Get-VM -Name VM2 | Get-Snapshot -Name 'Before Upgrade'
```

The output to the preceding command is as follows:

```
Name                     Description                     PowerState
----                     -----------                     ----------
Before Upgrade           Made before upgrading the v... PoweredOff
```

Snapshots can grow to the size of the original disks and can fill a datastore. The following example will show you the snapshot names, virtual machine names, snapshot sizes in GB, and creation dates for all of the snapshots that are larger than 10 GB:

```
PowerCLI C:\> Get-VM | Get-Snapshot |
>> Where-Object {$_.SizeGB -ge 10GB} |
>> Select-Object -Property Name,VM,SizeGB,Created
>>
```

In the next example, we will retrieve a list of all of the snapshots that are older than 3 days:

```
PowerCLI C:\> Get-VM | Get-Snapshot |
>> Where-Object {$_.Created -lt (Get-Date).AddDays(-3)} |
>> Select-Object -Property VM,Name,Description,Created
>>
```

Reverting to a snapshot

To revert a virtual machine to an existing snapshot, you can use the Set-VM cmdlet that we have seen earlier in the *Modifying the settings of a virtual machine* section. In the following example, we will revert the VM2 virtual machine to the snapshot named Before Upgrade:

```
PowerCLI C:\> $vm = Get-VM -Name VM2
PowerCLI C:\> $snapshot = Get-Snapshot -VM $vm -Name 'Before Upgrade'
PowerCLI C:\> Set-VM -VM $vm -Snapshot $snapshot –Confirm:$false
```

The output to the preceding command is as follows:

Name	PowerState	Num CPUs	MemoryGB
VM2	PoweredOff	1	1.000

Modifying snapshots

To modify the name or description of a snapshot, you can use the Set-Snapshot cmdlet. The Set-Snapshot cmdlet has the following syntax:

```
Set-Snapshot [-Snapshot] <Snapshot[]> [-Name <String>] [-Description
<String>] [-WhatIf] [-Confirm] [<CommonParameters>]
```

In the next example, we will modify the name and description of the 'Before patching' snapshot of the VM2 virtual machine:

```
PowerCLI C:\> Get-VM -Name VM2 |
>> Get-Snapshot -Name 'Before patching' |
>> Set-Snapshot -Name 'Before Microsoft patches' `
>> -Description 'Before installing the Microsoft May patches'
>>
```

The output to the preceding command is as follows:

```
Name                    Description                 PowerState
----                    -----------                 ----------
Before Microsoft ... Before installing the Micro... PoweredOn
```

Removing snapshots

Snapshots can use a considerable amount of disk space. Therefore, it is good practice to remove snapshots on a regular basis. To remove snapshots, you can use the Remove-Snapshot cmdlet. This cmdlet has the following syntax:

```
Remove-Snapshot [-Snapshot] <Snapshot[]> [-RemoveChildren]
[-RunAsync] [-WhatIf] [-Confirm] [<CommonParameters>]
```

You can use the Remove-Snapshot cmdlet to remove a single snapshot or use the -RemoveChildren parameter to remove a snapshot and all its children.

In the following example, we will remove the snapshot named 'Before Upgrade' and its child snapshots for virtual machine VM2:

```
PowerCLI C:\> Get-VM -Name VM2 |
>> Get-Snapshot -Name 'Before Upgrade' |
>> Remove-Snapshot -RemoveChildren -Confirm:$false
>>
```

Running commands on the guest OS

To run a command on the guest operating system of a virtual machine, you can use the `Invoke-VMScript` cmdlet. To use this cmdlet, the virtual machines must be powered on and must have the VMware Tools installed. You also need network connectivity to the ESXi server hosting the virtual machine on port 902. This cmdlet only supports the following guest operating systems:

- Windows XP 32-bit SP3
- Windows Server 2003 32-bit SP2
- Windows Server 2003 64-bit SP2
- Windows 7 64-bit
- Windows Server 2008 R2 64-bit
- Red Hat Enterprise 5 operating systems

The `Invoke-VMScript` cmdlet has the following syntax:

```
Invoke-VMScript [-ScriptText] <String> [-VM] <VirtualMachine[]>
[-HostCredential <PSCredential>] [-HostUser <String>] [-HostPassword
<SecureString>] [-GuestCredential <PSCredential>] [-GuestUser
<String>] [-GuestPassword <SecureString>] [-ToolsWaitSecs <Int32>]
[-ScriptType <ScriptType>] [-RunAsync] [-Server <VIServer[]>]
[-WhatIf] [-Confirm] [<CommonParameters>]
```

The `-ScriptType` parameter specifies the type of script. Valid values are `PowerShell`, `Bat`, and `Bash`. For Windows virtual machines, the default value is `PowerShell`, while for Linux virtual machines it is `Bash`.

The following example runs `'ipconfig /all'` on the guest operating system of the `VM2` virtual machine:

```
PowerCLI C:\> $GuestCredential = Get-Credential
PowerCLI C:\> Invoke-VMScript -VM VM2 -ScriptText 'ipconfig /all' `
>> -GuestCredential $GuestCredential
```

The output to the preceding command is as follows:

```
ScriptOutput
------------------------------------------------------------------
|   Windows IP Configuration
|
|      Host Name . . . . . . . . . . . . : VM2
```

```
|      Primary Dns Suffix  . . . . . . . . : blackmilktea.com
|      Node Type . . . . . . . . . . . . . : Hybrid
|      IP Routing Enabled. . . . . . . . . : No
|      WINS Proxy Enabled. . . . . . . . . : No
|      DNS Suffix Search List. . . . . . . : blackmilktea.com
|
| Ethernet adapter Local Area Connection:
|
|      Connection-specific DNS Suffix  . :
|      Description . . . . . . . . . . . . : vmxnet3 Ethernet Adapter
|      Physical Address. . . . . . . . . . : 00:50:56:A4:F5:F0
|      DHCP Enabled. . . . . . . . . . . . : No
|      Autoconfiguration Enabled . . . . . : Yes
|      IPv4 Address. . . . . . . . . . . . : 192.168.0.202(Preferred)
|      Subnet Mask . . . . . . . . . . . . : 255.255.255.0
|      Default Gateway . . . . . . . . . . : 192.168.0.1
|      DNS Servers . . . . . . . . . . . . : 192.168.0.2
|                                            192.168.0.3
|      NetBIOS over Tcpip. . . . . . . . . : Enabled
|
-------------------------------------------------------------------
```

Configuring Fault Tolerance

VMware Fault Tolerance is a feature that allows you to run a copy of a virtual machine on another host in the same cluster. The primary virtual machine and the secondary virtual machine are synchronized and run in virtual lockstep with each other. When the host of the primary virtual machine fails, the secondary virtual machine takes its place with the minimum possible interruption of service. Detailed instructions for configuring Fault Tolerance in your vSphere environment can be found on the *VMware vSphere Documentation* page at http://www.vmware.com/support/pubs/vsphere-esxi-vcenter-server-pubs.html under **ESXi and vCenter Server Product Documentation | vSphere Availability Guide**. You can download this guide in .html, .pdf, .epub, and .mobi formats. In this section, we will discuss how to turn Fault Tolerance on and off in a virtual machine.

Turning Fault Tolerance on

There are no PowerCLI cmdlets to turn Fault Tolerance on or off in a virtual machine, so we have to use the VMware vSphere API. In the next example, we will use the CreateSecondaryVM_Task method to create a secondary virtual machine for the VM2 virtual machine. The CreateSecondaryVM_Task method needs one parameter, which is the Managed Object Reference of the host where the secondary virtual machine is to be created and powered on. In this case, we don't specify a host but use $null as a placeholder. The secondary virtual machine will be created on a compatible host selected by the system.

```
PowerCLI C:\> $vm = Get-VM -Name VM2
PowerCLI C:\> $vm.ExtensionData.CreateSecondaryVM_Task($null)
```

The output to the preceding command is as follows:

Type	Value
Task	task-269

Turning Fault Tolerance off

To turn Fault Tolerance off for a virtual machine, we will use the VMware vSphere API TurnOffFaultToleranceForVM_Task method. In the following example, we will turn off Fault Tolerance for the VM2 virtual machine. The TurnOffFaultToleranceForVM_Task method does not have any parameters.

```
PowerCLI C:\> $vm = Get-VM -Name VM2
PowerCLI C:\> $vm.ExtensionData.TurnOffFaultToleranceForVM_Task()
```

The output to the preceding command is as follows:

Type	Value
Task	task-373

Opening the console of a virtual machine

PowerCLI 5.5 introduced the Open-VMConsoleWindow cmdlet that you can use to open the console of a virtual machine in a web browser. You can open the console in a new window or fullscreen. This cmdlet uses the **VMware Remote Console (VMRC)** browser plugin.

Supported browsers are as follows:

- Microsoft Internet Explorer Version 7 or later
- Mozilla Firefox Version 9 or later
- Google Chrome Version 16 or later

The syntax of the `Open-VMConsoleWindow` cmdlet is as follows:

```
Open-VMConsoleWindow [-VM] <RemoteConsoleVM[]> [-FullScreen]
[-UrlOnly] [-Server <VIConnection[]>] [-WhatIf] [-Confirm]
[<CommonParameters>]
```

The `-VM` parameter is required. The `-FullScreen` parameter will open the console in fullscreen mode. The `-UrlOnly` parameter does not open the console but returns the URL needed to open the console. This URL will stay valid for 30 seconds, after which the screen authentication ticket contained in the URL expires.

The command in the following example will open the console of the VM2 virtual machine:

```
PowerCLI C:\> Open-VMConsoleWindow -VM VM2
```

The **VM2** virtual machine has no operating system installed. That is what you will see in the following screenshot as the virtual machine tries to boot from a PXE boot server:

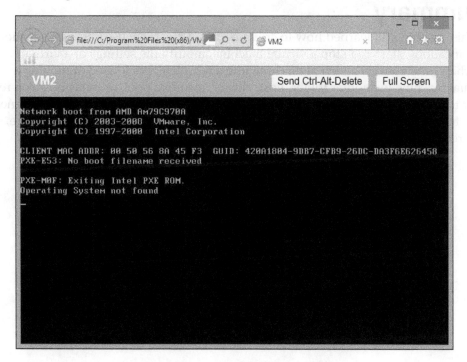

Removing a virtual machine

In the life cycle of a virtual machine, there comes a time when you may want to remove it. This may be because the application running on the virtual machine is not in use anymore or because the operating system running on the virtual machine is obsolete and you have moved the application to a new server. To remove a virtual machine, you can use the Remove-VM cmdlet, which has the following syntax:

```
Remove-VM [-DeletePermanently] [-RunAsync] [-VM] <VirtualMachine[]>
[-Server <VIServer[]>] [-WhatIf] [-Confirm] [<CommonParameters>]
```

If you use the -DeletePermanently parameter, the virtual machine will be removed from your vSphere inventory and from the datastores. If you omit the -DeletePermanently parameter, the virtual machine will only be removed from the vSphere inventory. Because the virtual machine's files remain on the datastores, you can register the virtual machine again.

In the following example, we will use the Remove-VM cmdlet to remove the VM6 virtual machine from the inventory and also remove its files from the datastore. A virtual machine must be powered off before you attempt to remove it.

```
PowerCLI C:\> Remove-VM -VM VM6 -DeletePermanently -Confirm:$false
```

Summary

In this chapter, you learned how to create a virtual machine, use OS customization specifications, start and stop a virtual machine, modify the settings of a virtual machine, and convert a virtual machine into a template. We looked at moving a virtual machine to another folder, host, cluster, resource pool, or datastore. You read how to update VMware Tools, and upgrade the virtual hardware. You also learned how to use snapshots, run commands in the guest OS, configure Fault Tolerance, and remove a virtual machine.

In the next chapter, we will look at managing virtual networks with PowerCLI.

6
Managing Virtual Networks with PowerCLI

ESXi servers need network connections for management, vMotion, fault tolerance logging traffic, iSCSI, and NAS/NFS access. Virtual machines need network connections for communicating with other virtual or physical computers. VMware vSphere provides two types of virtual switches that you can use to configure the networks: vSphere Standard Switches and vSphere Distributed Switches. The vSphere Standard Switches are specific for an ESXi server host. The vSphere Distributed Switches are created and centrally managed on a vCenter Server and are copied to every host that uses this vSphere Distributed Switch.

The topics that will be covered in the chapter are as follows:

- Using vSphere Standard Switches
- Using host network adapters
- Using standard port groups
- Using vSphere Distributed Switches
- Using distributed virtual port groups
- Configuring host networking
- Configuring the network of a virtual machine

Using vSphere Standard Switches

The vSphere Standard Switches are created on a specific host. If you are using vSphere clusters, then normally you will create the same vSphere Standard Switches on all of your hosts in a cluster, and give a switch the same configuration on all of the hosts. You can use PowerCLI to create and configure the switches on all of your hosts.

The next diagram shows two hosts, and each host has a vSphere Standard Switch:

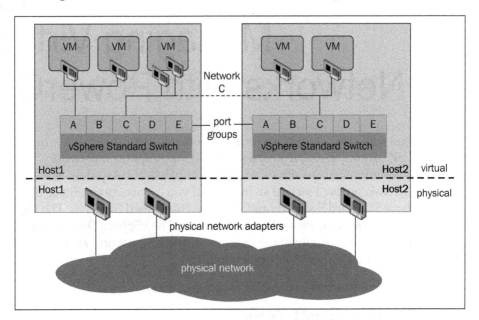

Creating vSphere Standard Switches

After deploying a new ESXi server, one vSphere Standard Switch is already created. This switch, called `vSwitch0`, has two port groups: **Management Network** and **VM Network**. Also, it is connected to a physical adapter `vmnic0`. You can use this switch to connect the host to a vCenter Server or to connect directly to this host using the vSphere Client.

The next screenshot of vSphere Web Client shows vSphere Standard Switch
vSwitch0 just after deploying the host 192.168.0.133.

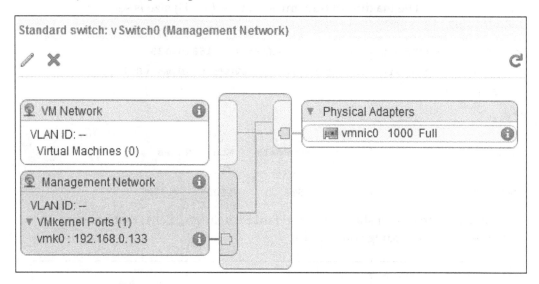

To create a new standard switch, you can use the New-VirtualSwitch cmdlet.
This cmdlet has the following syntax:

```
New-VirtualSwitch [-VMHost] <VMHost> [-Name] <String> [[-NumPorts]
  <Int32>] [[-Nic] <PhysicalNic[]>] [[-Mtu] <Int32>] [-Server
  <VIServer[]>] [-WhatIf] [-Confirm] [<CommonParameters>]
```

Following is the list of parameters that are required while using the New-
VirtualSwitch cmdlet:

- The -VMHost parameter is necessary, and it accepts input via the pipeline.

- The -Name parameter is also necessary.

- The -Numports parameter specifies the number of virtual switch ports.
  The port number displayed in the vSphere Client might differ from the
  value that you specified for the -NumPorts parameter.

> In ESXi 5.5 or later, standard virtual switches are always
> elastic, so the -NumPorts parameter is no longer
> applicable and its value is ignored.

The next PowerCLI command creates a new vSphere Standard Switch named vSwitch1 on host 192.168.0.133 and connects the switch to the network interface vmnic2. The **maximum transmission unit (MTU)** size is set to the default value of 1,500:

```
PowerCLI C:\> $VMHost = Get-VMHost -Name 192.168.0.133
PowerCLI C:\> New-VirtualSwitch -VMHost $VMHost -Name vSwitch1 `
>> -Nic vmnic2
>>
```

Name	NumPorts	Mtu	Notes
vSwitch1	1536	1500	

The following screenshot shows the Standard Switch, vSwitch1, that has been created with the preceding command:

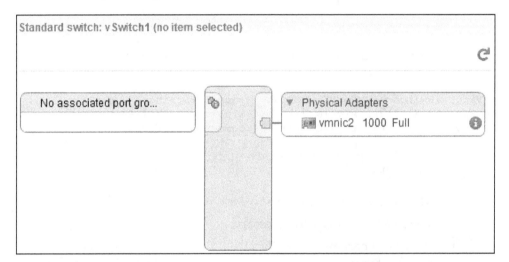

Configuring vSphere Standard Switches

You can use the Get-VirtualSwitch cmdlet to get a list of your virtual switches. As of writing this book, the cmdlet will return vSphere Standard and Distributed switches unless you specify the -Standard parameter to return only vSphere Standard Switches. VMware has the intention to modify this cmdlet to return only vSphere Standard Switches. To get a list of your vSphere Distributed Switches, it is better to use the Get-VDSwitch cmdlet. This will be discussed later in the chapter.

The `Get-VirtualSwitch` cmdlet has the following syntax:

```
Get-VirtualSwitch [[-VMHost] <VMHost[]>] [[-VM] <VirtualMachine[]>]
  [-Datacenter <Datacenter[]>] [-Name <String[]>] [-Standard]
  [-Distributed] [-Server <VIServer[]>] [<CommonParameters>]


Get-VirtualSwitch -Id <String[]> [-Server <VIServer[]>]
  [<CommonParameters>]


Get-VirtualSwitch -RelatedObject <VirtualSwitchRelatedObjectBase[]>
  [<CommonParameters>]
```

If you use the `Get-VirtualSwitch` cmdlet without parameters, then you will get a list of all of your switches from your hosts. To retrieve only the switches for a specific host, you have to specify the `-VMHost` parameter as shown in the following command line:

```
PowerCLI C:\> $VMHost = Get-VMHost -Name 192.168.0.133
PowerCLI C:\> Get-VirtualSwitch -VMHost $VMHost
```

The output of the preceding command is as follows:

Name	NumPorts	Mtu	Notes
vSwitch0	1536	1500	
vSwitch1	1536	1500	

If you only want to retrieve a specific virtual switch, you can specify the name of the switch as follows:

```
PowerCLI C:\> Get-VirtualSwitch -VMHost $VMHost -Name vSwitch1
```

The output of the preceding command is as follows:

Name	NumPorts	Mtu	Notes
vSwitch1	1536	1500	

To modify the settings of a vSphere Standard Switch, you can use the `Set-VirtualSwitch` cmdlet. You can use this cmdlet to change the number of ports, the MTU size, and the network interface cards for the virtual switch. The syntax of the `Set-VirtualSwitch` cmdlet is as follows:

```
Set-VirtualSwitch [-VirtualSwitch] <VirtualSwitch[]> [[-NumPorts]
  <Int32>] [[-Nic] <String[]>] [[-Mtu] <Int32>] [-Server <VIServer[]>]
  [-WhatIf] [-Confirm] [<CommonParameters>]
```

The –VirtualSwitch parameter is required. After changing the number of switch ports using the –NumPorts parameter, the ESXi host must be restarted for the changes to take effect. In ESXi 5.5 or later, standard virtual switches are always elastic, so the -NumPorts parameter is no longer applicable and its value is ignored.

The network interface cards specified as a value of the –Nic parameter will replace the old NICs. For example, you can use the following command to modify the MTU size of a switch to 9,000 for Jumbo Frames, and the network interface cards to vmnic2 and vmnic3:

```
PowerCLI C:\> Get-VirtualSwitch -VMHost $VMHost -Name vSwitch1 |
>> Set-VirtualSwitch -Mtu 9000 -Nic vmnic2,vmnic3 –Confirm:$false
>>
WARNING: The 'Nic' parameter of 'Set-VirtualSwitch' cmdlet is deprecated.
Use the 'Add-VirtualSwitchPhysicalNetworkAdapter' cmdlet instead.
```

Name	NumPorts	Mtu	Notes
vSwitch1	1536	9000	

After executing the previous command, both vmnic2 and vmnic3 will be **active adapters**.

As you can see in the warning message in the output of the preceding command, the –Nic parameter of the Set-VirtualSwitch cmdlet is deprecated. In the next section, we will look at the Add-VirtualSwitchPhysicalNetworkAdapter cmdlet that should be used instead.

Ethernet uses a frame size of 1,500 bytes by default. **Jumbo frames** are Ethernet frames that are larger than 1,500 bytes and are often 9,000 bytes per frame. In a reliable network, Jumbo frames have less overhead than the standard Ethernet frames and a better throughput. In an unreliable network, however, the chance of losing a frame is bigger for Jumbo frames than for the standard frame size. The loss of a frame requires the retransmission of a frame. In an unreliable network, it is better to use the standard frame sizes. If you use Jumbo frames, then all of the switches and routers between two communicating computers must support the Jumbo frame size. If there are switches or routers along the transmission path that have varying frame sizes, then you can end up with fragmentation problems. If a switch or router along the path does not support jumbo frames and it receives one, it will drop the frame.

Adding network adapters to a switch

To add a physical network adapter to a virtual switch, you should use the Add-Virt ualSwitchPhysicalNetworkAdapter cmdlet. This cmdlet has the following syntax:

```
Add-VirtualSwitchPhysicalNetworkAdapter [-VMHostPhysicalNic]
 <PhysicalNic[]> [-VirtualSwitch] <VirtualSwitch>
[-VirtualNicPortgroup <VirtualPortGroup[]>]
[-VMHostVirtualNic <HostVirtualNic[]>] [-Server <VIServer[]>]
[-WhatIf] [-Confirm] [<CommonParameters>]
```

The -VMHostPhysicalNic and -VirtualSwitch parameters are required.

The next example adds network adapter vmnic3 to the virtual switch vSwitch1 on the host 192.168.0.133:

```
PowerCLI C:\> $VMHost = Get-VMHost -Name 192.168.0.133

PowerCLI C:\> $NetworkAdapter = Get-VMHostNetworkAdapter
-VMHost $VMHost -Physical -Name vmnic3

PowerCLI C:\> Get-VirtualSwitch -Name vSwitch1 -VMHost $VMHost |

>> Add-VirtualSwitchPhysicalNetworkAdapter -VMHostPhysicalNic
 $NetworkAdapter -Confirm:$false

>>
```

Removing vSphere Standard Switches

To remove a vSphere Standard Switch, you can use the Remove-VirtualSwitch cmdlet. The syntax of this cmdlet is as follows:

```
Remove-VirtualSwitch [-VirtualSwitch] <VirtualSwitch[]>
[-Server <VIServer[]>] [-WhatIf] [-Confirm] [<CommonParameters>]
```

In the next example, we will remove vSwitch1 from the host 192.168.0.133:

```
PowerCLI C:\> $VMHost = Get-VMHost -Name 192.168.0.133

PowerCLI C:\> Get-VirtualSwitch -VMHost $VMHost -Name vSwitch1 |

>> Remove-VirtualSwitch -Confirm:$False

>>
```

Using host network adapters

A vSphere Standard or Distributed Switch can have virtual and physical network adapters. Physical network adapters are used to connect virtual switches to physical switches and have a name starting with vmnic. Virtual network adapters or VMKernel network adapters can be used to set various properties such as management traffic, vMotion, fault tolerance logging, IP address, and subnet mask. Virtual network adapters have a name starting with vmk. You can see virtual and physical network adapters in the screenshot given in the *Creating vSphere Standard Switches* section.

Creating host network adapters

To create a new virtual network adapter or VMkernel port, you can use the New-VMHostNetworkAdapter cmdlet. The cmdlet creates a port group if the -PortGroup parameter is used. The syntax of this cmdlet is as follows:

```
New-VMHostNetworkAdapter [[-VMHost] <VMHost>]
[[-PortGroup] <String>] [-PortId <String>]
[-VirtualSwitch] <VirtualSwitchBase> [[-IP] <String>]
[[-SubnetMask] <String>] [[-Mac] <String>] [-Mtu <Int32>]
[-ConsoleNic] [-VMotionEnabled [<Boolean>]]
[-FaultToleranceLoggingEnabled [<Boolean>]] [-IPv6ThroughDhcp]
[-AutomaticIPv6] [-IPv6 <String[]>] [-ManagementTrafficEnabled
[<Boolean>]] [-VsanTrafficEnabled [<Boolean>]] [-Server <VIServer[]>]
[-WhatIf] [-Confirm] [<CommonParameters>]
```

In the next example, we will create a new VMkernel port called vmk1 on the virtual switch vSwitch1 that is present on the host 192.168.0.133. A port group named VMKernelPortGroup1 is also created:

```
PowerCLI C:\> $VMHost = Get-VMHost -Name 192.168.0.133

PowerCLI C:\> $VirtualSwitch = $VMHost |

>> Get-VirtualSwitch -Name vSwitch1

>>

PowerCLI C:\> New-VMHostNetworkAdapter -VMHost $VMhost -PortGroup
VMKernelPortGroup1 -VirtualSwitch $VirtualSwitch -IP 192.168.0.150
-SubnetMask 255.255.255.0
```

Name	Mac	DhcpEnabled	IP	SubnetMask	Device
vmk1	00:50:56:65:bd:a1	False	192.168.0.150	255.255.255.0	vmk1

To fit the preceding output to the width of this page, I had to truncate DeviceName into Device. Also, there are other examples in this chapter in which the output is truncated.

Retrieving host network adapters

The Get-VMHostNetworkAdapter cmdlet can be used to retrieve the physical and virtual host network adapters. This cmdlet will retrieve the network adapters for vSphere Standard Switches and also for vSphere Distributed Switches. The syntax of the Get-VMHostNetworkAdapter cmdlet is as follows:

```
Get-VMHostNetworkAdapter [[-VMHost] <VMHost[]>] [-Physical]
[-VMKernel] [-Console] [[-Name] <String[]>] [-Id <String[]>]
[-Server <VIServer[]>] [<CommonParameters>]

Get-VMHostNetworkAdapter [[-VirtualSwitch] <VirtualSwitchBase[]>]
[-PortGroup <VirtualPortGroupBase[]>] [-Physical] [-VMKernel]
[-Console] [[-Name] <String[]>] [-Id <String[]>]
[-Server <VIServer[]>] [<CommonParameters>]
```

The first parameter set is for the vSphere Standard Switches and the second parameter set for the vSphere Distributed Switches.

In the next example, all of the host network adapters of the host 192.168.0.133 are retrieved:

```
PowerCLI C:\> $VMHost = Get-VMHost -Name 192.168.0.133
PowerCLI C:\> $VMHost | Get-VMHostNetworkAdapter
```

Name	Mac	DhcpEnabled	IP	SubnetMask
vmnic0	00:0c:29:da:a2:1b	False		
vmnic1	00:0c:29:da:a2:25	False		
vmnic2	00:0c:29:da:a2:2f	False		
vmnic3	00:0c:29:da:a2:39	False		
vmnic4	00:0c:29:da:a2:43	False		
vmnic5	00:0c:29:da:a2:4d	False		
vmnic6	00:0c:29:da:a2:57	False		
vmnic7	00:0c:29:da:a2:61	False		
vmk0	00:0c:29:da:a2:1b	True	192.168.0.133	255.255.255.0
vmk1	00:50:56:65:bd:a1	False	192.168.0.150	255.255.255.0

In the following example, we will retrieve all of the network adapters for the vSphere distributed switch VDSwitch1:

```
PowerCLI C:\> $VDSwitch = Get-VDSwitch -Name VDSwitch1
PowerCLI C:\> Get-VMHostNetworkAdapter -DistributedSwitch $VDSwitch

Name    Mac              DhcpEnabled IP SubnetMask DeviceName
----    ---              ----------- -- ---------- ----------
vmnic4  00:0c:29:da:a2:43 False                    vmnic4
```

Configuring host network adapters

To modify the settings of a host network adapter, you can use the Set-VMHostNetworkAdapter cmdlet. The syntax of this cmdlet is as follows:

```
Set-VMHostNetworkAdapter -PhysicalNic <PhysicalNic[]>
[-Duplex <String>] [-BitRatePerSecMb <Int32>] [-AutoNegotiate]
[-WhatIf] [-Confirm] [<CommonParameters>]

Set-VMHostNetworkAdapter -VirtualNic <HostVirtualNic[]> [-Dhcp]
[-IP <String>] [-SubnetMask <String>] [-Mac <String>] [-Mtu <Int32>]
[-VMotionEnabled [<Boolean>]] [-FaultToleranceLoggingEnabled
[<Boolean>]] [-ManagementTrafficEnabled [<Boolean>]]
[-VsanTrafficEnabled [<Boolean>]] [-IPv6ThroughDhcp [<Boolean>]]
[-AutomaticIPv6 [<Boolean>]] [-IPv6 <String[]>] [-IPv6Enabled
[<Boolean>]] [-WhatIf] [-Confirm] [<CommonParameters>]

Set-VMHostNetworkAdapter -VirtualNic <HostVirtualNic[]> -PortGroup
<DistributedPortGroup> [-WhatIf] [-Confirm] [<CommonParameters>]
```

The Set-VMHostNetworkAdapter cmdlet has three parameter sets. The first parameter set is for setting the network speed on the physical network adapters to half or full duplex or auto negotiate. The second parameter set is for setting the various properties of a virtual network adapter. The third parameter set is for migrating a host network adapter from a Standard Port Group to a Distributed Port Group.

Configuring network speed and the duplex setting

In the first example of the Set-VMHostNetworkAdapter cmdlet, we will set the speed of the physical network adapter vmnic2 of the host 192.168.0.133 to 1000 MB and full-duplex:

```
PowerCLI C:\> Get-VMHostNetworkAdapter -VMHost 192.168.0.133 -Name vmnic2
|
>> Set-VMHostNetworkAdapter -BitRatePerSecMb 1000 -Duplex full
-Confirm:$false
```

```
>>

Name    Mac                DhcpEnabled  IP  SubnetMask  DeviceName
----    ---                -----------  --  ----------  ----------
vmnic2  00:0c:29:da:a2:2f  False                        vmnic2
```

Configuring the management network

To enable a VMkernel port on an ESXi server for management traffic, you have to use the `Set-VMHostNetworkAdapter` `-ManagementTrafficEnabled` parameter. Using `$true` as the value for this parameter will enable management traffic and `$false` will disable it. In the following example, we will enable management traffic for the VMkernel port vmk1 of the host `192.168.0.133`:

```
PowerCLI C:\> Get-VMHostNetworkAdapter -VMHost 192.168.0.133 -Name vmk1 |
>> Set-VMHostNetworkAdapter -ManagementTrafficEnabled:$true
-Confirm:$false
>>

Name Mac               DhcpEnabled IP            SubnetMask    Device
---- ---               ----------- --            ----------    ------
vmk1 00:50:56:65:bd:a1 False       192.168.0.150 255.255.255.0 vmk1
```

Configuring vMotion

In the following example, we will enable vMotion on the VMkernel network adapter vmk2 for the host `192.168.0.133`:

```
PowerCLI C:\> Get-VMHostNetworkAdapter -VMHost 192.168.0.133 -Name
 vmk1 |
>> Set-VMHostNetworkAdapter -VMotionEnabled:$true -Confirm:$false
>>

Name Mac               DhcpEnabled IP            SubnetMask    Device
---- ---               ----------- --            ----------    ------
vmk1 00:50:56:65:bd:a1 False       192.168.0.150 255.255.255.0 vmk1
```

To disable vMotion, you have to modify `$true` in the preceding example to `$false`.

Removing host network adapters

To remove a host network adapter, you can use the `Remove-VMHostNetworkAdapter` cmdlet, which has the following syntax:

```
Remove-VMHostNetworkAdapter [-Nic] <HostVirtualNic[]> [-WhatIf]
[-Confirm] [<CommonParameters>]
```

In the following example, we will use the `Remove-VMHostNetworkAdapter` cmdlet to remove the host network adapter `vmk1` from the host `192.168.0.133`:

```
PowerCLI C:\> Get-VMHostNetworkAdapter -VMHost 192.168.0.133 -Name
 vmk1 |
>> Remove-VMHostNetworkAdapter -Confirm:$false
>>
```

Configuring NIC Teaming

NIC Teaming, also known as **Load Balancing and Failover (LBFO)**, allows you to combine multiple network adapters into one virtual NIC for fault tolerance and better performance. You can configure NIC Teaming for an entire virtual switch or per virtual port group. The `Get-NicTeamingPolicy` and `Set-NicTeamingPolicy` cmdlets that we will discuss in this section have two parameter sets, one for NIC Teaming at the virtual switch level and one for NIC Teaming at the virtual port group level. The syntax of the `Get-NicTeamingPolicy` cmdlet is as follows:

```
Get-NicTeamingPolicy [-VirtualSwitch] <VirtualSwitch[]>
[-Server <VIServer[]>] [<CommonParameters>]


Get-NicTeamingPolicy [-VirtualPortGroup] <VirtualPortGroup[]>
[-Server <VIServer[]>] [<CommonParameters>]
```

In the following example, we will retrieve the NIC Teaming policy for virtual switch `vSwitch1` of host `192.168.0.133`:

```
PowerCLI C:\> Get-VMHost -Name 192.168.0.133 |
>> Get-VirtualSwitch -Name vSwitch1 |
>> Get-NicTeamingPolicy
>>


VirtualSwitch ActiveNic StandbyNic UnusedNic FailbackEnabled NotifySw
------------- --------- ---------- --------- --------------- --------
vSwitch1      {vmnic2}                        True            True
```

In the following example, we will retrieve the NIC Teaming policy for the virtual port group Management Network of the host 192.168.0.133:

```
PowerCLI C:\> Get-VMHost -Name 192.168.0.133 |
>> Get-VirtualPortGroup -Name 'Management Network' |
>> Get-NicTeamingPolicy
>>


VirtualPortGroup    ActiveNic StandbyNic UnusedNic FailbackEnabled Not
----------------    --------- ---------- --------- --------------- ---
Management Network {vmnic0}                         True            Tru
```

To configure a NIC Teaming policy by using the Set-NicTeamingPolicy cmdlet, you have to use a Teaming policy, retrieved by the Get-NicTeamingPolicy cmdlet, as the input. You can pass this Teaming policy via the pipeline. The syntax of the Set-NicTeamingPolicy cmdlet is as follows:

```
Set-NicTeamingPolicy [-VirtualSwitchPolicy]
<NicTeamingVirtualSwitchPolicy[]> [-BeaconInterval <Int32>]
[-LoadBalancingPolicy <LoadBalancingPolicy>]
[-NetworkFailoverDetectionPolicy <NetworkFailoverDetectionPolicy>]
[-NotifySwitches [<Boolean>]] [-FailbackEnabled [<Boolean>]]
[-MakeNicActive <PhysicalNic[]>] [-MakeNicStandby <PhysicalNic[]>]
[-MakeNicUnused <PhysicalNic[]>] [-WhatIf] [-Confirm]
[<CommonParameters>]


Set-NicTeamingPolicy [-VirtualPortGroupPolicy]
<NicTeamingVirtualPortGroupPolicy[]> [-InheritLoadBalancingPolicy
[<Boolean>]] [-InheritNetworkFailoverDetectionPolicy [<Boolean>]]
[-InheritNotifySwitches [<Boolean>]] [-InheritFailback [<Boolean>]]
[-InheritFailoverOrder [<Boolean>]] [-LoadBalancingPolicy
<LoadBalancingPolicy>] [-NetworkFailoverDetectionPolicy
<NetworkFailoverDetectionPolicy>] [-NotifySwitches [<Boolean>]]
[-FailbackEnabled [<Boolean>]] [-MakeNicActive <PhysicalNic[]>]
[-MakeNicStandby <PhysicalNic[]>] [-MakeNicUnused <PhysicalNic[]>]
[-WhatIf] [-Confirm] [<CommonParameters>]
```

In the next example, we will add the physical network adapter vmnic1 to the virtual switch vSwitch0 on the host 192.168.0.133. Then, we will configure NIC Teaming for the virtual port group Management Network and add vmnic1 to the active NICs:

```
PowerCLI C:\> $VMHost = Get-VMHost -Name 192.168.0.133
PowerCLI C:\> $Switch = $VMHost | Get-VirtualSwitch -Name vSwitch0
```

```
PowerCLI C:\> $Switch | Set-VirtualSwitch -Nic vmnic0,vmnic1
-Confirm:$false


Name                            NumPorts   Mtu   Notes
----                            --------   ---   -----
vSwitch0                        1536       1500


PowerCLI C:\> $Policy = $VMHost |
>> Get-VirtualPortGroup -Name 'Management Network' |
>> Get-NicTeamingPolicy
>>
PowerCLI C:\> Set-NicTeamingPolicy -VirtualPortGroupPolicy $Policy
-MakeNicActive vmnic1


VirtualPortGroup    ActiveNic         StandbyNic UnusedNic FailbackEnab
----------------    ---------         ---------- --------- ------------
Management Network {vmnic1, vmnic0}                        True
```

In the screenshot of the vSphere Web Client, you can see the teamed **Physical Adapters** vmnic0 and vmnic1 after executing the commands from the previous example:

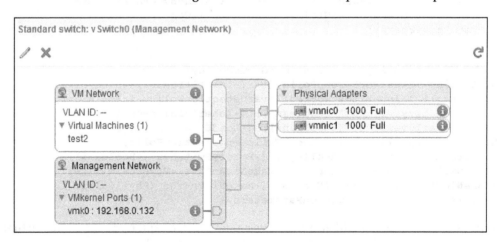

Using standard port groups

Port groups are collections of ports that have the same properties, such as the same virtual switch, VLAN ID, Teaming policy, policies for filtering, tagging, and traffic shaping. Port groups are identified by a network label name. You should give all port groups in a datacenter, which are connected to the same network, the same network label. This will make virtual machine configurations portable across hosts. Using the vSphere PowerCLI cmdlets, you can only specify a network label name for the port group and a VLAN ID.

A **Virtual Local Area Network** (**Virtual LAN** or **VLAN**) is a virtual computer network independent of physical location. All the computers in a VLAN can receive broadcasts from the others and are usually in the same IP subnet.

Creating standard port groups

The New-VirtualPortGroup cmdlet will create a new port group for a vSphere Standard Switch. The syntax of this cmdlet is as follows:

```
New-VirtualPortGroup [-Name] <String> [-VirtualSwitch]
<VirtualSwitch> [-VLanId <Int32>] [-Server <VIServer[]>]
[-WhatIf] [-Confirm] [<CommonParameters>]
```

In the following example, we will create a new standard port group named VLAN 10 Port Group for the virtual switch vSwitch1 on all of the hosts in the cluster Cluster01. The standard port group connected to VLAN 10:

```
PowerCLI C:\> Get-Cluster -Name Cluster01 |
>> Get-VMHost |
>> Get-VirtualSwitch -Name vSwitch1 |
>> New-VirtualPortGroup -Name "VLAN 10 Port Group" -VLanId 10
>>
```

Name	Key	VLanId	PortBinding	NumPorts
VLAN 10 Port Group	key-vim.host.PortGr...	10		
VLAN 10 Port Group	key-vim.host.PortGr...	10		

Configuring standard port groups

To get a list of all of your standard port groups or to retrieve just one port group, you can use the `Get-VirtualPortGroup` cmdlet. The syntax of this cmdlet is as follows:

```
Get-VirtualPortGroup [[-VMHost] <VMHost[]>] [-VM <VirtualMachine[]>]
[-VirtualSwitch <VirtualSwitchBase[]>] [-Name <String[]>]
[-Datacenter <Datacenter[]>] [-Standard] [-Distributed]
[-Tag <Tag[]>] [-Server <VIServer[]>] [<CommonParameters>]

Get-VirtualPortGroup -Id <String[]> [-Server <VIServer[]>]
[<CommonParameters>]

Get-VirtualPortGroup -RelatedObject
<VirtualPortGroupRelatedObjectBase[]> [<CommonParameters>]
```

If you use the `Get-VirtualPortGroup` cmdlet without parameters, then you will get a list of all the port groups in your environment. You can specify a datacenter, host, virtual machine, virtual switch, or the name of a port group to filter for specific port groups.

To retrieve the VLAN 10 Port Group we just created from all of the hosts in cluster Cluster01, you can use the following command line:

```
PowerCLI C:\> Get-Cluster -Name Cluster01 |
>> Get-VMHost |
>> Get-VirtualPortGroup -Name "VLAN 10 Port Group"
>>
```

Name	Key	VLanId	PortBinding	NumPorts
VLAN 10 Port Group	key-vim.host.PortGr...	10		
VLAN 10 Port Group	key-vim.host.PortGr...	10		

The `Set-VirtualPortGroup` cmdlet can be used to change the name and the VLAN ID of a port group.

> If you change the name of a port group, any virtual machine using this port group will not be updated. These virtual machines will continue to show the previous network label and will no longer be connected to any virtual port group.

The `Set-VirtualPortGroup` cmdlet has the following syntax:

```
Set-VirtualPortGroup [-Name <String>] [-VLanId <Int32>]
[-VirtualPortGroup] <VirtualPortGroup[]> [-WhatIf] [-Confirm]
[<CommonParameters>]
```

The next example will rename VLAN 10 Port Group to VLAN 11 Port Group and change the VLAN ID to 11 on all of the hosts in the cluster Cluster01:

```
PowerCLI C:\> Get-Cluster -Name Cluster01 |
>> Get-VMHost |
>> Get-VirtualPortGroup -Name "VLAN 10 Port Group" |
>> Set-VirtualPortGroup -Name "VLAN 11 Port Group" -VLanId 11
>>


Name                Key                    VLanId PortBinding NumPorts
----                ---                    ------ ----------- --------
VLAN 11 Port Group key-vim.host.PortGr... 11
VLAN 11 Port Group key-vim.host.PortGr... 11
```

Removing standard port groups

The `Remove-VirtualPortGroup` cmdlet will remove a standard port group for you. The syntax of this cmdlet is as follows:

```
Remove-VirtualPortGroup [-VirtualPortGroup] <VirtualPortGroup[]>
[-WhatIf] [-Confirm] [<CommonParameters>]
```

In the next example, we will remove VLAN 11 Port Group from all of the hosts in cluster Cluster01:

```
PowerCLI C:\> Get-Cluster -Name Cluster01 |
>> Get-VMHost |
>> Get-VirtualPortGroup -Name "VLAN 11 Port Group" |
>> Remove-VirtualPortGroup -Confirm:$false
>>
```

Using vSphere Distributed Switches

The vSphere Distributed Switches are virtual switches that span across multiple hosts. This makes it easier to configure hosts that need similar network configurations. It also ensures that virtual machines will get the same network configuration when they migrate to another host. You need a vSphere Enterprise Plus license and a vCenter Server to be able to use vSphere Distributed Switches.

In vSphere PowerCLI, there are separate sets of cmdlets for working with vSphere Standard Switches and vSphere Distributed Switches. In the past, the VMware PowerCLI team tried to integrate both types of switches into one set of cmdlets. This is why, for example, the Get-VirtualSwitch cmdlet has a -Distributed parameter. However, this parameter is now obsolete, and VMware made a new set of cmdlets specific for vSphere Distributed Switches. The vSphere PowerCLI VDS snap-in that provides support for managing Distributed Switches and port groups was introduced in PowerCLI 5.1 Release 2. In this section, you will learn more about these new cmdlets.

In the following diagram, you see a vSphere Distributed Switch that spans two hosts:

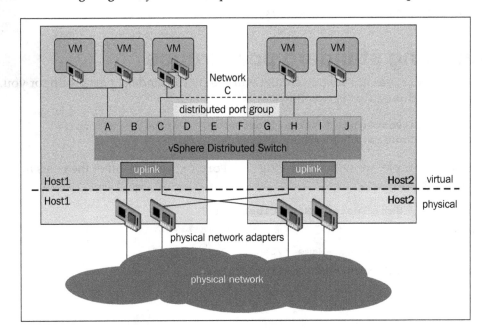

Creating vSphere Distributed Switches

The New-VDSwitch cmdlet creates new vSphere Distributed Switches. This cmdlet has the following syntax:

```
New-VDSwitch [-ContactDetails <String>] [-ContactName <String>]
[-LinkDiscoveryProtocol <LinkDiscoveryProtocol>]
[-LinkDiscoveryProtocolOperation <LinkDiscoveryOperation>]

[-MaxPorts <Int32>] [-Mtu <Int32>] [-Notes <String>]
[-NumUplinkPorts <Int32>] [-Version <String>] -Name <String>
-Location <VIContainer> [-RunAsync] [-Server <VIServer[]>]
[-WhatIf] [-Confirm] [<CommonParameters>]

New-VDSwitch -ReferenceVDSwitch <VDSwitch> -Name <String> -Location
<VIContainer> [-WithoutPortGroups] [-RunAsync] [-Server <VIServer[]>]
[-WhatIf] [-Confirm] [<CommonParameters>]

New-VDSwitch -BackupPath <String> [-KeepIdentifiers] [-Name <String>]
-Location <VIContainer> [-WithoutPortGroups] [-RunAsync]
[-Server <VIServer[]>] [-WhatIf] [-Confirm] [<CommonParameters>]
```

If you compare the preceding syntax with the syntax of the New-VirtualSwitch cmdlet, then you will see that the New-VDSwitch cmdlet has many more possibilities to configure the virtual switch during creation. In vSphere 5.1 and later versions, you can even specify a reference vSphere Distributed Switch or a backup profile from where a new switch can be created.

Creating a new vSphere Distributed Switch from scratch

To create a new vSphere Distributed Switch from scratch, you have to specify at least the -Name and the -Location parameters. The location can be a datacenter or a folder.

In the next example. we will create a new vSphere Distributed Switch named VDSwitch1 in datacenter New York:

```
PowerCLI C:\> $Datacenter = Get-Datacenter -Name "New York"
PowerCLI C:\> New-VDSwitch -Name "VDSwitch1" -Location $Datacenter
```

Name	NumPorts	Mtu	Version	Vendor
VDSwitch1	0	1500	5.5.0	VMware

Cloning a vSphere Distributed Switch

We can now clone the VDSwitch1 to a new switch VDSwitch2. Of course, this is not very useful because VDSwitch1 is not configured yet. We will clone the switch just to show you how to do it:

```
PowerCLI C:\> New-VDSwitch -Name "VDSwitch2" `
>> -ReferenceVDSwitch "VDSwitch1" -Location $Datacenter
>>
```

Name	NumPorts	Mtu	Version	Vendor
VDSwitch2	0	1500	5.5.0	VMware

If you want to clone a vSphere distributed switch without cloning the port groups, then you can use the -WithoutPortGroups parameter.

> Cloning a vSphere Distributed Switch and the New-VDSwitch -ReferenceVDSwitch parameter are only supported in VMware vSphere 5.1 and later versions.

Creating a vSphere Distributed Switch from an export

Later in this chapter, we will see how to create an export of the configuration of a vSphere Distributed Switch. If you have an export, then you can use it to recreate a switch or to create a new one. The next example will create a new vSphere Distributed Switch named VDSwitch3 in the datacenter New York from an export of the configuration of VDSwitch1:

```
PowerCLI C:\> New-VDSwitch -BackupPath C:\VDSwitch1Config.zip `
>> -Name VDSwitch3 -Location (Get-Datacenter -Name "New York")

Importing vSphere distributed switch - Switch name: 'VDSwitch1', Switch
version: 5.5.0, Number of port groups: 1, Number of resource pools: 8,
Number of uplinks: 1, Notes: VDSwitch1 Configuration
```

Name	NumPorts	Mtu	Version	Vendor
VDSwitch3	0	1500	5.5.0	VMware

Also, for importing an export you can use the -WithoutPortGroups parameter to prevent importing the port groups.

Creating a vSphere Distributed Switch from an export and creating the `New-VDSwitch -BackupPath` parameter are only supported in VMware vSphere 5.1 and later versions.

Retrieving vSphere Distributed Switches

You can retrieve vSphere Distributed Switches with the `Get-VDSwitch` cmdlet. The syntax of this cmdlet is as follows:

```
Get-VDSwitch [[-Name] <String[]>] [-Location <FolderContainer[]>]
[-VMHost <VMHost[]>] [-VM <VirtualMachine[]>] [-Server <VIServer[]>]
[<CommonParameters>]

Get-VDSwitch -Id <String[]> [-Server <VIServer[]>]
[<CommonParameters>]

Get-VDSwitch -RelatedObject <VDSwitchRelatedObjectBase[]>
[<CommonParameters>]
```

If you use the `Get-VDSwitch` cmdlet without parameters, then it will return all of the vSphere Distributed Switches in your environment. You can use the `-Location` parameter to specify a datacenter or folder in which you want to search for vSphere Distributed Switches.

The next example will retrieve all of the vSphere Distributed Switches in the datacenter New York:

```
PowerCLI C:\> Get-Datacenter -Name "New York" | Get-VDSwitch
```

Name	NumPorts	Mtu	Version	Vendor
VDSwitch1	0	1500	5.5.0	Vmware
VDSwitch2	0	1500	5.5.0	VMware
VDSwitch3	0	1500	5.5.0	VMware

You can specify a value for the `-Name` parameter to retrieve a specific vSphere Distributed Switch. In the following example, we will retrieve the vSphere Distributed Switch VDSwitch1:

```
PowerCLI C:\> Get-VDSwitch -Name VDSwitch1
```

Name	NumPorts	Mtu	Version	Vendor
VDSwitch1	0	1500	5.5.0	VMware

Configuring vSphere Distributed Switches

The selection you make using `Get-VDSwitch` can be used as an input of the `Set-VDSwitch` cmdlet to modify the configuration or version of one or more vSphere Distributed Switches, to roll back the configuration to its previous state, or to import the configuration from a backup profile.

> Rolling back the configuration of a vSphere Distributed Switch and importing the configuration of a vSphere Distributed Switch from a backup are available only on vSphere 5.1 and later versions.

The `Set-VDSwitch` cmdlet has the following syntax:

```
Set-VDSwitch [-Name <String>] [-ContactDetails <String>]
[-ContactName <String>] [-LinkDiscoveryProtocol
<LinkDiscoveryProtocol>] [-LinkDiscoveryProtocolOperation
<LinkDiscoveryOperation>] [-MaxPorts <Int32>] [-Mtu <Int32>]
[-Notes <String>] [-NumUplinkPorts <Int32>] [-Version <String>]
[-VDSwitch] <VDSwitch[]> [-RunAsync] [-Server <VIServer[]>] [-WhatIf]
[-Confirm] [<CommonParameters>]

Set-VDSwitch -BackupPath <String> [-WithoutPortGroups] [-VDSwitch]
<VDSwitch[]> [-RunAsync] [-Server <VIServer[]>] [-WhatIf] [-Confirm]
[<CommonParameters>]

Set-VDSwitch -RollBackConfiguration [-VDSwitch] <VDSwitch[]>
[-RunAsync] [-Server <VIServer[]>] [-WhatIf] [-Confirm]
[<CommonParameters>]
```

In the next example, we will set almost every property for `VDSwitch1` that you can set using PowerShell. We will use a PowerShell technique called **splatting** to create a parameter list for the `Set-VDSwitch` cmdlet. The parameter list will be a hash table called `$Parameters`. By using the **splat operator** `@`, you can add the parameters in the `$Parameters` hash table to the `Set-VDSwitch` cmdlet call.

> When you use splatting, you have to use the name of the variable containing the parameter's hash table without the dollar sign, that is, `@Parameters` and not `@$Parameters`.

```
PowerCLI C:\> $VDSwitch = Get-VDSwitch -Name vDSWitch1

PowerCLI C:\> $Parameters = @{

>>    NumUplinkPorts = 2

>>    MaxPorts = 1024

>>    LinkDiscoveryProtocol = 'LLDP'
```

```
>>    LinkDiscoveryProtocolOperation = 'Both'
>>    ContactName = 'vsphereadmin@blackmilktea.com'
>>    ContactDetails = 'New York office'
>>    Notes = 'VDSwitch for New York datacenter'
>> }
>> $VDSwitch | Set-VDSwitch @Parameters
>> Get-VDSwitch -Name vDSWitch1 | Format-List -Property *
>>
```

Name	NumPorts	Mtu	Version	Vendor
VDSwitch1	0	1500	5.5.0	VMware

```
LinkDiscoveryProtocol          : LLDP
LinkDiscoveryProtocolOperation : Both
VlanConfiguration              :
Name                           : VDSwitch1
ExtensionData                  : VMware.Vim.
VmwareDistributedVirtualSwitch
NumPorts                       : 0
Key                            : 6c 48 12 50 ca 61 ec be-4d a8 bb 95 d0
0f bd a7
Mtu                            : 1500
Notes                          : VDSwitch for New York datacenter
Datacenter                     : New York
NumUplinkPorts                 : 4
ContactName                    : vsphereadmin@blackmilktea.com
ContactDetails                 : New York office
Version                        : 5.5.0
Vendor                         : VMware
Folder                         : network
MaxPorts                       : 1024
Id                             : VmwareDistributedVirtualSwitch-dvs-182
Uid                            : /VIServer=root@192.168.0.132:443/Distrib
utedSwitch=VmwareDistributedVirtualSwitch-dvs-49/
Client                         : VMware.VimAutomation.Vds.Impl.
V1.VDClientImpl
```

The following screenshot of the vSphere Web Client shows the settings of the Distributed Switch VDSwitch1 after executing the previous commands:

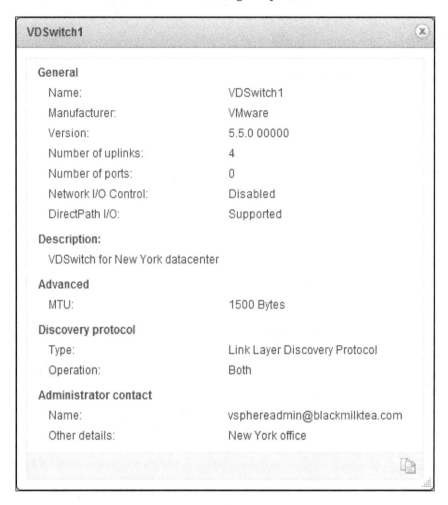

Rolling back the configuration of a vSphere Distributed Switch

If you made a mistake in the configuration of a vSphere Distributed Switch, then you can roll back the configuration to its previous state using the Set-VDSwitch – RollbackConfiguration parameter.

In the following example, we will modify the MTU size of the switch VDSwitch1 to 9,000, and then use the -RollbackConfiguration parameter to revert to the previous value of 1,500:

```
PowerCLI C:\> Get-VDSwitch -Name VDSwitch1 |
>> Set-VDSwitch -MTU 9000
>>
```

Name	NumPorts	Mtu	Version	Vendor
VDSwitch1	0	9000	5.5.0	VMware

```
PowerCLI C:\> Get-VDSwitch -Name VDSwitch1 |
>> Set-VDSwitch -RollbackConfiguration
>>
```

Name	NumPorts	Mtu	Version	Vendor
VDSwitch1	0	1500	5.5.0	

Importing the configuration of a vSphere Distributed Switch from a backup

You can import the configuration of a vSphere Distributed Switch from a backup created with the Export-VDSwitch cmdlet. Later in this chapter, you will learn how to create a backup. In this section, we will show you how to restore the configuration from a backup.

You have to use the Set-VDSwitch -BackupPath parameter to specify the path to the configuration .zip file. You can also use the -WithoutPortGroups parameter if you don't want to restore the port groups.

In the next example, we will import the configuration of VDSwitch1 from a backup file called 'c:\myVDSwitch1Config.zip':

```
PowerCLI C:\> Get-VDSwitch -Name 'VDSwitch1' |
>> Set-VDSwitch -BackupPath 'c:\myVDSwitch1Config.zip'
>>
```

```
Restoring vSphere distributed switch configuration - Switch name:
'VDSwitch1', Switch version: 5.5.0, Number of port groups: 0, Number
of resource pools: 8, Number of uplinks: 1, Notes: My VDSwitch1
configuration
```

Name	NumPorts	Mtu	Version	Vendor
VDSwitch1	0	1500	5.5.0	VMware

Upgrading a vSphere Distributed Switch

In every new VMware vSphere version, VMware introduces new features to the
vSphere Distributed Switch. To be able to use these new features, you have to
upgrade your switches to the new version.

In the next example, we will upgrade the version of the VDSwitch4 switch to 5.5.0:

```
PS C:\> $VDSwitch = Get-VDSwitch -Name VDSwitch4
PS C:\> $VDSwitch
```

Name	NumPorts	Mtu	Version	Vendor
VDSwitch4	0	1500	4.1.0	VMware

```
PS C:\> $VDSwitch | Set-VDSwitch -Version 5.5.0
```

Name	NumPorts	Mtu	Version	Vendor
VDSwitch4	0	1500	5.5.0	VMware

Adding hosts to vSphere Distributed Switches

After creating a vSphere Distributed Switch, you have to add hosts to the switch.
Normally, you add at least all of the hosts that are in the same cluster. Because
a vSphere Distributed Switch is created in a datacenter or a folder, a vSphere
Distributed Switch is not limited to one cluster. You can add hosts of multiple
clusters to the same switch.

The `Add-VDSwitchVMHost` cmdlet will add hosts to a vSphere Distributed Switch. The syntax of this cmdlet is as follows:

```
Add-VDSwitchVMHost -VDSwitch <VDSwitch> -VMHost <VMHost[]>
[-Server <VIServer[]>] [-RunAsync] [-WhatIf] [-Confirm]
[<CommonParameters>]
```

In the next example, we will add all of the hosts of the cluster `"Cluster01"` to the vSphere Distributed Switch `"VDSwitch1"`:

```
PowerCLI C:\> $VMHost = Get-Cluster Cluster01 | Get-VMHost
PowerCLI C:\> Add-VDSwitchVMHost -VDSwitch VDSwitch1 -VMHost $VMHost
```

Adding host physical network adapters to a vSphere Distributed Switch

Adding hosts to a vSphere Distributed Switch does not add physical network adapters to the switch. For each host, you have to add network adapters to the vSphere Distributed Switch to give the switch connectivity to the external network.

The `Add-VDSwitchPhysicalNetworkAdapter` cmdlet will connect a host's physical network adapter to a vSphere Distributed Switch. The syntax of this cmdlet is as follows:

```
Add-VDSwitchPhysicalNetworkAdapter [-VMHostNetworkAdapter]
<PhysicalNic[]> [-DistributedSwitch] <DistributedSwitch> [-Server
<VIServer[]>] [-WhatIf] [-Confirm] [<CommonParameters>]
```

The following example will add the physical network adapter vmnic4 of the host `192.168.0.133` to the vSphere Distributed Switch VDSwitch1:

```
PowerCLI C:\> $NetworkAdapter = Get-VMHost -Name 192.168.0.133 |
>> Get-VMHostNetworkAdapter -Name vmnic4 -Physical
>>
PowerCLI C:\> Add-VDSwitchPhysicalNetworkAdapter `
>> -DistributedSwitch VDSwitch1 `
>> -VMHostNetworkAdapter $NetworkAdapter -Confirm:$false
>>
```

Removing host physical network adapters from a vSphere Distributed Switch

Removing a physical network adapter from a vSphere Distributed Switch can be done using the Remove-VDSwitchPhysicalNetworkAdapter cmdlet. The syntax of this cmdlet is as follows:

```
Remove-VDSwitchPhysicalNetworkAdapter [-VMHostNetworkAdapter]
<PhysicalNic[]> [-WhatIf] [-Confirm] [<CommonParameters>]
```

You have to specify only a network adapter as the value of the -VMHostNetworkAdapter parameter; then the cmdlet will remove that network adapter from the switch to which it is connected.

In the following example, the physical network adapter vmnic4 from the host 192.168.0.133 will be removed from the vSphere Distributed Switch VDSwitch1:

```
PowerCLI C:\> Get-VMhost -Name 192.168.0.133 |
>> Get-VMHostNetworkAdapter -Physical -Name vmnic4 |
>> Remove-VDSwitchPhysicalNetworkAdapter -Confirm:$false
>>
```

Removing hosts from a vSphere Distributed Switch

You can use the Remove-VDSwitchVMHost cmdlet to remove a host from a vSphere Distributed Switch. This cmdlet has the following syntax:

```
Remove-VDSwitchVMHost -VDSwitch <VDSwitch> -VMHost <VMHost[]> [-Server
<VIServer[]>] [-RunAsync] [-WhatIf] [-Confirm] [<CommonParameters>]
```

In the next example, we will remove the host 192.168.0.133 from the vSphere Distributed Switch VDSwitch1:

```
PowerCLI C:\> Get-VDSwitch -Name VDSwitch1 |
>> Remove-VDSwitchVMHost -VMHost 192.168.0.133 -Confirm:$false
>>
```

Exporting the configuration of vSphere Distributed Switches

If you export the configuration of a vSphere Distributed Switch, then you can create a .zip file that can be used as a backup for the configuration of the vSphere Distributed Switch. You can use this .zip file to recreate or clone the vSphere Distributed Switch.

The Export-VDSwitch cmdlet that you can use to create the .zip file has the following syntax:

```
Export-VDSwitch [-VDSwitch] <VDSwitch[]> [-WithoutPortGroups]
[-Description <String>] [-Destination <String>] [-Force]
[-Server <VIServer[]>] [<CommonParameters>]
```

The next PowerCLI example will export the configuration of the vSphere Distributed Switch VDSwitch1 into a file called VDSwitch1Config.zip:

```
PowerCLI C:\> Get-VDSwitch -Name VDSwitch1 |
>> Export-VDSwitch -Description "VDSwitch1 Configuration" `
>> -Destination "c:\VDSwitch1Config.zip"
>>


Mode            LastWriteTime      Length Name
----            -------------      ------ ----
-a---        1/9/2014   6:51 PM      4374 VDSwitch1Config.zip
```

> Exporting the configuration of a vSphere Distributed Switch and the Export-VDSwitch cmdlet are only supported in VMware vSphere 5.1 and later versions.

Removing vSphere Distributed Switches

To remove a vSphere Distributed Switch, you can use the Remove-VDSwitch cmdlet. This cmdlet has the following syntax:

```
Remove-VDSwitch [-VDSwitch] <VDSwitch[]> [-RunAsync]
[-Server <VIServer[]>] [-WhatIf] [-Confirm] [<CommonParameters>]
```

In the next example, we will remove the vSphere Distributed Switch VDSwitch1:

```
PowerCLI C:\> Get-VDSwitch -Name VDSwitch1 |
>> Remove-VDSwitch -Confirm:$false
>>
```

Using distributed virtual port groups

In this section, you will learn how to use port groups on Distributed Virtual Switches.

Creating distributed virtual port groups

You can use the New-VDPortgroup cmdlet to create distributed virtual port groups from scratch, from the reference port groups, or from an export of a Distributed Virtual Switch. The syntax of the New-VDPortgroup cmdlet is as follows:

```
New-VDPortgroup [-VDSwitch] <VDSwitch> -Name <String>
[-Notes <String>] [-NumPorts <Int32>] [-VlanId <Int32>]
[-VlanTrunkRange <VlanRangeList>] [-PortBinding
<DistributedPortGroupPortBinding>] [-RunAsync]
[-Server <VIServer[]>] [-WhatIf] [-Confirm] [<CommonParameters>]

New-VDPortgroup [-VDSwitch] <VDSwitch> [-Name <String>]
-ReferencePortgroup <VDPortgroup> [-RunAsync] [-Server <VIServer[]>]
[-WhatIf] [-Confirm] [<CommonParameters>]

New-VDPortgroup [-VDSwitch] <VDSwitch> [-Name <String>] -BackupPath
<String> [-KeepIdentifiers] [-RunAsync] [-Server <VIServer[]>]
[-WhatIf] [-Confirm] [<CommonParameters>]
```

The New-VDPortgroup cmdlet has three parameter sets. The first parameter set is the default one, the second parameter set can be used to create a port group from a reference port group, and the third one can be used to create a port group from an export.

The first example creates a new distributed virtual port group on the vSphere Distributed Switch VDSwitch1 with 64 ports and VLAN ID 10:

```
PowerCLI C:\> Get-VDSwitch -Name VDSwitch1 |
>> New-VDPortgroup -Name "VLAN 10 Port Group" -NumPorts 64 -VLanId 10
>>

Name                    NumPorts PortBinding
----                    -------- -----------
VLAN 10 Port Group      64       Static
```

Creating distributed virtual port groups from a reference group

In the following example, we will create a new distributed virtual port group named VLAN 10 Port group 2 using the port group VLAN 10 Port Group as a reference:

```
PowerCLI C:\> $Portgroup = Get-VDPortgroup -Name 'VLAN 10 Port Group'
PowerCLI C:\> Get-VDSwitch -Name VDSwitch1 |
>> New-VDPortgroup -Name 'VLAN 10 Port group 2' -ReferencePortgroup
$Portgroup
>>


Name                         NumPorts PortBinding
----                         -------- -----------
VLAN 10 Port group 2         64       Static
```

 Creating distributed virtual port groups from a reference group and the New-VDPortgroup -ReferencePortgroup parameter are only supported in VMware vSphere 5.1 and later versions.

Creating distributed virtual port groups from an export

This is the last example of this section. In this one, we will create a new distributed virtual port group named VLAN 10 Port group 3 using an export. Later in this chapter, we will show you how to create an export of a distributed virtual port group.

```
PowerCLI C:\> Get-VDSwitch -Name VDSwitch1 |
>> New-VDPortgroup -Name 'VLAN 10 Port group 3' -BackupPath c:\users\
robert\vlan10portgroup.zip
>>


Restoring vSphere distributed port group configuration - Name: VLAN 10
Port Group, VLAN: 'Access: 10', Type: standard, Port binding: static,
Port allocation: elastic, Notes:


Name                         NumPorts PortBinding
----                         -------- -----------
VLAN 10 Port group 3         64       Static
```

Creating distributed virtual port groups from an export and the `New-VDPortgroup -BackupPath` parameter are only supported in VMware vSphere 5.1 and later versions.

Configuring distributed virtual port groups

You can use the `Get-VDPortgroup` cmdlet to retrieve all of your distributed virtual port groups or to retrieve a specific one. The syntax of this cmdlet is as follows:

```
Get-VDPortgroup [[-Name] <String[]>]
[-NetworkAdapter <NetworkAdapter[]>] [-VDSwitch <VDSwitch[]>]
[-VMHostNetworkAdapter <HostVirtualNic[]>] [-Server <VIServer[]>]
[-Tag <Tag[]>] [<CommonParameters>]

Get-VDPortgroup -Id <String[]> [-Server <VIServer[]>]
[<CommonParameters>]

Get-VDPortgroup -RelatedObject <VDPortgroupRelatedObjectBase[]>
[<CommonParameters>]
```

In the following example, we will retrieve all of our distributed virtual port groups:

```
PowerCLI C:\> Get-VDPortGroup

Name                        NumPorts PortBinding
----                        -------- -----------
VDSwitch1-DVUplinks-182     4        Static
VLAN 10 Port Group          64       Static
VLAN 10 Port group 2        64       Static
VLAN 10 Port group 3        64       Static
```

The `Set-VDPortgroup` cmdlet can be used to modify the configuration of a distributed virtual port group, to roll back the distributed virtual port group to its last valid configuration, or to import the configuration from a `.zip` file created earlier with the `Export-VDPortgroup` cmdlet. The syntax of the `Set-VDPortgroup` cmdlet is as follows:

```
Set-VDPortgroup [-Name <String>] [-Notes <String>] [-NumPorts
<Int32>] [-VlanId <Int32>] [-VlanTrunkRange <VlanRangeList>]
[-PrivateVlanId <Int32>] [-PortBinding
<DistributedPortGroupPortBinding>] [-DisableVlan] [-VDPortgroup]
<VDPortgroup[]> [-RunAsync] [-Server <VIServer[]>] [-WhatIf]
[-Confirm] [<CommonParameters>]


Set-VDPortgroup -RollbackConfiguration [-VDPortgroup] <VDPortgroup[]>
[-RunAsync] [-Server <VIServer[]>] [-WhatIf] [-Confirm]
[<CommonParameters>]
```

```
Set-VDPortgroup -BackupPath <String> [-VDPortgroup] <VDPortgroup[]>
[-RunAsync] [-Server <VIServer[]>] [-WhatIf] [-Confirm]
[<CommonParameters>]
```

Renaming a distributed virtual port group

In the following example, we will rename distributed virtual port group VLAN 10
Port Group 2 to VLAN 20 Port Group, modify the number of ports to 128, and change
the VLAN ID to 20:

```
PowerCLI C:\> Get-VDPortgroup -Name 'VLAN 10 Port Group 2' |
>> Set-VDPortgroup -Name 'VLAN 20 Port Group' -NumPorts 128 -VlanId 20
>>
```

```
Name                         NumPorts PortBinding
----                         -------- -----------
VLAN 20 Port Group           128      Static
```

In the following screenshot of the vSphere Web Client, the port group is shown after
it is renamed to VLAN 20 Port Group:

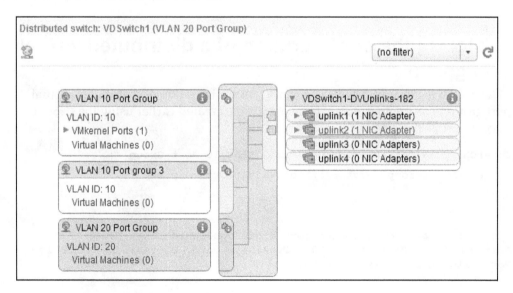

Rolling back the configuration of a distributed virtual port group

In the following example, we will roll back the configuration of distributed virtual port group VLAN 10 Port Group to its last valid configuration using the following command:

```
PowerCLI C:\> Get-VDPortgroup -Name 'VLAN 10 Port Group' |
>> Set-VDPortgroup -RollbackConfiguration
>>

Name                          NumPorts PortBinding
----                          -------- -----------
VLAN 10 Port Group            64       Static
```

 Rolling back the configuration of a distributed virtual port group and the Set-VDPortgroup -RollbackConfiguration parameter are only supported in VMware vSphere 5.1 and later versions.

Restoring the configuration of a distributed virtual port group

In the following example, we will restore the configuration of distributed virtual port group VLAN 10 Port Group from a .zip file created earlier using the Export-VDPortgroup cmdlet:

```
PowerCLI C:\> Get-VDPortgroup -Name 'VLAN 10 Port Group' |
>> Set-VDPortgroup -BackupPath c:\Vlan10PortGroup.zip
>>

Applying vSphere distributed port group configuration - Name: VLAN 10
Port Group, VLAN: 'Access: 10', Type: standard, Port binding: static,
Port allocation: elastic, Notes:

Name                          NumPorts PortBinding
----                          -------- -----------
VLAN 10 Port Group            64       Static
```

Restoring the configuration of a distributed virtual port group and the `Set-VDPortgroup -BackupPath` parameter are only supported in VMware vSphere 5.1 and later versions.

Configuring Network I/O Control

The virtual Distributed Switch cmdlets don't have a method to configure **Network I/O Control**. However, in PowerCLI you can use all of the VMware vSphere public APIs. It is not difficult to use them to enable or disable Network I/O Control.

Enabling Network I/O Control

In the following example, we will enable Network I/O Control for switch `VDSwitch1` using the `EnableNetworkResourceManagement()` method from the API:

```
PowerCLI C:\> $VDSwitch = Get-VDSwitch -Name VDSwitch1

PowerCLI C:\>
$VDSwitch.ExtensionData.EnableNetworkResourceManagement($true)
```

Disabling Network I/O Control

Disabling Network I/O Control for `VDSwitch1` can be done by replacing `$true` in the previous example with `$false`:

```
PowerCLI C:\> $VDSwitch = Get-VDSwitch -Name VDSwitch1

PowerCLI C:\>
$VDSwitch.ExtensionData.EnableNetworkResourceManagement($false)
```

Exporting the configuration of distributed virtual port groups

You can make an export from one or more distributed virtual port groups with the `Export-VDPortGroup` cmdlet, and later use this export to create new port groups or to restore the configuration of port groups. The syntax of the `Export-VDPortGroup` cmdlet is as follows:

```
Export-VDPortGroup [-VDPortGroup] <VDPortgroup[]> [-Description
<String>] [-Destination <String>] [-Force] [-Server <VIServer[]>]
[<CommonParameters>]
```

In the next example, we will create an export of VLAN 10 Port Group:

```
PowerCLI C:\> Get-VDPortGroup -Name 'VLAN 10 Port Group' |
>> Export-VDPortGroup -Destination C:\Vlan10PortGroup.zip
>>
```

```
Mode            LastWriteTime       Length Name
----            -------------       ------ ----
-a---       1/9/2014    6:57 PM        1865 Vlan10PortGroup.zip
```

 The Export-VDPortGroup cmdlet is supported only in VMware vSphere 5.1 and later versions.

Migrating a host network adapter from a standard port group to a distributed port group

In the next example, we will use the Set-VMHostNetworkAdapter cmdlet, which we have seen before, to migrate the virtual network adapter vmk1 to the distributed port group VLAN 10 Port Group:

```
PowerCLI C:\> Get-VMHostNetworkAdapter -Name vmk1 |
>> Set-VMHostNetworkAdapter -PortGroup 'VLAN 10 Port Group'
-Confirm:$false
>>
```

```
Name Mac             DhcpEnabled IP          SubnetMask    Device
---- ---             ----------- --          ----------    ------
vmk1 00:50:56:65:bd:a1 False        192.168.0.150 255.255.255.0 vmk1
```

Removing distributed virtual port groups

To remove a distributed virtual port group, you can use the Remove-VDPortGroup cmdlet. The syntax of this cmdlet is as follows:

```
Remove-VDPortGroup [-VDPortGroup] <VDPortgroup[]> [-RunAsync]
[-Server <VIServer[]>] [-WhatIf] [-Confirm] [<CommonParameters>]
```

In the following example, we will remove the port group named VLAN 10 Port Group:

```
PowerCLI C:\> Get-VDPortGroup -Name 'VLAN 10 Port Group' |
>> Remove-VDPortGroup -Confirm:$false
>>
```

Configuring host networking

The Get-VMHostNetwork cmdlet will retrieve information about the network on a specific host. This cmdlet has the following syntax:

```
Get-VMHostNetwork [-Server <VIServer[]>] [-VMHost] <VMHost[]>
[<CommonParameters>]
```

In the next example, we will retrieve the information about the network on the host 192.168.0.133:

```
PowerCLI C:\> Get-VMHost -Name 192.168.0.133 | Get-VMHostNetwork |
>> Format-List *
>>
```

```
VMHostId               : HostSystem-host-167
VMHost                 : 192.168.0.133
VMKernelGateway        : 192.168.0.1
VMKernelGatewayDevice  :
ConsoleGateway         :
ConsoleGatewayDevice   :
DnsAddress             : {192.168.0.1}
DnsFromDhcp            : True
DnsDhcpDevice          : vmk0
DomainName             : sitecomwl306
HostName               : localhost
SearchDomain           : {localdomain, sitecomwl306}
VirtualSwitch          : {vSwitch0, vSwitch1}
PhysicalNic            : {vmnic0, vmnic1, vmnic2, vmnic3...}
ConsoleNic             : {}
VirtualNic             : {vmk0, vmk1}
Uid                    : /VIServer=root@192.168.0.132:443/
VMHost=HostSystem-host-167/VMHostNetwork=/
```

```
IPv6Enabled              : True
ConsoleV6Gateway         :
ConsoleV6GatewayDevice   :
VMKernelV6Gateway        :
VMKernelV6GatewayDevice  :
ExtensionData            : VMware.Vim.HostNetworkInfo
ExtensionData2           : VMware.Vim.HostNetworkSystem
Name                     :
Id                       : HostNetworkSystem-networkSystem-167
Client                   : VMware.VimAutomation.ViCore.Impl.V1.VimClient
```

The hosts I use as examples in this book are all virtual ESXi servers running in my home lab. As you can see from the preceding output, the hostname is still `localhost` and the domain is `sitecomwl306`. That is my SiteCom wireless LAN. Let's try to change the hostname and domain.

The `Set-VMHostNetwork` cmdlet will modify the network settings of a host. The syntax of this cmdlet is as follows:

```
Set-VMHostNetwork [-Network] <VMHostNetworkInfo[]>
[-ConsoleGateway <String>] [-VMKernelGateway <String>]
[-VMKernelGatewayDevice <String>] [-ConsoleGatewayDevice<String>]
[-DomainName <String>] [-HostName <String>] [-DnsFromDhcp
[<Boolean>]] [-DnsDhcpDevice <Object>] [-DnsAddress <String[]>]
[-SearchDomain <String[]>] [-IPv6Enabled [<Boolean>]]
[-ConsoleV6Gateway <String>] [-ConsoleV6GatewayDevice <String>]
[-VMKernelV6Gateway <String>] [-VMKernelV6GatewayDevice <String>]
[-WhatIf] [-Confirm]  [<CommonParameters>]
```

In this example, we will change the host name of the host `192.168.0.133` into `ESX1`, and modify the domain name to `blackmilktea.com`. To be able to do this, we have to disable `DnsFromDhcp` because the domain name and host name cannot be explicitly set if `DnsFromDhcp` is enabled:

```
PowerCLI C:\> Get-VMHost -Name 192.168.0.133 | Get-VMHostNetwork |
>> Set-VMHostNetwork -HostName ESX1 -DomainName blackmilktea.com
-DnsFromDhcp:$false
>>
```

HostName	DomainName	DnsFro mDhcp	ConsoleGateway	ConsoleGatewayD evice	Dns
ESX1	blackmilk...	False			

Configuring the network of a virtual machine

To configure the network of a virtual machine guest operating system, you can use the Get-VMGuestNetworkInterface and Set-VMGuestNetworkInterface cmdlets. Both cmdlets are experimental and might be changed or removed in a future PowerCLI release. The cmdlets use the VMware Tools. So, if these tools are not installed inside the guest operating system or when they are not running, the cmdlets will not work. Because the cmdlets use the VMware Tools, you can configure a guest's network even if the network is not running or is disconnected.

In the help of Get-VMGuestNetworkInterface and Set-VMGuestNetworkInterface cmdlets, the following requirements for using these cmdlets are specified:

- This cmdlet supports only Windows XP 32 SP3, Windows Server 2003 32-bit SP2, Windows Server 2003 64-bit SP2, Windows 7 64-bit, Windows Server 2008 R2 64-bit, and the Redhat Enterprise 5 operating systems.

- To run this cmdlet against vCenter Server/ESX/ESXi versions earlier than 5.0, you need to meet the following requirements:

  ° You must run the cmdlet on the 32-bit version of Windows PowerShell.

  ° You must have access to the ESX that hosts the virtual machine over TCP port 902.

  ° For vCenter Server/ESX/ESXi versions earlier than 4.1, you need the VirtualMachine.Interact.ConsoleInteract privilege. For vCenter Server/ESX/ESXi 4.1 and later, you need the VirtualMachine. Interact.GuestControl privilege.

- To run this cmdlet against vCenter Server/ESXi 5.0 and later, you need VirtualMachine.GuestOperations.Execute and VirtualMachine. GuestOperations.Modify privileges.

The syntax of the Get-VMGuestNetworkInterface cmdlet is as follows:

```
Get-VMGuestNetworkInterface [-Name <String[]>] [[-VM]
<VirtualMachine[]>] [-VMGuest <VMGuest[]>] [-Server <VIServer[]>]
[-ToolsWaitSecs <Int32>] [-GuestPassword <SecureString>]
[-GuestUser <String>] [-GuestCredential <PSCredential>]
[-HostPassword <SecureString>] [-HostUser <String>]
[-HostCredential <PSCredential>] [<CommonParameters>]
```

In the next example, we will retrieve the network configuration for the virtual machine VM1. First, we have to enter a username and password with administrative rights in the guest operating system:

```
PowerCLI C:\> $Credential = Get-Credential


cmdlet Get-Credential at command pipeline position 1
Supply values for the following parameters:
Credential
PowerCLI C:\> $GuestNic = Get-VM -Name VM1 |
>> Get-VMGuestNetworkInterface -GuestCredential $Credential
>>
PowerCLI C:\> $GuestNic


VM  Name                    IP            IPPolicy SubnetMask
--  ----                    --            -------- ----------
VM1 Local Area Connection 192.168.0.201 Static   255.255.255.0
```

The syntax of the Set-VMGuestNetworkInterface cmdlet is as follows:

```
Set-VMGuestNetworkInterface -VmGuestNetworkInterface
<VMGuestNetworkInterface[]> [-WinsPolicy <DhcpPolicy>]
[-Wins <String[]>] [-DnsPolicy <DhcpPolicy>] [-Dns <String[]>]
[-IPPolicy <DhcpPolicy>] [[-Gateway] <Object>] [[-Netmask] <String>]
[[-Ip] <IPAddress>] [-ToolsWaitSecs <Int32>]
[-GuestPassword <SecureString>] [-GuestUser <String>]
[-GuestCredential <PSCredential>] [-HostPassword <SecureString>]
[-HostUser <String>] [-HostCredential <PSCredential>] [-WhatIf]
[-Confirm] [<CommonParameters>]
```

In the following example, we will set the IP address of virtual machine VM1 to 192.168.0.251:

```
PowerCLI C:\> $GuestNic | Set-VMGuestNetworkInterface -IP 192.168.0.251
-GuestCredential $Credential


VM  Name                    IP            IPPolicy SubnetMask
--  ----                    --            -------- ----------
VM1 Local Area Connection 192.168.0.251 Static   255.255.255.0
```

Summary

In this chapter, we covered virtual networking. We showed you how to work with vSphere Standard Switches and vSphere Distributed Switches using PowerCLI. You learned to use port groups, to use host network adapters, and how to configure the management network of a host and the network of a virtual machine.

In the next chapter, you will learn all about managing storage with PowerCLI.

7
Managing Storage with PowerCLI

Your virtual machines need storage for their configuration files, disks, swap files, and snapshot files. These files can be placed on datastores that reside on a host's **local storage**, **Network File System (NFS)**, **Internet Small Computer System Interface (iSCSI)**, **Fibre Channel (FC)** or **Fibre Channel over Ethernet (FCoE)**, and **Storage Area Networks (SANs)**. Datastores can be grouped into Datastore Clusters to create pools of datastores for storage aggregation, easy initial placement of disks, and load balancing using **Storage DRS**. In this chapter, we will discuss how to manage storage with PowerCLI.

The topics that will be covered in this chapter are as follows:

- Rescanning for new storage devices
- Creating datastores
- Retrieving datastores
- Setting the multipathing policy
- Configuring the vmhba paths to a SCSI device
- Working with Raw Device Mappings
- Configuring Storage I/O Control
- Configuring Storage DRS
- Upgrading datastores to VMFS-5
- Removing datastores

Rescanning for new storage devices

After creating a **Logical Unit Number** (**LUN**) on your Fibre Channel storage system and presenting the LUN to your ESXi servers, you have to rescan the **HBAs** on the ESXi servers before you can create a datastore on the LUN. An ESXi host will not see a newly attached LUN before a rescan is performed. You can use the Get-VMHostStorage cmdlet to rescan the HBAs of a host. The Get-VMHostStorage cmdlet has the following syntax:

```
Get-VMHostStorage [-VMHost] <VMHost[]> [-Refresh] [-RescanAllHba]
[-RescanVmfs] [-Server <VIServer[]>] [<CommonParameters>]

Get-VMHostStorage -Id <String[]> [-Server <VIServer[]>]
[<CommonParameters>]
```

The -VMHost and -Id parameters are required.

In the next example, we will rescan all of the HBAs of the hosts of the cluster Cluster01:

```
PowerCLI C:\> Get-Cluster -Name Cluster01 |
>> Get-VMHost | Get-VMHostStorage -RescanAllHba
>>
```

The following is the output of the preceding command:

```
SoftwareIScsiEnabled
--------------------
False
False
```

Creating datastores

You can use the New-Datastore cmdlet to create a new datastore. The New-Datastore cmdlet has two parameter sets, one for creating VMFS datastores and one for creating NFS datastores. The syntax of the New-Datastore cmdlet is as follows:

```
New-Datastore [-Server <VIServer[]>] [-VMHost] <VMHost[]> [-Name]
<String> -Path <String> [-Vmfs] [-BlockSizeMB <Int32>]
[-FileSystemVersion <String>] [-WhatIf] [-Confirm]
[<CommonParameters>]

New-Datastore [-Server <VIServer[]>] [-VMHost] <VMHost[]> [-Name]
<String> -Path <String> [-Nfs] -NfsHost <String> [-ReadOnly]
[-WhatIf] [-Confirm] [<CommonParameters>]
```

The -VMHost, -Name, -Path, and -NfsHost parameters are required.

Creating NFS datastores

In the first example, we will create an NFS datastore. To indicate that we want to create an NFS datastore, we have to use the -Nfs parameter. The datastore will be created on the host 192.168.0.133 with the name Cluster01_Nfs01. The IP address of the NFS server is 192.168.0.201, and the remote path of the NFS mount point is /fs01/cluster01/nfs01:

```
PowerCLI C:\> New-Datastore -Nfs -VMHost 192.168.0.133 -Name
Cluster01_Nfs01 -NfsHost 192.168.0.201 -Path /fs01/cluster01/nfs01
```

Name	FreeSpaceGB	CapacityGB
Cluster01_Nfs01	976.292	1,000.000

Getting SCSI LUNs

Before we can create a VMFS datastore, we need to know the **canonical name** of the **SCSI logical unit** that will contain the new VMFS datastore.

The Get-ScsiLun cmdlet retrieves the SCSI devices available on the vCenter Server system and their canonical names. The syntax of the Get-ScsiLun cmdlet is as follows:

```
Get-ScsiLun [[-CanonicalName] <String[]>] [-VmHost] <VMHost[]>
[-Key <String[]>] [-LunType <String[]>] [-Server <VIServer[]>]
[<CommonParameters>]

Get-ScsiLun -Id <String[]> [-Server <VIServer[]>]
[<CommonParameters>]

Get-ScsiLun [[-CanonicalName] <String[]>] [-Hba] <Hba[]> [-Key
<String[]>] [-LunType <String[]>] [-Server <VIServer[]>]
[<CommonParameters>]

Get-ScsiLun [[-CanonicalName] <String[]>] [-Datastore] <Datastore[]>
[-Key <String[]>] [-LunType <String[]>] [-Server <VIServer[]>]
[<CommonParameters>]
```

The –VmHost, -Id, -Hba, and -Datastore parameters are required. These four parameter sets are needed for retrieving the SCSI LUNs for hosts, SCSI device IDs, storage adapters, and datastores.

In the next example, we will get all of the SCSI LUNs of the host 192.168.0.133 and select the Vendor, Model, RuntimeName, and CanonicalName properties:

```
PowerCLI C:\> Get-VMHost -Name 192.168.0.133 | Get-ScsiLun |
```

```
>> Select-Object -Property Vendor,Model,RuntimeName,CanonicalName
>>


RuntimeName      CanonicalName
-----------      -------------

3PARdata VV       vmhba0:C0:T3:L54 naa.60002ac000000000000002f400004ca6

HP      HSVX700 vmhba0:C0:T0:L10 naa.600a0b80001111550000f4f44041944d

HP      HSVX700 vmhba0:C0:T0:L2  naa.600a0b800011115500025315052494d

HP      HSVX700 vmhba0:C0:T0:L25 naa.600a0b8000111155000059ba3f0d204e

3PARdata VV       vmhba0:C0:T2:L51 naa.60002ac0000000000000035000004bee
```

Creating VMFS datastores

To create a VMFS datastore, we have to use the New-datastore -Vmfs parameter to indicate that we want to create a VMFS datastore. We have to specify a name for the datastore and a host on which we want to create the datastore. Finally, we have to specify the canonical name of the SCSI logical unit that will contain the new VMFS datastore. This is shown in the following code:

```
PowerCLI C:\> New-Datastore -Vmfs -VMHost 192.168.0.133 -Name
Cluster01_Vmfs01 -Path naa.600a0b80001111550000d2c418e29350
```

The following is the output of the preceding command:

```
Name                              FreeSpaceGB     CapacityGB
----                              -----------     ----------

Cluster01_Vmfs01                      248,801        249,750
```

If you create the VMFS datastore on a host that is part of a cluster, the new datastore will be mounted on all hosts of the cluster.

Creating software iSCSI VMFS datastores

To create a datastore on an iSCSI SAN, you can use hardware iSCSI initiators or software iSCSI initiators. Hardware iSCSI initiators are similar to Fibre Channel HBAs. In this section, we will discuss how to create VMFS datastores using software iSCSI initiators. Before you can connect your ESXi hosts to an iSCSI LUN, your storage administrators will have to create a LUN and expose it to your ESXi servers. To set up software iSCSI initiators, you have to enable software iSCSI on your hosts using the Set-VMHostStorage cmdlet.

The syntax of this cmdlet is as follows:

```
Set-VMHostStorage -VMHostStorage <VMHostStorageInfo[]>
-SoftwareIScsiEnabled [<Boolean>] [-WhatIf] [-Confirm]
[<CommonParameters>]
```

The `-VMHostStorage` and `-SoftwareIScsiEnable` parameters are required.

Then, you can create an iSCSI HBA target. First, you have to find the iSCSI HBA using the `Get-VMHostHba` cmdlet, which has the following syntax:

```
Get-VMHostHba [[-VMHost] <VMHost[]>] [[-Device] <String[]>]
[-Type <HbaType[]>] [-Server <VIServer[]>] [<CommonParameters>]
```

This cmdlet has no required parameters.

To create the iSCSI HBA target, you can use the `New-IScsiHbaTarget` cmdlet. The syntax for the `New-IScsiHbaTarget` cmdlet is as follows:

```
New-IScsiHbaTarget -IScsiHba <IScsiHba[]> [-Address] <String[]>
[[-Port] <Int32>] [-Type <IScsiHbaTargetType>] [[-IScsiName]
<String>] [-ChapType <ChapType>] [-ChapName <String>] [-ChapPassword
<String>] [-MutualChapEnabled [<Boolean>]] [-MutualChapName <String>]
[-MutualChapPassword <String>] [-InheritChap [<Boolean>]]
[-InheritMutualChap [<Boolean>]] [-Server <VIServer[]>] [-WhatIf]
[-Confirm] [<CommonParameters>]
```

The `-IScsiHba` and `-Address` parameters are required.

After creating the iSCSI HBA target, we have to rescan the HBAs. The iSCSI HBA has to be bound to a VMkernel port group. In the following script, we will create a dedicated switch and VMkernel port group for iSCSI. There are no cmdlets to bind an iSCSI HBA to a VMkernel port group, so we have to fall back to the vSphere API's `IscsiManager BindVnic()` method.

After the binding, we have an iSCSI LUN that we can use to create a datastore. The following script performs all of the necessary steps. The script first defines the variables we use, and then it retrieves the VMHost object of the host on which the iSCSI datastore will be created. Software iSCSI will be enabled on this host. Then, an iSCSI target will be created and a rescan of the HBAs will be performed on the host. A new virtual switch and a VMkernel port group will be created. The VMkernel port group will be bound to the iSCSI HBA. Finally, the new iSCSI datastore will be created.

```
# Define the variables
$HostName = '192.168.0.133'
$iSCSITarget = '192.168.0.135'
```

```
$VirtualSwitchName = 'vSwitch2'
$NicName = 'vmnic3'
$PortGroupName = 'iSCSI Port group 1'
$ChapType = 'Preferred'
$ChapUser = 'Cluster01User'
$ChapPassword = 'Cluster01Password'
$DatastoreName = 'Cluster01_iSCSI01'

# Retrieve the host to add the iSCSI datastore to
$VMHost = Get-VMHost -Name $HostName

# Enable software iSCSI support on the host
$VMHost | Get-VMHostStorage | Set-VMHostStorage
-SoftwareIScsiEnabled:$true

# Create an iSCSI target
$VMHostHba = $VMHost | Get-VMHostHba -Type iSCSI
$VMHostHba |
New-IScsiHbaTarget -Address $iSCSITarget -ChapType $ChapType -ChapName
$ChapUser -ChapPassword $ChapPassword

# Rescan all HBAs
$VMHost | Get-VMHostStorage -RescanAllHba

# Create a new virtual switch and a vmkernel port group
$vSwitch = New-VirtualSwitch -VMHost $VMHost -Name $VirtualSwitchName
-Nic $NicName
$NetworkAdapter = New-VMHostNetworkAdapter -VirtualSwitch $vSwitch
-PortGroup $PortGroupName

# Bind the vmkernel port group to the iSCSI HBA
$IscsiManager = Get-View -Id $vmhost.ExtensionData.Configmanager.
IscsiManager
$IscsiManager.BindVnic($VMHostHba.Device, $NetworkAdapter.Name)

# Create the iSCSI datastore
$ScsiLun = $VMHost |
Get-ScsiLun |
Where-Object {$_.RuntimeName -like "$($VMHostHba.Device)*"}
New-Datastore -Vmfs -VMHost $VMHost -Name $DatastoreName -Path
$ScsiLun.CanonicalName
```

Retrieving datastores

You can use the `Get-Datastore` cmdlet to retrieve a specific datastore or a list of all of your datastores. The syntax of the `Get-Datastore` cmdlet is as follows:

```
Get-Datastore [-Server <VIServer[]>] [[-Name] <String[]>]
[-Location <VIObject[]>] [-RelatedObject
<DatastoreRelatedObjectBase[]>] [-Refresh] [-Tag <Tag[]>]
[<CommonParameters>]

Get-Datastore [-Server <VIServer[]>] -Id <String[]> [-Refresh]
[<CommonParameters>]
```

The `-Id` parameter is required.

In the next example, we will retrieve the datastore with the name `Cluster01_Vmfs01`:

```
PowerCLI C:\> Get-Datastore -Name Cluster01_Vmfs01
```

The following is the output of the preceding command:

Name	FreeSpaceGB	CapacityGB
Cluster01_Vmfs01	248,801	249,750

Setting the multipathing policy

If you use Fibre Channel or iSCSI storage devices, the use of multipathing and having multiple paths between your hosts and the SAN are highly recommended. Depending on the recommendations made by your storage vendor, you have to set the multipathing policy to either **Fixed**, **Most Recently Used (MRU)**, or **Round Robin (RR)**.

 More information about multipathing policies can be found in the VMware Knowledge Base article *Multipathing policies in ESXi 5.x and ESXi/ESX 4.x (1011340)*, at http://kb.vmware.com/kb/1011340.

You can use the `Get-ScsiLun` cmdlet to retrieve the current multipathing policy for your LUNs as follows:

```
PowerCLI C:\> Get-VMHost -Name 192.168.0.133 | Get-ScsiLun |
>> Where-Object {$_.LunType -eq 'disk'} |
```

```
>> Select-Object -Property CanonicalName,LunType,MultipathPolicy
>>
```

The following is the output of the preceding command:

```
CanonicalName                         LunType  MultipathPolicy
-------------                         -------  ---------------
naa.600a0b80001111550000f35b93e19350  disk     MostRecentlyUsed
naa.600a0b80001111550000a8adc7e19350  disk     MostRecentlyUsed
naa.600a0b80001111550000893247e29350  disk     MostRecentlyUsed
naa.600a0b80001111550000b6182ca14450  disk     MostRecentlyUsed
naa.600a0b80001111550000d2c418e29350  disk     MostRecentlyUsed
```

If you want to modify the multipathing policy, you can use the Set-ScsiLun
cmdlet's -MultipathPolicy parameter to do so. The syntax of the Set-ScsiLun
cmdlet is as follows:

```
Set-ScsiLun [[-MultipathPolicy] <ScsiLunMultipathPolicy>]
[[-PreferredPath] <ScsiLunPath>] [-ScsiLun] <ScsiLun[]>
[-CommandsToSwitchPath <Int32>] [-BlocksToSwitchath <Int32>]
[-NoCommandsSwitch] [-NoBlocksSwitch] [-WhatIf] [-Confirm]
[<CommonParameters>]
```

The -ScsiLun parameter is required. The -MultipathPolicy parameter has four
valid parameter values: Fixed, RoundRobin, MostRecentlyUsed, and Unknown.

In the next example, we will set the multipathing policy for all of the disk LUNs of
the host 192.168.0.133 to RoundRobin:

```
PowerCLI C:\> Get-VMHost -Name 192.168.0.133 | Get-ScsiLun |
>> Where-Object {$_.LunType -eq 'disk'} |
>> Set-ScsiLun -MultipathPolicy RoundRobin |
>> Select-Object -Property CanonicalName,LunType,MultipathPolicy
>>
```

The following is the output of the preceding command:

```
CanonicalName                         LunType MultipathPolicy
-------------                         ------- ---------------
naa.600a0b80001111550000f35b93e19350  disk     RoundRobin
naa.600a0b80001111550000a8adc7e19350  disk     RoundRobin
naa.600a0b80001111550000893247e29350  disk     RoundRobin
naa.600a0b80001111550000b6182ca14450  disk     RoundRobin
naa.600a0b80001111550000d2c418e29350  disk     RoundRobin
```

Configuring the vmhba paths to a SCSI device

For each vmhba path to a storage device, you can indicate that the path is active or not active. You can also indicate that the path is the preferred path to the SCSI device.

Retrieving the vmhba paths to a SCSI device

You can use the `Get-ScsiLunPath` cmdlet to retrieve the list of vmhba paths to a specified SCSI device. The syntax of the `Get-ScsiLunPath` cmdlet is as follows:

```
Get-ScsiLunPath [[-Name] <String[]>] [-ScsiLun] <ScsiLun[]>
[<CommonParameters>]
```

The `-ScsiLun` parameter is required, and it accepts input from the pipeline.

In the next example, we will retrieve the vmhba paths of the LUN with `CanonicalName naa.600a0b80001111550000f35b93e19350` from the host `192.168.0.133`:

```
PowerCLI C:\> Get-VMHost -Name 192.168.0.133 | Get-ScsiLun |
>> Where-Object {$_.CanonicalName -eq 'naa.600a0b80001111550000f35b9
3e19350'} |
>> Get-ScsiLunPath
>>
```

The following is the output of the preceding command:

Name	SanID	State	Preferred
fc.5001...	50:01:43:81:09:CF:CD:40	Standby	False
fc.5001...	50:01:43:81:09:CF:CD:24	Active	False
fc.5001...	50:01:43:81:09:CF:CD:44	Standby	False
fc.5001...	50:01:43:81:09:CF:CD:20	Standby	False

Modifying the vmhba paths to a SCSI device

You can use the `Set-ScsiLunPath` cmdlet to enable or disable a vmhba path and to set the preferred path. The syntax of the `Set-ScsiLunPath` cmdlet is as follows:

```
Set-ScsiLunPath [[-Active] [<Boolean>]] [-ScsiLunPath]
<ScsiLunPath[]> [-Preferred] [-WhatIf] [-Confirm]
[<CommonParameters>]
```

The `-ScsiLunPath` parameter is required.

In the following example, we will set the vmhba path with `SanId`
`50:01:43:81:09:CF:CD:40` to `Active` and `Preferred`:

```
PowerCLI C:\> Get-VMHost -Name 192.168.0.133 | Get-ScsiLun |
>> Where-Object {$_.CanonicalName -eq
'naa.600a0b80001111550000f35b93e19350'} |
>> Get-ScsiLunPath |
>> Where-Object {$_.SanId -eq '50:01:43:81:09:CF:CD:40'} |
>> Set-ScsiLunPath -Active:$true -Preferred
>>
```

The following is the output of the preceding command:

```
Name          SanID                             State     Preferred
----          -----                             -----     ---------
fc.5001...    50:01:43:81:09:CF:CD:40           Active    True
```

If you give the `-Active` parameter the value `$false`, you will disable the vmhba
path. This is done using the following command line:

```
PowerCLI C:\> Get-VMHost -Name scomp0975.wurnet.nl | Get-ScsiLun |
>> Where-Object {$_.CanonicalName -eq 'naa.600a0b80001111550000f35b9
3e19350'} |
>> Get-ScsiLunPath |
>> Where-Object {$_.SanId -eq '50:01:43:81:09:CF:CD:24'} |
>> Set-ScsiLunPath -Active:$false
>>

Name          SanID                             State       Preferred
----          -----                             -----       ---------
fc.5001...    50:01:43:81:09:CF:CD:24           Disabled    True
```

Working with Raw Device Mappings

A **Raw Device Mapping (RDM)** is a storage device that is presented directly
to a virtual machine. RDMs are available in two compatibility modes: physical
and virtual. The most important difference is that the virtual compatibility mode
RDMs can be a part of a VMware vSphere snapshot. Snapshots of a physical
compatibility-mode RDM can only be taken on the storage array.

There are some use cases for RDMs. The most common use case is the quorum disk in a Microsoft Windows cluster. A quorum disk must be in the physical compatibility mode.

 For more information about using Microsoft Windows Clusters on VMware vSphere, you should read the *Setup for Failover Clustering and Microsoft Cluster Service* guide. You can find this guide on https://www.vmware.com/support/pubs/. VMware Knowledge Base article *Microsoft Clustering on VMware vSphere: Guidelines for supported configurations (1037959)* can be found at http://kb.vmware.com/kb/1037959.

To add a RDM to a virtual machine, you can use the New-Harddisk cmdlet. You have already seen the syntax of this cmdlet in *Chapter 5, Managing Virtual Machines with PowerCLI*. The value of the -DiskType parameter specifies what type of disk it will be. The valid values are rawVirtual, rawPhysical, flat, and unknown.

You also need to specify a value for the New-Harddisk -DeviceName parameter. You can retrieve the device name from the LUN number by using the Get-ScsiLun cmdlet. In the next example, we will retrieve all of the LUNs of the host 192.168.0.133 and display the RuntimeName and ConsoleDeviceName properties:

```
PowerCLI C:\> Get-VMHost -Name 192.168.0.133 | Get-ScsiLun |
>> Select-Object -Property RuntimeName,ConsoleDeviceName
>>
```

The following is the output of the preceding command:

```
RuntimeName       ConsoleDeviceName
-----------       -----------------
vmhba0:C0:T0:L0   /vmfs/devices/genscsi/naa.5001438109cfcd00
vmhba0:C0:T0:L1
/vmfs/devices/disks/naa.600a0b80001111550000b6182ca14450
vmhba0:C0:T0:L2
/vmfs/devices/disks/naa.600a0b80001111550000f35b93e19350
vmhba0:C0:T0:L3
/vmfs/devices/disks/naa.600a0b80001111550000a8adc7e19350
vmhba0:C0:T0:L4
/vmfs/devices/disks/naa.600a0b80001111550000893247e29350
vmhba0:C0:T0:L5
/vmfs/devices/disks/naa.600a0b80001111550000d2c418e29350
```

In the following example, we will add a physical RDM to virtual machine VM1. If the LUN number of the RDM is 4, the device name is /vmfs/devices/disks/naa.600a 0b8000l111550000893247e29350:

```
PowerCLI C:\> New-HardDisk -VM VM1 -DiskType RawPhysical -DeviceName
/vmfs/devices/disks/naa.600a0b80001111550000893247e29350
```

The following is the output of the preceding command:

```
CapacityGB Persistence          Filename
---------- -----------          --------
500.000    IndependentPersis... [Cluster01_Vmfs01] VM1/VM1_1.vmdk
```

Configuring Storage I/O Control

Storage I/O Control (**SIOC**) is a feature of VMware vSphere Enterprise Plus that provides I/O prioritization of virtual machines running on a group of VMware vSphere hosts that have access to the same datastore. If the latencies of a datastore come above a certain threshold, Storage I/O Control will throttle the I/O bandwidth of the virtual machines that use this datastore (according to their respective share value). The default value for the latency threshold is 30 milliseconds. You should keep this default value unless you have a good reason to change it. One good reason can be the use of SSDs, where a latency threshold of 10 - 15 milliseconds is recommended.

You can enable or disable Storage I/O Control using the -StorageIOControlEnabled parameter of the Set-Datastore cmdlet. You can also specify a value for the threshold with the -CongestionThresholdMillisecond parameter. The syntax of the Set-datastore cmdlet is as follows:

```
Set-Datastore [-Datastore] <Datastore[]> [[-Name] <String>]
[-CongestionThresholdMillisecond <Int32>] [-StorageIOControlEnabled
[<Boolean>]] [-Server <VIServer[]>] [-WhatIf] [-Confirm]
[<CommonParameters>]

Set-Datastore [-Datastore] <Datastore[]> -MaintenanceMode [<Boolean>]
[-EvacuateAutomatically] [-RunAsync] [-Server <VIServer[]>] [-WhatIf]
[-Confirm] [<CommonParameters>]
```

The -Datastore and -MaintenanceMode parameters are required. The first parameter set is for updating the datastore. The second parameter set is for enabling and disabling maintenance mode.

In the next example, we will enable Storage I/O Control for the datastore
`Cluster01_Vmfs01`:

```
PowerCLI C:\> Set-Datastore -Datastore Cluster01_Vmfs01
-StorageIOControlEnabled:$true
```

The following is the output of the preceding command:

Name	FreeSpaceGB	CapacityGB
Cluster01_Vmfs01	44.706	99.750

If you want to enable Storage I/O Control for all of your datastores that don't have
Storage I/O Control enabled yet, you can use the following command:

```
PowerCLI C:\> Get-Datastore |
>> Where-Object {-not $_.StorageIOControlEnabled} |
>> Set-Datastore -StorageIOControlEnabled:$true
>>
```

To disable Storage I/O Control for the datastore `Cluster01_Vmfs01`, we have to give
the value `$false` to the `-StorageIOControlEnabled` parameter:

```
PowerCLI C:\> Set-Datastore -Datastore Cluster01_Vmfs01
-StorageIOControlEnabled:$false
```

Name	FreeSpaceGB	CapacityGB
Cluster01_Vmfs01	44.706	99.750

Retrieving Storage I/O Control settings

`StorageIOControlEnabled` and `CongestionThresholdMillisecond` are properties
of the `NasDatastoreImpl` and `VmfsDatastoreImpl` objects that are returned by the
`Get-Datastore` cmdlet. It is easy to retrieve these properties by piping the output of
the `Get-Datastore` cmdlet to the `Select-Object` cmdlet:

```
PowerCLI C:\> Get-Datastore |
>> Select-Object -Property Name,StorageIOControlEnabled,
>> CongestionThresholdMillisecond
>>
```

The following is the output of the preceding command:

Name	StorageIOControlEnabled	CongestionThresholdMillisec
Cluster01_Nfs01	False	30
Cluster01_Vmfs01	True	30

Configuring Storage DRS

vSphere **Storage Distributed Resource Scheduler (Storage DRS)** is a vSphere feature first introduced in vSphere 5.0. It gives you the possibility to combine datastores in a **Datastore Cluster**. You can then manage the Datastore Cluster instead of the individual datastores. When you create a new virtual machine and put the disks on a Datastore Cluster, Storage DRS will place the disks on the optimal datastore based on utilized disk space and datastore performance. Storage DRS can also migrate disks to another datastore in the same Datastore Cluster when the utilized disk space or latency of a datastore becomes too high. You can also make **Affinity Rules** to separate disks and virtual machines over multiple datastores or keep them together on the same datastore. If you put a datastore in **Datastore Maintenance Mode**, Storage DRS will move all of the disks on this datastore to other datastores in the same Datastore Cluster.

The first thing that you have to do, if you want to use Storage DRS, is to create one or more datastore clusters. If you have multiple types of datastores, such as gold, silver, and bronze, you might want to create a Datastore Cluster for each type.

Creating a Datastore Cluster

You can create a Datastore Cluster with the New-DatastoreCluster cmdlet, which has the following syntax:

```
New-DatastoreCluster [-Name] <String> -Location <VIContainer>
[-Server <VIServer[]>] [-WhatIf] [-Confirm] [<CommonParameters>]
```

The New-DatastoreCluster cmdlet has two required parameters: -Name and -Location. The value of the -Location parameter must be a datacenter or a folder. The following command will create a new Datastore Cluster named Gold-Datastore-Cluster in datacenter New York:

```
PowerCLI C:\> New-DatastoreCluster -Name Gold-Datastore-Cluster
  -Location (Get-Datacenter -Name 'New York')
```

The following is the output of the preceding command:

```
Name                    CapacityGB   FreeSpaceGB   SdrsAutomationLevel
----                    ----------   -----------   -------------------
Gold-Datastore-Cluster       0.000         0.000              Disabled
```

Retrieving Datastore Clusters

The `Get-DatastoreCluster` cmdlet will retrieve all of your Datastore Clusters or one or more specific Datastore Clusters. The syntax of the `Get-DatastoreCluster` cmdlet is as follows:

```
Get-DatastoreCluster [-Id <String[]>] [[-Name] <String[]>]
[-Location <VIContainer[]>] [-VM <VirtualMachine[]>] [-Template
<Template[]>] [-Datastore <Datastore[]>] [-Server <VIServer[]>]
[<CommonParameters>]
```

This cmdlet has no required parameters. If you don't specify a parameter, the `New-DatastoreCluster` cmdlet will retrieve all of your Datastore Clusters. You can use one of the parameters to retrieve Datastore Clusters based on the ID, name, location, virtual machines, templates, datastores, or vCenter Server. In the next example, we will retrieve all of our Datastore Clusters:

```
PowerCLI C:\> Get-DatastoreCluster
```

```
Name                    CapacityGB   FreeSpaceGB   SdrsAutomationLevel
----                    ----------   -----------   -------------------
Gold-Datastore-Cluster       0.000         0.000              Disabled
```

Modifying Datastore Clusters

After creating a Datastore Cluster, Storage DRS is disabled. To enable Storage DRS, you have to use the `Set-DatastoreCluster` cmdlet. The syntax of this cmdlet is as follows:

```
Set-DatastoreCluster -DatastoreCluster <DatastoreCluster[]>
[-IOLatencyThresholdMillisecond <Int32>] [-IOLoadBalanceEnabled
[<Boolean>]] [-Name <String>] [-SdrsAutomationLevel
<DrsAutomationLevel>] [-SpaceUtilizationThresholdPercent <Int32>]
[-Server <VIServer[]>] [-WhatIf] [-Confirm] [<CommonParameters>]
```

The `-DatastoreCluster` parameter is required.

To enable Storage DRS, you have to use the -SdrsAutomationLevel parameter. This parameter has three possible values: Disabled, Manual, and FullyAutomated. If you use Manual, Storage DRS will give you recommendations for the placement of disks on the datastores. You will have to apply the recommendations to move the disks. If you choose FullyAutomated, Storage DRS will automatically move disks if the utilized disk space or latency of a datastore becomes too high.

If you want to enable load balancing based on I/O metrics, you have to use the -IOLoadBalanceEnabled parameter and pass it the value $true.

In the following example, we will enable Storage DRS and set the automation level to FullyAutomated for Gold-Datastore-Cluster. We will also enable load balancing based on I/O metrics:

```
PowerCLI C:\> Set-DatastoreCluster -DatastoreCluster
Gold-Datastore-Cluster -SdrsAutomationLevel FullyAutomated
-IOLoadBalanceEnabled:$true

Name                     CapacityGB   FreeSpaceGB   SdrsAutomationLevel
----                     ----------   -----------   -------------------
Gold-Datastore-Cluster        0.000         0.000        FullyAutomated
```

In the next screenshot of the vSphere Web Client, you will see the Datastore Cluster **Gold-Datastore-Cluster** after executing the preceding command:

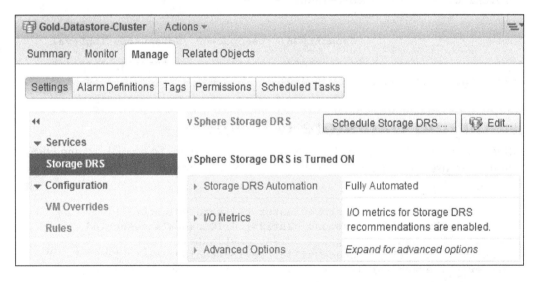

Adding datastores to a Datastore Cluster

The `Move-Datastore` cmdlet will move datastores into a Datastore Cluster or to a folder or datacenter. The syntax of the `Move-Datastore` cmdlet is as follows:

```
Move-Datastore [-Datastore] <Datastore[]> [-Destination] <VIObject>
[-Server <VIServer[]>] [-WhatIf] [-Confirm] [<CommonParameters>]
```

The `-Datastore` and `-Destination` parameters are required.

In the following example, we will move the `Cluster01_Vmfs01` datastore into the Datastore Cluster `Gold-Datastore-Cluster`:

```
PowerCLI C:\> Move-Datastore -Datastore Cluster01_Vmfs01
-Destination (Get-DatastoreCluster -Name Gold-Datastore-Cluster)
```

In the following screenshot of the vSphere Web Client, you will see the datastore **Cluster01_Vmfs01** after it is moved into the Datastore Cluster **Gold-datastore-Cluster**:

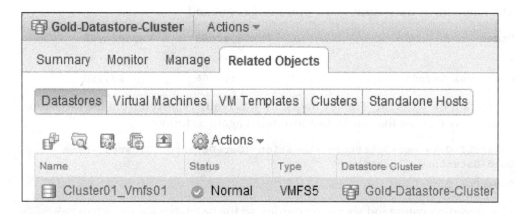

Retrieving the datastores in a Datastore Cluster

If you want to know which datastores are in a Datastore Cluster, you can use the `Get-Datastore -Location` parameter. In the following example, we will retrieve all of the datastores in the `Gold-Datastore-Cluster` Datastore Cluster:

```
PowerCLI C:\> Get-Datastore -Location (Get-DatastoreCluster -Name
Gold-Datastore-Cluster)
```

The following is the output of the preceding command:

```
Name                           FreeSpaceGB     CapacityGB
----                           -----------     ----------
Cluster01_Vmfs01                    44.706         99.750
```

Removing datastores from a Datastore Cluster

To remove a datastore from a Datastore Cluster, you have to move the datastore to a folder or a datacenter. In the next example, we will move the `Cluster01_Vmfs01` datastore from the `Gold-Datastore-Cluster` Datastore Cluster to the `New York` datacenter:

```
PowerCLI C:\> Move-Datastore -Datastore Cluster01_Vmfs01 -Destination
(Get-Datacenter -Name 'New York')
```

The following is the output of the preceding command:

```
Name                           FreeSpaceGB     CapacityGB
----                           -----------     ----------
Cluster01_Vmfs01                    44.706         99.750
```

To check if the `Cluster_Vmfs01` datastore was really removed from the Datastore Cluster, we can use the Get-Datastore cmdlet again as follows:

```
PowerCLI C:\> Get-Datastore -Location (Get-DatastoreCluster -Name
Gold-Datastore-Cluster)
PowerCLI C:\>
```

The preceding command shows no output, so the `Gold-Datastore-Cluster` Datastore Cluster no longer contains any datastores.

Removing Datastore Clusters

To remove a Datastore Cluster, you can use the `Remove-DatastoreCluster` cmdlet. The syntax of this cmdlet is as follows:

```
Remove-DatastoreCluster [-DatastoreCluster] <DatastoreCluster[]>
[-Server <VIServer[]>] [-WhatIf] [-Confirm] [<CommonParameters>]
```

The `-DatastoreCluster` parameter is required.

In the following example, we will remove the `Gold-Datastore-Cluster` Datastore Cluster:

```
PowerCLI C:\> Remove-DatastoreCluster
-DatastoreCluster Gold-datastore-Cluster -Confirm:$false
```

Upgrading datastores to VMFS-5

With vSphere 5, VMware upgraded the VMFS filesystem to version 5. VMFS-5 came with the following new features: Unified 1MB File Block Size, Large Single Extent Volumes of 64 TB, Smaller 8 KB Sub-Block, Small File Support, Increased File Count limit > 120,000, **VMware vSphere Storage APIs for Array Integration (VAAI)**, primitive **Atomic Test & Set (ATS)**, enhancement for file locking, **GUID Partition Table (GPT)**, and a new starting sector of 2048.

If you upgraded your vSphere environment from version 4 or earlier to version 5, your datastores are probably still on VMFS-3. There are two options for going to VMFS-5. The first option is to create new VMFS-5 datastores and move your virtual machines to the new datastores. When your old VMFS-3 datastores are empty, you can remove them. The advantage of this method is that the new datastores will have all of the new VMFS-5 features. However, it is a lot of work and you need enough free space on your storage system to create at least one new datastore.

The second option is to upgrade your datastores to VMFS-5. Upgrading your datastores can be done online without downtime for your virtual machines. However, upgraded datastores will not have all of the new features. Upgraded datastores will keep the block size they had before the upgrade, still have the old Sub-Block Size of 64 KB, keep the file limit of 30,720, continue to use the **Master Boot Record (MBR)** partition type, and start on sector 128.

You can retrieve the VMFS version of your datastores with the following command:

```
PowerCLI C:\> Get-Datastore |
>> Where-Object {$_.GetType().Name -eq 'VmfsDatastoreImpl'} |
>> Select-Object -Property Name,FileSystemVersion
>>
```

The following is the output of the preceding command:

```
Name                                          FileSystemVersion
----                                          -----------------
Cluster01_Vmfs01                                          5.60
```

In the next screenshot of the vSphere Web Client, you will see the datastore **Cluster01_Vmfs01** with filesystem version **VMFS 3.58** before it is upgraded to VMFS-5:

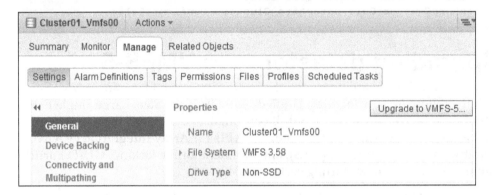

If you want to upgrade your datastores to VMFS-5, you can use the following PowerCLI script to upgrade all of your datastores. The script uses the Get-Datastore cmdlet to retrieve all of your datastores. Then, it uses the Where-Object cmdlet in the pipeline to filter for VMFS datastores that have a version lower than 5. The ForEach-Object cmdlet is used to process all of the datastores that are found. Then, the script retrieves the HostStorageSystem object of a host connected to the datastore. The UpgradeVmfs() method of this HostStorageSystem object is used to upgrade the datastore. The following script is used to update the datastore:

```
Get-Datastore |
Where-Object {$_.GetType().Name -eq 'VmfsDatastoreImpl'
-and $_.FileSystemVersion -lt 5} |
ForEach-Object {
  $Datastore = $_
  # Get the HostStorageSystem of the first host that the
  # datastore is connected to
  # The UpgradeVmfs() method of this object is used to
  # upgrade the datastore
  $HostStorageSystem = $Datastore |
    Get-VMHost | Select-Object -First 1 |
    Get-VMHostStorage | Get-View

  # Construct the path to the volume to upgrade
  # For example:
  # /vmfs/volumes/4e97fa06-7fa61558-937e-984be163eb88
  $Volume = '/' + $Datastore.ExtensionData.Info.Url.TrimStart('ds:/').
TrimEnd('/')
```

```
# Upgrade the datastore
$HostStorageSystem.UpgradeVmfs($Volume)
}
```

Removing datastores

To remove a datastore, you can use the `Remove-Datastore` cmdlet. The syntax of this cmdlet is as follows:

```
Remove-Datastore [-Datastore] <Datastore[]> [-VMHost] <VMHost>
[-Server <VIServer[]>] [-RunAsync] [-WhatIf] [-Confirm]
[<CommonParameters>]
```

The required parameters of the `Remove-Datastore` cmdlet are `-Datastore` and `-VMHost`.

In the next example, we will remove the `Cluster01_Vmfs01` datastore, which we created at the beginning of this chapter:

```
PowerCLI C:\> Remove-Datastore -Datastore Cluster01_Vmfs01 -VMHost
192.168.0.133 -Confirm:$false
```

If you try to remove a datastore, it is possible that you get an error message similar to the following error message:

```
Remove-datastore : 1/18/2014 7:37:46 PM     Remove-Datastore
    The resource '51ceb90c-6cb03821-3504-ac162daa6ca0' is in use.
```

Before you can remove a datastore, there are some requirements that must be fulfilled:

- There must be no virtual machines residing on the datastore
- The datastore must not be part of a Datastore Cluster
- The datastore must not be managed by Storage DRS
- Storage I/O Control must be disabled for the datastore
- The datastore must not be used for vSphere HA heartbeat

After fulfilling all of these requirements, you will not get the `The resource is in use` error anymore when you remove a datastore.

We have not discussed the use of datastores for vSphere HA heartbeat yet. We will do this in *Chapter 8, Managing High Availability and Clustering with PowerCLI.*

Summary

In this chapter, we covered how to manage storage. We showed you how to create and remove datastores, configure software iSCSI initiators, work with RDMs, configure Storage I/O Control, create and remove Datastore Clusters, add datastores to a datastore cluster, and upgrade your datastores to VMFS-5.

In the next chapter, you will learn all about managing High Availability and clustering with PowerCLI.

8

Managing High Availability and Clustering with PowerCLI

Availability of the applications running in your environment is an important advantage of virtualization. In the case of a host or operating system failure, VMware vSphere **High Availability (HA)** will restart the affected virtual machines. This ensures that your servers are available as much as possible.

VMware vSphere **Distributed Resources Scheduler (DRS)** provides initial placement of a virtual machine on an appropriate host during power on, automated load balancing to maximize performance, and distribution of virtual machines across hosts to comply with affinity and anti-affinity rules.

To save power and money, **Distributed Power Management (DPM)** will consolidate your virtual machines on fewer hosts in your cluster and power down the unused hosts when not all of the resources are needed.

To use DRS or DPM, you need a VMware vSphere Enterprise or Enterprise Plus license.

The topics that will be covered in this chapter are:

- Creating vSphere HA and DRS clusters
- Retrieving clusters
- Modifying cluster settings
- Moving hosts to clusters
- Moving clusters
- Using DRS rules

- Using DRS recommendations
- Using resource pools
- Using Distributed Power Management (DPM)
- Removing clusters

Creating vSphere HA and DRS clusters

In *Chapter 4, Managing vSphere Hosts with PowerCLI*, you already saw how to create a vSphere cluster with the default settings using the New-Cluster cmdlet. In the default settings, HA and DRS are disabled. You will now see how to create a cluster with HA and DRS enabled. First, the syntax of the New-Cluster cmdlet will be repeated so you don't have to look back at *Chapter 4, Managing vSphere Hosts with PowerCLI*:

```
New-Cluster [-HARestartPriority <HARestartPriority>]
[-HAIsolationResponse <HAIsolationResponse>] [-VMSwapfilePolicy
<VMSwapfilePolicy>] [-Name] <String> -Location <VIContainer> [-HAEnabled]
[-HAAdmissionControlEnabled] [-HAFailoverLevel <Int32>] [-DrsEnabled]
[-DrsMode <DrsMode>] [-DrsAutomationLevel <DrsAutomationLevel>]
[-VsanDiskClaimMode <VsanDiskClaimMode>] [-VsanEnabled] [-Server
<VIServer[]>] [-WhatIf] [-Confirm] [<CommonParameters>]
```

The -Name and -Location parameters are required.

In the next example, an HA- and DRS-enabled cluster named Cluster02 will be created in the New York datacenter. The new cluster will have the DRS migration automation level as "fully automated". The HA admission control will be enabled and the cluster will have a configured failover capacity of one host. The VM restart priority will be high and the host isolation response will be "leave powered on". The swap file location for virtual machines will be the virtual machine directory.

Because you will use almost every parameter of the New-Cluster cmdlet, you will use splatting to create a hash table with all of the parameters and their values. Splatting was explained in *Chapter 6, Managing Virtual Networks with PowerCLI*, so I hope you still remember this great PowerShell feature. It makes your code more readable because you don't have to create a single long command. Consider the following command lines:

```
PowerCLI C:\> $Parameters = @{
>>    Name = 'Cluster02'
>>    Location = (Get-Datacenter -Name 'New York')
>>    DrsEnabled = $true
>>    DrsAutomationLevel = 'FullyAutomated'
>>    HAEnabled = $true
>>    HAAdmissionControlEnabled = $true
```

```
>>    HAFailoverLevel = 1
>>    HAIsolationResponse = 'DoNothing'
>>    HARestartPriority = 'High'
>>    VMSwapfilePolicy = 'WithVM'
>> }
>> New-Cluster @Parameters
>>
```

Name	HAEnabled	HAFailover Level	DrsEnabled	DrsAutomationLevel
Cluster02	True	1	True	FullyAutomated

In the next image, you will see a screenshot from the vSphere Web Client showing the HA and DRS settings of Cluster02 after running the preceding PowerCLI commands to create the cluster:

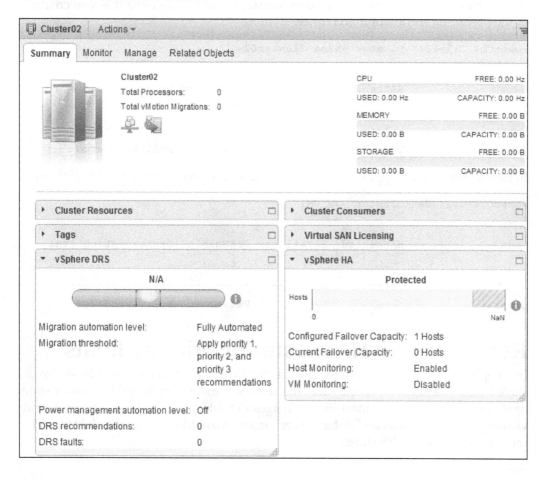

Retrieving clusters

To retrieve one or more of the clusters available on your vCenter Server system, you can use the Get-Cluster cmdlet. The syntax of the Get-Cluster cmdlet is:

```
Get-Cluster [-VM <VirtualMachine[]>] [-VMHost <VMHost[]>] [-Location
<VIContainer[]>] [[-Name] <String[]>] [-NoRecursion] [-Server
<VIServer[]>] [<CommonParameters>]

Get-Cluster -Id <String[]> [-Server <VIServer[]>] [<CommonParameters>]
```

The -Location parameter enables you to filter for clusters in a specific location such as a datacenter or folder. The -Name, -Id, -VM, and -VMHost parameters specify filters that you can use to retrieve clusters with a specific name or ID, or clusters containing the specified virtual machines or hosts.

In the first example, you will retrieve the cluster named Cluster02 that you created in the preceding section of this chapter.

```
PowerCLI C:\> Get-Cluster -Name Cluster02
```

Name	HAEnabled	HAFailover Level	DrsEnabled	DrsAutomationLevel
Cluster02	True	1	True	FullyAutomated

In the second example, you will retrieve the cluster on which virtual machine VM1 runs:

```
PowerCLI C:\> Get-Cluster -VM VM1
```

Name	HAEnabled	HAFailover Level	DrsEnabled	DrsAutomationLevel
Cluster01	True	1	False	FullyAutomated

Retrieving the HA master or primary hosts

In a vSphere HA cluster, one of the hosts is the master host and all other hosts are slave hosts. The master host monitors the state of the slave hosts and the power state of all the protected virtual machines, manages the lists of cluster hosts and protected virtual machines, acts as a vCenter Server management interface to the cluster, and reports the cluster health state.

The `Get-HAPrimaryVMHost` cmdlet will retrieve the master host on a vCenter 5.0 or later HA cluster and will retrieve the primary HA hosts on an earlier than vCenter 5.0 cluster. The syntax of the `Get-HAPrimaryVMHost` cmdlet is:

```
Get-HAPrimaryVMHost [[-Cluster] <Cluster[]>] [-Server <VIServer[]>]
[<CommonParameters>]
```

In the example, the master host on the cluster `Cluster01` is retrieved using the following command lines:

```
PowerCLI C:\> Get-Cluster -Name Cluster01 | Get-HAPrimaryVMHost

Name                ConnectionState PowerState NumCpu CpuUsageMhz
----                --------------- ---------- ------ -----------
192.168.0.133       Connected       PoweredOn       2          69
```

Retrieving cluster configuration issues

If your cluster is incorrectly configured, the vSphere Web Client will show you the issues in the **Summary** tab. In the next screenshot of the vSphere Web Client, you will see two cluster configuration issues: **Insufficient capacity in cluster Cluster01 to satisfy resource configuration in New York** and **vCenter Server is unable to find a master vSphere HA agent in cluster Cluster01 in New York**:

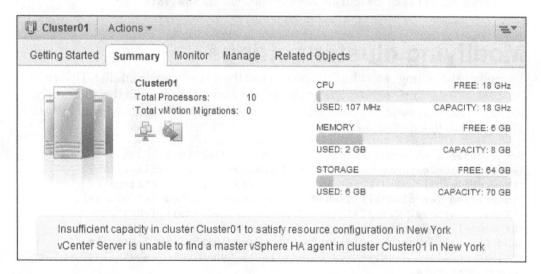

You can easily find any cluster configuration issues with PowerCLI. The next PowerCLI script displays the cluster name, creation time, and the full formatted message of all of the cluster configuration issues in your environment.

The script uses the `Get-Cluster` cmdlet to retrieve all of the clusters. It pipes the output to the `Get-View` cmdlet to return the vSphere View objects of the clusters. The vSphere View objects are piped to the `Select-Object` cmdlet to expand the `ConfigIssue` property. Another `Select-Object` cmdlet is used in the pipeline to retrieve the cluster name using a calculated property, the creation time, and the full formatted message. Finally, the output is piped to `Format-Table -AutoSize` to display it in a compact table format:

```
PowerCLI C:\> Get-Cluster | Get-View |
>> Select-Object -ExpandProperty ConfigIssue |
>> Select-Object -Property @{Name="Cluster";Expression={$_.
ComputeResource.Name}},
>> CreatedTime,FullFormattedMessage | Format-Table -AutoSize
>>


Cluster    CreatedTime            FullFormattedMessage
-------    -----------            --------------------
Cluster01 1/8/2014 06:03:36 PM   vCenter Server is unable to find a master
vSphere HA agent in cluster Cluster01 in New York

Cluster01 1/19/2014 05:48:27 AM Insufficient capacity in cluster
Cluster01 to satisfy resource configuration in New York
```

Modifying cluster settings

To modify the settings of a cluster, you can use the `Set-Cluster` cmdlet. This cmdlet has basically the same parameters as the `New-Cluster` cmdlet with the addition of the `-Profile` parameter that enables you to associate a host profile with a cluster. The syntax of the `Set-Cluster` cmdlet is:

```
Set-Cluster [-HARestartPriority <HARestartPriority>]
[-HAIsolationResponse <HAIsolationResponse>] [-VMSwapfilePolicy
<VMSwapfilePolicy>] [-Cluster] <Cluster[]> [[-Name] <String>]
[-HAEnabled [<Boolean>]] [-HAAdmissionControlEnabled [<Boolean>]]
[-HAFailoverLevel <Int32>] [-DrsEnabled [<Boolean>]] [-DrsMode
<DrsMode>] [-DrsAutomationLevel <DrsAutomationLevel>] [-VsanEnabled
[<Boolean>]] [-VsanDiskClaimMode <VsanDiskClaimMode>] [-Profile
<VMHostProfile>] [-Server <VIServer[]>] [-RunAsync] [-WhatIf] [-Confirm]
[<CommonParameters>]
```

Disabling HA

The next example will disable HA for `Cluster02`. This might be useful when you perform network maintenance that may cause isolation responses.

```
PowerCLI C:\> Get-Cluster -Name Cluster02 | Set-Cluster -HAEnabled $false
-Confirm:$false
```

Name	HAEnabled	HAFailover Level	DrsEnabled	DrsAutomationLevel
----	---------	----------	----------	------------------
Cluster02	False	1	True	FullyAutomated

Disabling or enabling host monitoring

To disable host monitoring, you have to use the vSphere API. The next script will disable host monitoring for `Cluster02`. In the script, a `ClusterConfigSpecEx` object is created. Also, a `ClusterDasConfigInfo` object for the `dasConfig` property of the `ClusterConfigSpecEx` object is created. The `hostMonitoring` property of the `ClusterDasConfigInfo` object is set to `disabled`. Finally, the `ReconfigureComputeResource_Task()` method is called using the `ClusterConfigSpecEx` object as the first parameter.

The second parameter of the `ReconfigureComputeResource_Task()` method is named `modify`. If the value of the `modify` parameter is set to `$true`, the changes specified in the `ClusterConfigSpecEx` object will be applied incrementally to the cluster object. If the value of the `modify` parameter is `$false`, the configuration of the cluster will match the specification exactly. In this case, any unset properties of the specification will result in unset or default properties of the configuration of the cluster.

The `ReconfigureComputeResource_Task()` method creates a vSphere task and runs asynchronously:

```
# Disabling host monitoring
$Cluster = Get-Cluster -Name Cluster02
$spec = New-Object VMware.Vim.ClusterConfigSpecEx
$spec.dasConfig = New-Object VMware.Vim.ClusterDasConfigInfo
$spec.dasConfig.hostMonitoring = "disabled"
$Cluster.ExtensionData.ReconfigureComputeResource_Task($spec, $true)
```

If you want to enable host monitoring, you have to modify `"disabled"` in line 5 of the preceding script to `"enabled"`.

Associating a host profile with a cluster

In *Chapter 4, Managing vSphere Hosts with PowerCLI*, you already saw how to attach or associate a host profile to a cluster using the `Apply-VMHostProfile` cmdlet. The next example will show you how to associate a host profile to a cluster using the `Set-Cluster` cmdlet:

```
PowerCLI C:\> Set-Cluster -Cluster Cluster02 -Profile Cluster-Profile
-Confirm:$false
```

If you want to remove the association, you can use `$null` as the value for the `-Profile` parameter.

Enabling VM and application monitoring

VM and application monitoring will restart a virtual machine if VMware Tools' heartbeats are not received for a specific time frame. This time frame, called the `failureInterval`, is configurable. You can also specify the minimum time the virtual machine must be up, called `minUpTime`, the maximum number of times, called `maxFailures`, and a virtual machine will be restarted in a certain time window, called `maxFailureWindow`. In the vSphere client, there are three predefined settings to monitor sensitivity called low, medium, and high.

The preset values for the low, medium, and high monitoring sensitivities are:

Monitoring Sensitivity	Low	Medium	High
failureInterval	120	60	30
minUpTime	480	240	120
maxFailures	3	3	3
maxFailureWindow	604800	86400	3600

Of course, you can use your own custom values. If you don't want to use **Maximum resets time window**, you have to use the value `-1` for the `maxFailureWindow` property.

In the next screenshot of the vSphere Web Client, you will see the VM Monitoring settings of a cluster with **VM and Application Monitoring** enabled and **Monitoring Sensitivity** set to **High**.

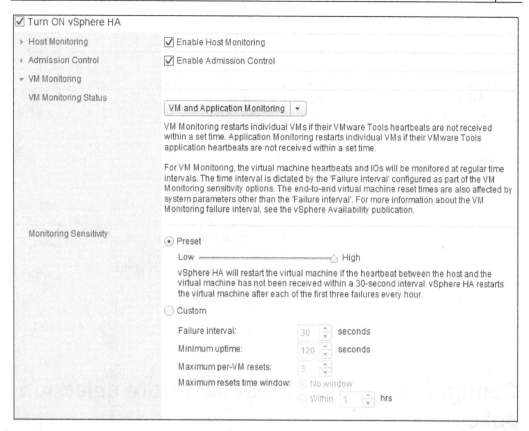

☑ Turn ON vSphere HA

▸ Host Monitoring   ☑ Enable Host Monitoring

▸ Admission Control   ☑ Enable Admission Control

▾ VM Monitoring

VM Monitoring Status

VM and Application Monitoring ▾

VM Monitoring restarts individual VMs if their VMware Tools heartbeats are not received
within a set time. Application Monitoring restarts individual VMs if their VMware Tools
application heartbeats are not received within a set time.

For VM Monitoring, the virtual machine heartbeats and IOs will be monitored at regular time
intervals. The time interval is dictated by the 'Failure interval' configured as part of the VM
Monitoring sensitivity options. The end-to-end virtual machine reset times are also affected by
system parameters other than the 'Failure interval'. For more information about the VM
Monitoring failure interval, see the vSphere Availability publication.

Monitoring Sensitivity

⦿ Preset

Low ─────────────────────────◌ High

vSphere HA will restart the virtual machine if the heartbeat between the host and the
virtual machine has not been received within a 30-second interval. vSphere HA restarts
the virtual machine after each of the first three failures every hour.

◌ Custom

Failure interval: 30   seconds

Minimum uptime: 120 seconds

Maximum per-VM resets: 3

Maximum resets time window: ◌ No window
                               ◌ Within 1   hrs

You cannot use the Set-Cluster cmdlet to enable or disable VM and application monitoring. You have to use the vSphere API again to do this. In the next script, you will create the ClusterConfigSpecEx and ClusterDasConfigInfo objects as you have seen before. The vmMonitoring property of the ClusterDasConfigInfo object will get the value vmAndAppMonitoring. You will also create a ClusterDasVmSettings object as the value of the defaultVmSettings property of the ClusterDasConfigInfo object. A ClusterDasVmToolsMonitoringSettings object is created as the value of the vmToolsMonitoringSettings property of the ClusterDasVmSettings object. The properties of the ClusterVmToolsMonitoringSettings object will get a value that corresponds with the medium monitoring sensitivity. Finally, the ReconfigureComputeResource_Task() method is called to reconfigure the cluster.

```
# Enabling VM and application monitoring
$Cluster = Get-Cluster -Name Cluster02
$spec = New-Object VMware.Vim.ClusterConfigSpecEx
```

```
$spec.dasConfig = New-Object VMware.Vim.ClusterDasConfigInfo
$spec.dasConfig.vmMonitoring = "vmAndAppMonitoring"
$spec.dasConfig.defaultVmSettings = New-Object VMware.Vim.
ClusterDasVmSettings
$spec.dasConfig.defaultVmSettings.vmToolsMonitoringSettings = New-
Object VMware.Vim.ClusterVmToolsMonitoringSettings
$spec.dasConfig.defaultVmSettings.vmToolsMonitoringSettings.enabled =
$true
$spec.dasConfig.defaultVmSettings.vmToolsMonitoringSettings.
vmMonitoring = "vmAndAppMonitoring"
$spec.dasConfig.defaultVmSettings.vmToolsMonitoringSettings.
failureInterval = 60
$spec.dasConfig.defaultVmSettings.vmToolsMonitoringSettings.minUpTime
= 240
$spec.dasConfig.defaultVmSettings.vmToolsMonitoringSettings.
maxFailures = 3
$spec.dasConfig.defaultVmSettings.vmToolsMonitoringSettings.
maxFailureWindow = 86400
$Cluster.ExtensionData.ReconfigureComputeResource_Task($spec, $true)
```

The possible values for the vmMonitoring property are vmMonitoringDisabled (the default value), vmMonitoringOnly, or vmAndAppMonitoring.

Configuring the heartbeat datastore selection policy

Datastore heartbeating is a vSphere HA feature introduced in vSphere 5.0. In the case of a lost network connection between the HA master and the slaves, datastore heartbeating is used to validate whether a host has failed or just the network between the hosts is lost. If the master concludes that a slave host has failed because there are no datastore heartbeats, the virtual machines of the failed host will be restarted on other hosts in the cluster. If a host still has datastore heartbeats, the master concludes that the slave is **isolated** or **partitioned**. Depending on the configured host isolation response for the cluster, the virtual machines on the isolated host will be left powered on, shut down, or powered off.

vCenter Server selects two datastores per host for datastore heartbeating, according to the datastore heartbeating policy defined for the cluster. The policy can be one of the following: automatically select datastores accessible from the host, use datastores only from the specified list, or use datastores from the specified list and complement automatically if needed.

In the next table, you will see the three datastore heartbeating policies and the possible values for the HBDatastoreCandidatePolicy property used by the vSphere API:

HBDatastoreCandidatePolicy	Description
allFeasibleDs	Automatically select datastores accessible from the host
userSelectedDs	Use datastores only from the specified list
allFeasibleDsWithUserPreference	Use datastores from the specified list and complement automatically if needed

In the first example, you will retrieve the datastore heartbeating policy for Cluster01:

```
PowerCLI C:\> $Cluster = Get-Cluster -Name Cluster01

PowerCLI C:\> $Cluster.ExtensionData.Configuration.DasConfig.
HBDatastoreCandidatePolicy

allFeasibleDsWithUserPreference
```

In the following example, you will retrieve the datastores used for datastore heartbeating in cluster Cluster01:

```
PowerCLI C:\> $cluster.ExtensionData.RetrieveDasAdvancedRuntimeInfo().
HeartbeatDatastoreInfo |
>> Select-Object -ExpandProperty Datastore |
>> Get-VIObjectByVIView
>>
```

There are no PowerCLI cmdlets to configure datastore heartbeating, so you have to use the vSphere API. In the next example, you will configure the "automatically select datastores accessible from the host" datastore heartbeating policy for cluster Cluster01. First, you create the ClusterConfigSpecEx and ClusterDasConfigInfo objects as a value of the dasConfig property of the ClusterConfigSpecEx object. Then, you give the hBDatastoreCandidatePolicy property of the ClusterDasConfigInfo object the allFeasibleDs value. Finally, you call the ReconfigureComputeResource_Task() method to reconfigure the cluster.

```
# Automatically select datastores accessible from the host
# for datastore heartbeating
$Cluster = Get-Cluster -Name Cluster01
$spec = New-Object VMware.Vim.ClusterConfigSpecEx
$spec.dasConfig = New-Object VMware.Vim.ClusterDasConfigInfo
```

```
$spec.dasConfig.hBDatastoreCandidatePolicy = "allFeasibleDs"
$Cluster.ExtensionData.ReconfigureComputeResource_Task($spec, $true)
```

The next screenshot of the vSphere Web Client will show you the **Datastore Heartbeating** settings of `Cluster01` set to **Automatically select datastores accessible from the host** after running the preceding PowerCLI commands:

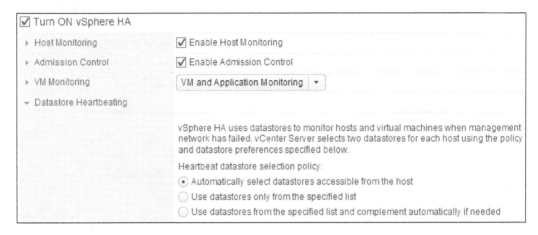

In the next example, you will configure the "use datastores only from the specified list" datastore heartbeating policy for `Cluster01`. The new thing in this example is that you have to specify the Managed Object References of the datastores that you selected for the datastore heartbeating. Therefore, an array of two `ManagedObjectReference` objects is specified as the value of the `heartbeatDatastore` property of the `ClusterDasConfigInfo` object. The array is filled with the MoRefs of the selected datastores. The `hBDatastoreCandidatePolicy` property of the `ClusterDasConfigInfo` object is given the `userSelectedDs` value. Finally, the `ReconfigureComputeResource_Task()` method is called to reconfigure the cluster.

```
# Use datastores only from the specified list
# for datastore heartbeating
$Cluster = Get-Cluster -Name Cluster01
$Datastore1 = Get-Datastore -Name Datastore1
$Datastore2 = Get-Datastore -Name Datastore2
$spec = New-Object VMware.Vim.ClusterConfigSpecEx
$spec.dasConfig = New-Object VMware.Vim.ClusterDasConfigInfo
$spec.dasConfig.heartbeatDatastore = New-Object VMware.Vim.
ManagedObjectReference[] (2)
$spec.dasConfig.heartbeatDatastore[0] = New-Object VMware.Vim.
ManagedObjectReference
$spec.dasConfig.heartbeatDatastore[0].type = "Datastore"
```

```
$spec.dasConfig.heartbeatDatastore[0].Value = $Datastore1.
ExtensionData.MoRef.Value
$spec.dasConfig.heartbeatDatastore[1] = New-Object VMware.Vim.
ManagedObjectReference
$spec.dasConfig.heartbeatDatastore[1].type = "Datastore"
$spec.dasConfig.heartbeatDatastore[1].Value = $Datastore2.
ExtensionData.MoRef.Value
$spec.dasConfig.hBDatastoreCandidatePolicy = "userSelectedDs"
$Cluster.ExtensionData.ReconfigureComputeResource_Task($spec, $true)
```

In the last example of configuring datastore heartbeating, you will configure the "use datastores from the specified list and complement automatically if needed" datastore heartbeating policy for Cluster01. The example is almost the same as the preceding example. The difference is that you now give the hBDatastoreCandidatePolicy property of the ClusterDasConfigInfo object the allFeasibleDsWithUserPreference value:

```
# Use datastores from the specified list and complement
# automatically if needed for datastore heartbeating
$Cluster = Get-Cluster -Name Cluster01
$Datastore1 = Get-Datastore -Name Datastore1
$Datastore2 = Get-Datastore -Name Datastore2
$spec = New-Object VMware.Vim.ClusterConfigSpecEx
$spec.dasConfig = New-Object VMware.Vim.ClusterDasConfigInfo
$spec.dasConfig.heartbeatDatastore = New-Object VMware.Vim.
ManagedObjectReference[] (2)
$spec.dasConfig.heartbeatDatastore[0] = New-Object VMware.Vim.
ManagedObjectReference
$spec.dasConfig.heartbeatDatastore[0].type = "Datastore"
$spec.dasConfig.heartbeatDatastore[0].Value = $Datastore1.
ExtensionData.MoRef.Value
$spec.dasConfig.heartbeatDatastore[1] = New-Object VMware.Vim.
ManagedObjectReference
$spec.dasConfig.heartbeatDatastore[1].type = "Datastore"
$spec.dasConfig.heartbeatDatastore[1].Value = $Datastore2.
ExtensionData.MoRef.Value
$spec.dasConfig.hBDatastoreCandidatePolicy =
"allFeasibleDsWithUserPreference"
$Cluster.ExtensionData.ReconfigureComputeResource_Task($spec, $true)
```

Moving hosts to clusters

You can use the Move-VMHost cmdlet to move a host to a cluster. The host has to already be added to your vSphere inventory. If it isn't, you can use the Add-VMHost cmdlet to add the host to your inventory, as shown in *Chapter 4, Managing vSphere Hosts with PowerCLI*. The host also has to be in maintenance mode or you will get the error message: **The operation is not allowed in the current state**.

The syntax of the Move-VMHost cmdlet is:

```
Move-VMHost [-VMHost] <VMHost[]> [-Destination] <VIContainer> [-Server
<VIServer[]>] [-RunAsync] [-WhatIf] [-Confirm] [<CommonParameters>]
```

The -VMHost and -Destination parameters are required.

You can also use the Move-VMhost cmdlet to move a host to another VIContainer object such as a datacenter or a folder.

In the next example, you will first put host 192.168.0.134 in maintenance mode, move the host to Cluster02, and finally exit maintenance mode:

```
PowerCLI C:\> $VMHost = Get-VMHost -Name 192.168.0.134
PowerCLI C:\> $VMHost | Set-VMHost -State Maintenance
```

Name	ConnectionState	PowerState	NumCpu	CpuUsageMhz
192.168.0.134	Maintenance	PoweredOn	2	226

```
PowerCLI C:\> $VMHost | Move-VMHost -Destination (Get-Cluster -Name
Cluster02) -Confirm:$false
```

Name	ConnectionState	PowerState	NumCpu	CpuUsageMhz
192.168.0.134	Maintenance	PoweredOn	2	226

```
PowerCLI C:\> $VMHost | Set-VMHost -State Connected
```

Name	ConnectionState	PowerState	NumCpu	CpuUsageMhz
192.168.0.134	Connected	PoweredOn	2	619

Moving clusters

You can use the `Move-Cluster` cmdlet to move a cluster to a folder. The folder must be in the same datacenter as the cluster. The syntax of the `Move-Cluster` cmdlet is:

```
Move-Cluster [-Cluster] <Cluster[]> [-Destination] <VIContainer> [-Server
<VIServer[]>] [-RunAsync] [-WhatIf] [-Confirm] [<CommonParameters>]
```

The `-Cluster` and `-Destination` parameters are required.

Besides a folder, you can specify the datacenter to which the cluster belongs as the value of the `-Destination` parameter. In this case, the cluster is moved to the host system folder of the datacenter. It is not possible to move a cluster to another datacenter.

In the next example, `Cluster01` is moved to the `Accounting` folder:

```
PowerCLI C:\> Move-Cluster -Cluster Cluster01 -Destination Accounting
```

Name	HAEnabled	HAFailover Level	DrsEnabled	DrsAutomationLevel
Cluster01	True	1	True	FullyAutomated

Using DRS rules

To control the placement of virtual machines on hosts in a cluster, you can use DRS affinity rules or anti-affinity rules. There are two types of affinity rules:

- **VM-VM affinity rules**: These rules specify affinity or anti-affinity between virtual machines. An affinity rule specifies that DRS should or must keep a group of virtual machines together on the same host. A use case of the affinity rules can be performance, because virtual machines on the same hosts have the fastest network connection possible. An anti-affinity rule specifies that DRS should or must keep a group of virtual machines on separate hosts. This prevents you from losing all of the virtual machines in the group if a host crashes.

- **VM-Host affinity rules**: These rules specify affinity or anti-affinity between a group of virtual machines and a group of hosts. An affinity rule specifies that the group of virtual machines should or must run on the group of hosts. An anti-affinity rule specifies that the group of virtual machines should or must not run on the group of hosts.

In PowerCLI, there are cmdlets to use VM-VM affinity rules. To use VM-Host affinity rules, you have to, unfortunately, use the vSphere API.

Creating VM-VM DRS rules

To create a VM-VM DRS rule, you can use the `New-DrsRule` cmdlet that has the following syntax:

```
New-DrsRule [-Name] <String> [-Cluster] <Cluster[]> [-Enabled
[<Boolean>]] -KeepTogether [<Boolean>] -VM <VirtualMachine[]> [-RunAsync]
[-Server <VIServer[]>] [-WhatIf] [-Confirm] [<CommonParameters>]
```

The `-Name`, `-Cluster`, `-KeepTogether`, and `-VM` parameters are required.

If the value of the `-KeepTogether` parameter is `$true`, the new DRS rule is an affinity rule. If the value is `$false`, the new DRS rule is an anti-affinity rule.

If the value of the `-Enabled` parameter is `$true`, the new DRS rule is enabled. If the value is `$false`, it is disabled.

In the next example, you will create a new, enabled DRS VM-VM affinity rule named `Keep VM1 and VM2 together` for `Cluster01`. The DRS rule will keep the two virtual machines `VM1` and `VM2` together on the same host.

```
PowerCLI C:\> New-DrsRule -Name 'Keep VM1 and VM2 together' -Cluster
Cluster01 -VM VM1,VM2 -KeepTogether:$true -Enabled:$true
```

```
Name                        Enabled Type         VMIDs
----                        ------- ----         -----
Keep VM1 and VM2 together   True    VMAffinity   {VirtualMachine-vm-129,
VirtualMachine-vm-105}
```

In the next screenshot, you will see the window of the vSphere Web Client, which you can use to create a DRS rule filled with the same settings as in the preceding PowerCLI command.

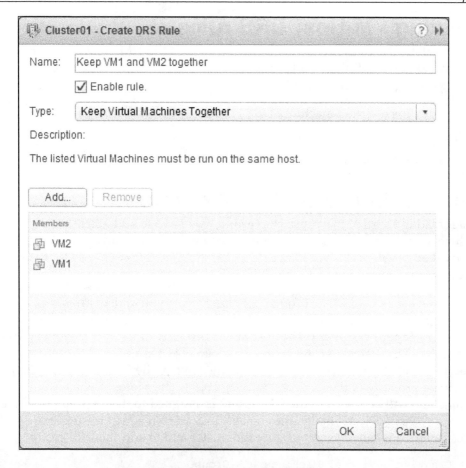

In the second example, you will create a new DRS VM-VM anti-affinity rule named `Separate VM3 and VM4` for `Cluster01`:

```
PowerCLI C:\> New-DrsRule -Name 'Separate VM3 and VM4' -Cluster Cluster01
-VM VM3,VM4 -KeepTogether:$false -Enabled:$true


Name                    Enabled Type            VMIDs
----                    ------- ----            -----

Separate VM3 and VM4 True     VMAntiAffinity {VirtualMachine-vm-107,
VirtualMachine-vm-126}
```

Creating VM-Host DRS rules

Unfortunately, there are no PowerCLI cmdlets to create a VM-Host affinity rule. You have to use the vSphere API to do this. There are three steps involved in creating a VM-Host affinity rule:

1. Creating a virtual machines DRS group
2. Creating a host DRS group
3. Creating a virtual machines to hosts DRS rules

Creating virtual machines DRS groups

While creating a virtual machines DRS group, you have to add at least one virtual machine to this group. In the next example, you will create a virtual machines DRS group called `Cluster01 VMs should run on host 192.168.0.133` for `Cluster01` and add virtual machine `VM1` to this DRS group.

First you create a `ClusterConfigSpecEx` object. Then you add an array containing one `ClusterGroupSpec` object to the `GroupSpec` property of the `ClusterConfigSpecEx` object. The `operation` property of the `ClusterGroupSpec` object is given the value `add`. A `ClusterVmGroup` object is assigned to the `info` property of the `ClusterGroupSpec` object. The name of the DRS group is assigned to the `name` property of the `ClusterVmGroup` object. The MoRef of the virtual machine that will be added to the DRS group is assigned to the `vm` property of the `ClusterVmGroup` object. Finally, the cluster's `ReconfigureComputeResource_Task()` method is called to reconfigure the cluster and to add the DRS group:

```
# Creating a Virtual Machines DRS Group
$Cluster = Get-Cluster -Name Cluster01
$VM = Get-VM -Name VM1 -Location $Cluster
$DRSGroupName = 'Cluster01 VMs should run on host 192.168.0.133'
$spec = New-Object VMware.Vim.ClusterConfigSpecEx
$spec.groupSpec = New-Object VMware.Vim.ClusterGroupSpec[] (1)
$spec.groupSpec[0] = New-Object VMware.Vim.ClusterGroupSpec
$spec.groupSpec[0].operation = 'add'
$spec.groupSpec[0].info = New-Object VMware.Vim.ClusterVmGroup
$spec.groupSpec[0].info.name = $DRSGroupName
$spec.groupSpec[0].info.vm += $VM.ExtensionData.MoRef
$Cluster.ExtensionData.ReconfigureComputeResource_Task($spec, $true)
```

Creating hosts DRS groups

Creating a hosts DRS group is similar to creating a virtual machine DRS group. Instead of adding a `ClusterVmGroup` object to the `info` property of the `ClusterGroupSpec` object, you have to add a `ClusterHostGroup` object. The `host` property of `ClusterHostGroup` will get the MoRef of the host you want to add to the DRS group assigned. You have to add at least one host to a hosts DRS group.

In the following example, you will create a hosts DRS group called `Cluster01 192.168.0.133 Hosts DRS Group` and you will add host `192.168.0.133` to this group:

```
# Creating a Hosts DRS Group
$Cluster = Get-Cluster -Name Cluster01
$VMHost = Get-VMHost -Name 192.168.0.133 -Location $Cluster
$DRSGroupName = 'Cluster01 192.168.0.133 Hosts DRS Group'
$spec = New-Object VMware.Vim.ClusterConfigSpecEx
$spec.groupSpec = New-Object VMware.Vim.ClusterGroupSpec[] (1)
$spec.groupSpec[0] = New-Object VMware.Vim.ClusterGroupSpec
$spec.groupSpec[0].operation = "add"
$spec.groupSpec[0].info = New-Object VMware.Vim.ClusterHostGroup
$spec.groupSpec[0].info.name = $DRSGroupName
$spec.groupSpec[0].info.host += $VMHost.ExtensionData.MoRef
$Cluster.ExtensionData.ReconfigureComputeResource_Task($spec, $true)
```

Retrieving DRS groups

There are no cmdlets to retrieve DRS groups. You will have to use the vSphere API. The DRS groups are in the `ConfigurationEx.Group` property of a vSphere `ClusterComputeResource` object.

The next example will show you how to retrieve the DRS groups of `Cluster01`:

```
PowerCLI C:\> Get-Cluster -Name Cluster01 |
>> ForEach-Object { $_.ExtensionData.ConfigurationEx.Group }
>>


Vm            : {VirtualMachine-vm-129}
LinkedView    :
Name          : Cluster01 VMs should run on host 192.168.0.133
UserCreated   :
DynamicType   :
```

```
DynamicProperty :

Host              : {HostSystem-host-109}
LinkedView        :
Name              : Cluster01 192.168.0.133 Hosts DRS Group
UserCreated       :
DynamicType       :
DynamicProperty   :
```

Modifying DRS groups

If you want to modify a DRS group, the only thing you can do is add or remove virtual machines or hosts to or from the DRS group. There are no PowerCLI cmdlets to do this, so you have to use the vSphere API.

Adding virtual machines to a DRS group

In the first example, you will add virtual machines VM2, VM4, and VM7 to the DRS group Cluster01 VMs should run on host 192.168.0.133. Because the structure of the ClusterConfigSpecEx objects is always the same, I will explain only what is unique in this example. In this case, the operation is edit. The DRS group is assigned to the info property. All of the new group members are added to the info.vm property.

```
# Adding virtual machines to a DRS group
$Cluster = Get-Cluster -Name Cluster01
$GroupName = "Cluster01 VMs should run on host 192.168.0.133"
$VMs = Get-VM -Name VM2,VM4,VM7
$spec = New-Object VMware.Vim.ClusterConfigSpecEx
$spec.groupSpec = New-Object VMware.Vim.ClusterGroupSpec[] (1)
$spec.groupSpec[0] = New-Object VMware.Vim.ClusterGroupSpec
$spec.groupSpec[0].operation = "edit"
$spec.groupSpec[0].info = $Cluster.ExtensionData.ConfigurationEx.Group |
   Where-Object {$_.Name -eq $GroupName}
foreach ($VM in $VMs)
{
   $spec.groupSpec[0].info.vm += $VM.ExtensionData.MoRef
}
$Cluster.ExtensionData.ReconfigureComputeResource_Task($spec, $true)
```

Removing virtual machines from a DRS group

In the second example about modifying DRS groups, the virtual machines VM4 and VM7 will be removed from DRS group Cluster01 VMs should run on host 192.168.0.133.

This example looks a lot like the preceding one. The difference is that virtual machines are removed from the info.vm property using the Where-Object cmdlet and the -notcontains operator. Only the virtual machines that are not in the list of virtual machines to be removed are assigned to the info.vm property.

```
# Removing virtual machines from a DRS group
$Cluster = Get-Cluster -Name Cluster01
$GroupName = "Cluster01 VMs should run on host 192.168.0.133"
$VMs = Get-VM -Name VM4,VM7
$VMsMorefs = $VMs | ForEach-Object {$_.ExtensionData.MoRef}
$spec = New-Object VMware.Vim.ClusterConfigSpecEx
$spec.groupSpec = New-Object VMware.Vim.ClusterGroupSpec[] (1)
$spec.groupSpec[0] = New-Object VMware.Vim.ClusterGroupSpec
$spec.groupSpec[0].operation = "edit"
$spec.groupSpec[0].info = New-Object VMware.Vim.ClusterVmGroup
$spec.groupSpec[0].info.name = $GroupName
$spec.groupSpec[0].info.vm = $Cluster.ExtensionData.ConfigurationEx.
Group |
   Where-Object {$_.Name -eq $GroupName} |
   Select-Object -ExpandProperty vm |
   Where-Object {$VMsMorefs -notcontains $_}
$Cluster.ExtensionData.ReconfigureComputeResource_Task($spec, $true)
```

 Remember that you cannot remove all of the virtual machines or hosts from a DRS group. A DRS group needs at least one group member.

Adding and removing hosts to or from a DRS group is similar to adding or removing virtual machines to or from a DRS group. I leave this to you as an exercise to solve (Hint: use Get-VMHost instead of Get-VM).

 More information about the VMware.VIM.* objects used in the preceding examples can be found in the VMware vSphere API reference documentation: http://pubs.vmware.com/vsphere-55/topic/com.vmware.wssdk.apiref.doc/right-pane.html

Removing DRS groups

Removing DRS groups is similar to preceding DRS groups operations. To remove a DRS group, the operation is `remove` and `removeKey` is the DRS group's name.

```
# Removing a DRS group
$Cluster = Get-Cluster -Name Cluster01
$GroupName = "Cluster01 VMs should run on host 192.168.0.133"
$spec = New-Object VMware.Vim.ClusterConfigSpecEx
$spec.groupSpec = New-Object VMware.Vim.ClusterGroupSpec[] (1)
$spec.groupSpec[0] = New-Object VMware.Vim.ClusterGroupSpec
$spec.groupSpec[0].operation = "remove"
$spec.groupSpec[0].removeKey = $GroupName
$Cluster.ExtensionData.ReconfigureComputeResource_Task($spec, $true)
```

Creating virtual machines to hosts DRS rules

Finally, you have to relate the virtual machines DRS group to the hosts DRS group in a virtual machines to hosts DRS rule. There are four possible relations:

- Must run on hosts in group
- Should run on hosts in group
- Must not run on hosts in group
- Should not run on hosts in group

In the example given, you will create a `Should run on hosts in group` virtual machines to hosts DRS rule to give preference to virtual machine VM1 to run on host 192.168.0.133.

First, a `ClusterConfigSpecEx` object is created. An array of one `ClusterRuleSpec` object is assigned to the `rulesSpec` property of the `ClusterConfigSpecEx` object. The `operation` property of `rulesSpec` is set to add. A `ClusterVmHostRuleInfo` object is assigned to the `info` property of `rulesSpec`. The `enabled` property of the `ClusterVmHostRuleInfo` object is set to $true. The `name` property is given the name of the DRS rule. Because it is a "should run on hosts in group" DRS rule, the mandatory property is set to $false. The `userCreated` property is set to $true. The `vmGroupName` and `affineHostGroupName` properties are assigned the names of the related DRS groups. Finally, the cluster's `ReconfigureComputeResource_Task()` method is called to create the DRS rule:

```
# Creating a Virtual Machines to Hosts DRS rule
$Cluster = Get-Cluster -Name Cluster01
$spec = New-Object VMware.Vim.ClusterConfigSpecEx
```

```
$spec.rulesSpec = New-Object VMware.Vim.ClusterRuleSpec[] (1)
$spec.rulesSpec[0] = New-Object VMware.Vim.ClusterRuleSpec
$spec.rulesSpec[0].operation = "add"
$spec.rulesSpec[0].info = New-Object VMware.Vim.ClusterVmHostRuleInfo
$spec.rulesSpec[0].info.enabled = $true
$spec.rulesSpec[0].info.name = "Cluster01 VM1 should run on host
192.168.0.133 DRS Rule"
$spec.rulesSpec[0].info.mandatory = $false
$spec.rulesSpec[0].info.userCreated = $true
$spec.rulesSpec[0].info.vmGroupName = "Cluster01 VMs should run on
host 192.168.0.133"
$spec.rulesSpec[0].info.affineHostGroupName = "Cluster01 192.168.0.133
Hosts DRS Group"
$Cluster.ExtensionData.ReconfigureComputeResource_Task($spec, $true)
```

If you want to create a "must run on hosts in group" DRS rule, you only have to change the line `$spec.rulesSpec[0].info.mandatory = $false` in the preceding code to the following:

```
$spec.rulesSpec[0].info.mandatory = $true
```

If you want to create a "must not run on hosts in group" or "should not run on hosts in group" DRS group, you have to assign the DRS hosts group name to `$spec.rulesSpec[0].info.antiAffineHostGroupName` instead of `$spec.rulesSpec[0].info.affineHostGroupName`.

In the next screenshot of the vSphere Web Client, you will see the virtual machines to hosts DRS rule `Cluster01 VM1 should run on host 192.168.0.133 DRS Rule` created with the preceding PowerCLI commands:

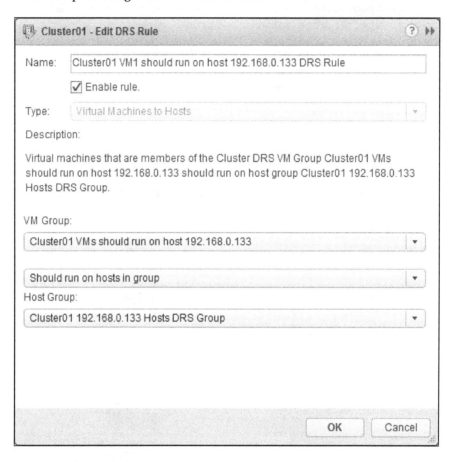

Retrieving DRS rules

You can use the `Get-DrsRule` cmdlet to retrieve the DRS rules of the specified clusters. The syntax of this cmdlet is:

```
Get-DrsRule [[-Name] <String[]>] [-Cluster] <Cluster[]> [[-VM]
<VirtualMachine[]>] [-Type <ResourceSchedulingRuleType[]>] [-Server
<VIServer[]>] [<CommonParameters>]
```

```
Get-DrsRule [[-Name] <String[]>] [-Cluster] <Cluster[]> [[-VM]
<VirtualMachine[]>] [-VMHost <VMHost[]>] [-Server <VIServer[]>]
[<CommonParameters>]
```

The `-Cluster` parameter is required. You cannot use the `-Type` and `-VMHost` parameters in the same command, because they are in different parameter sets.

If you don't specify the `-Type` or `-Host` parameters, you will only retrieve the VM-VM affinity or VM-VM anti-affinity rules:

```
PowerCLI C:\> Get-DrsRule -Cluster Cluster01
```

Name	Enabled	Type	VMIDs
Keep VM1 and VM2 together VirtualMachine-vm-105}	True	VMAffinity	{VirtualMachine-vm-129,
Separate VM3 and VM4 VirtualMachine-vm-126}	True	VMAntiAffinity	{VirtualMachine-vm-107,

If you also want to retrieve the VM-Host DRS rules, you have to specify all of the possible types as a value of the `-Type` parameter:

```
PowerCLI C:\> Get-DrsRule -Cluster Cluster01 -Type VMAffinity,VMAntiAffin
ity,VMHostAffinity
```

Name	Enabled	Type	VMIDs
Keep VM1 and VM2 together VirtualMachine-vm-105}	False	VMAffinity	{VirtualMachine-vm-129,
Keep VMs on Host	True	VMHostAffinity	{VirtualMachine-vm-129}
Seperate VM1 and DC1 VirtualMachine-vm-129}	True	VMAntiAffinity	{VirtualMachine-vm-111,

You can also retrieve all of the DRS rules that involve certain virtual machines using the `-VM` parameter:

```
PowerCLI C:\> Get-DrsRule -Cluster Cluster01 -VM VM2
```

Name	Enabled	Type	VMIDs
Keep VM1 and VM2 together VirtualMachine-vm-105}	False	VMAffinity	{VirtualMachine-vm-129,

To retrieve all of the DRS rules that involve specific hosts, use the `-VMHost` parameter using the following command:

```
PowerCLI C:\> Get-DrsRule -Cluster Cluster01 -VMHost 192.168.0.133
```

Name	Enabled	Type	VMIDs
Keep VMs on Host	True	VMHostAffinity	{VirtualMachine-vm-129}

Modifying DRS rules

To modify a DRS rule, you can use the `Set-DrsRule` cmdlet. The syntax of this cmdlet is:

```
Set-DrsRule [[-Enabled] [<Boolean>]] [-Rule] <DrsRule[]> [-Name <String>]
[-VM <VirtualMachine[]>] [-RunAsync] [-Server <VIServer[]>] [-WhatIf]
[-Confirm] [<CommonParameters>]
```

The `-Rule` parameter is required.

In the following example, the DRS rule `Keep VM1 and VM2 together` of `Cluster01` will be disabled:

```
PowerCLI C:\> Get-DrsRule -Name 'Keep VM1 and VM2 together' -Cluster
Cluster01 |
>> Set-DrsRule -Enabled:$false
>>
```

Name	Enabled	Type	VMIDs
Keep VM1 and VM2 together	False	VMAffinity	{VirtualMachine-vm-129, VirtualMachine-vm-105}

Removing DRS rules

The `Remove-DrsRule` cmdlet can be used to remove a DRS rule. The syntax of the `Remove-DrsRule` cmdlet is:

```
Remove-DrsRule [-Rule] <DrsRule[]> [-RunAsync] [-WhatIf] [-Confirm]
[<CommonParameters>]
```

The `-Rule` parameter is required.

In the next example, the DRS rule `Keep VM1 and VM2 together` of `Cluster01` is removed:

```
PowerCLI C:\> Get-DrsRule -Cluster Cluster01 -Name 'Keep VM1 and VM2
together' |
>> Remove-DrsRule -Confirm:$false
```

Using DRS recommendations

To retrieve the available DRS recommendations from the provided clusters, you can use the `Get-DrsRecommendation` cmdlet. This is useful if you configured `DrsAutomationLevel` on your cluster as `Manual` or `PartiallyAutomated`. The syntax of the `Get-DrsRecommendation` cmdlet is:

```
Get-DrsRecommendation [[-Cluster] <Cluster[]>] [-Refresh] [-Priority
<Int32[]>] [-Server <VIServer[]>] [<CommonParameters>]
```

In the next example, you will retrieve all of the DRS recommendations for all of the clusters:

```
PowerCLI C:\ > Get-DrsRecommendation


Priority Recommendation                 Reason
-------- --------------                  ------
2        Migrate VM 'VM1' from host... Fix soft VM/host affinity r...
```

To apply a DRS recommendation, you can use the `Apply-DrsRecommendation` cmdlet. This cmdlet has the following syntax:

```
Apply-DrsRecommendation [-DrsRecommendation] <DrsRecommendation[]>
[-RunAsync] [-WhatIf] [-Confirm] [<CommonParameters>]
```

The `-DrsRecommendation` property is required.

In the following example, all of the DRS recommendations will be applied:

```
PowerCLI C:\> Get-DrsRecommendation | Apply-DrsRecommendation
```

If you have several DRS recommendations and you don't want to apply them all, you can use a filter to select the DRS recommendations you want to apply:

```
PowerCLI C:\> Get-DrsRecommendation |
>> Where-Object {$_.Recommendation -like "*VM1*" } |
>> Apply-DrsRecommendation
```

Using resource pools

The virtual machines in a vSphere cluster share the resources of the ESXi hosts in the cluster. Resource pools are a way to divide the resources of the cluster into different pools. Virtual machines in a resource pool share the resources of their resource pool. This can be useful to always give a group of virtual machines the resources they need or to limit the amount of resources for a group of virtual machines.

Each cluster has a root resource pool called `Resources`. The resource pools you create are children of the `Resources` root resource pool or of other resource pools in the cluster.

Resource pools and virtual machines have settings that will be explained in the next table:

Setting	Description
Shares	A relative importance against sibling resource pools or virtual machines. Shares can have a level (Custom, High, Low, or Normal) or an amount.
Limit	The maximum allowed resources.
Reservation	The minimum available resources.
Expandable reservation (resource pool only)	If a resource pool has expandable reservation, it can use resources of the parent resource pool, if the parent resource pool has unreserved resources.

You already saw the `Move-VM` cmdlet that can be used to move virtual machines into resource pools in *Chapter 5*, *Managing Virtual Machines with PowerCLI*.

Creating resource pools

You can use the `New-ResourcePool` cmdlet to create a resource pool. The syntax of the `New-ResourcePool` cmdlet is:

```
New-ResourcePool -Location <VIContainer> -Name <String>
[-CpuExpandableReservation [<Boolean>]] [-CpuLimitMhz <Int64>]
[-CpuReservationMhz <Int64>] [-CpuSharesLevel <SharesLevel>]
[-MemExpandableReservation [<Boolean>]] [-MemLimitMB <Int64>]
[-MemLimitGB <Decimal>] [-MemReservationMB <Int64>] [-MemReservationGB
<Decimal>] [-MemSharesLevel <SharesLevel>] [-NumCpuShares <Int32>]
[-NumMemShares <Int32>] [-Server <VIServer[]>] [-WhatIf] [-Confirm]
[<CommonParameters>]
```

The `-Location` and `-Name` parameters are required. The value of the `-Location` parameter can be a resource pool, cluster, or host.

In the following example, a new resource pool called `ResourcePool2` will be created for `Cluster01`. Because the parameter list is quite long, splatting is used to make the code more readable.

```
PowerCLI C:\> $Parameters = @{
>> Location = (Get-Cluster -Name Cluster01)
>> Name = 'ResourcePool2'
>> CpuExpandableReservation = $true
>> CpuReservationMhz = 500
>> CpuSharesLevel = 'normal'
>> MemExpandableReservation = $true
>> MemReservationMB = 512
>> MemSharesLevel = 'high'
>> }
>> New-ResourcePool @Parameters
>>
```

Name	CpuShares Level	CpuReser vationMHz	CpuLimit MHz	MemShares Level	MemReser vationGB	MemLi mitGB
ResourcePool2	Normal	500	-1	High	0.500	-1.000

Retrieving resource pools

To retrieve resource pools, you can use the `Get-ResourcePool` cmdlet. The syntax of the `Get-ResourcePool` cmdlet is:

```
Get-ResourcePool [-VM <VirtualMachine[]>] [-Location <VIContainer[]>]
[[-Name] <String[]>] [-NoRecursion] [-Server <VIServer[]>]
[<CommonParameters>]

Get-ResourcePool -Id <String[]> [-Server <VIServer[]>]
[<CommonParameters>]

Get-ResourcePool -RelatedObject <ResourcePoolRelatedObjectBase[]>
[<CommonParameters>]
```

If you don't specify parameters, all of the resource pools in your environment will be retrieved. You can use the different parameters to filter the resource pools. In the next example, you will retrieve all of the resource pools of Cluster01:

```
PowerCLI C:\> Get-Cluster -Name Cluster01 | Get-ResourcePool
```

Name	CpuShares Level	CpuReser vationMHz	CpuLimit MHz	MemShares Level	MemReser vationGB	MemLi mitGB
Resources	Normal	6560	6560	Normal	0.753	0.753
ResourcePool2	Normal	500	-1	High	0.500	-1.000

Modifying resource pools

The Set-ResourcePool cmdlet can be used to modify the settings of a resource pool. The syntax of this cmdlet is:

```
Set-ResourcePool [-ResourcePool] <ResourcePool[]> [-Name <String>]
[-CpuExpandableReservation [<Boolean>]] [-CpuLimitMhz <Int64>]
[-CpuReservationMhz <Int64>] [-CpuSharesLevel <SharesLevel>]
[-MemExpandableReservation [<Boolean>]] [-MemLimitMB <Int64>]
[-MemLimitGB <Decimal>] [-MemReservationMB <Int64>] [-MemReservationGB
<Decimal>] [-MemSharesLevel <SharesLevel>] [-NumCpuShares <Int32>]
[-NumMemShares <Int32>] [-Server <VIServer[]>] [-WhatIf] [-Confirm]
[<CommonParameters>]
```

The -ResourcePool parameter is the only required parameter.

You cannot specify a new location for a resource pool using the Set-ResourcePool cmdlet, but the rest of the parameters of the Set-ResourcePool cmdlet are the same as for the New-ResourcePool cmdlet.

In the next example, the ResourcePool2 memory limit and CPU limit will be modified:

```
PowerCLI C:\> Set-ResourcePool -ResourcePool Resourcepool2 -MemLimitGB 4
-CpuLimitMhz 6000
```

Name	CpuShares Level	CpuReser vationMHz	CpuLimit MHz	MemShares Level	MemReser vationGB	MemLi mitGB
ResourcePool2	Normal	500	6000	High	0.500	4.000

Moving resource pools

To move a resource pool to a new location, you can use the `Move-ResourcePool` cmdlet, which has the following syntax:

```
Move-ResourcePool [-ResourcePool] <ResourcePool[]> [-Destination]
<VIContainer> [-Server <VIServer[]>] [-WhatIf] [-Confirm]
[<CommonParameters>]
```

The `-ResourcePool` and `-Destination` parameters are required. You cannot move a resource pool between different hosts or clusters.

In the next example, a new resource pool named `ResourcePool1` is created and then the existing resource pool `ResourcePool2` is relocated and made a child of the `ResourcePool1` resource pool:

```
PowerCLI C:\> New-ResourcePool -Name ResourcePool1 -Location (Get-Cluster
-Name Cluster01)
```

Name	CpuShares Level	CpuReser vationMHz	CpuLimit MHz	MemShares Level	MemReser vationGB	MemLi mitGB
ResourcePool1	Normal	0	-1	Normal	0.000	-1.000

```
PowerCLI C:\> Move-ResourcePool -ResourcePool ResourcePool2 -Destination
(Get-ResourcePool -Name ResourcePool1)
```

Name	CpuShares Level	CpuReser vationMHz	CpuLimit MHz	MemShares Level	MemReser vationGB	MemLi mitGB
ResourcePool2	Normal	500	6000	High	0.500	4.000

If you want to see the hierarchy of the resource pools, you can look at the `Parent` property of the resource pools:

```
PowerCLI C:\> Get-ResourcePool -Location (Get-Cluster -Name Cluster01) |
>> Select-Object -Property Name,Parent | Format-Table-AutoSize
>>
```

Name	Parent
Resources	Cluster01
ResourcePool1	Resources
ResourcePool2	ResourcePool1

In the example output, you can see that the Resources resource pool is a child of the Cluster01 cluster, the ResourcePool1 resource pool is a child of the Resources resource pool, and the ResourcePool2 resource pool is a child of the ResourcePool1 resource pool.

Configuring resource allocation between virtual machines

You can also specify shares, limits, and reservations for virtual machines. You can use the Get-VMResourceConfiguration cmdlet to retrieve the current resource configuration of virtual machines. The syntax of the Get-VMResourceConfiguration cmdlet is:

```
Get-VMResourceConfiguration [-Server <VIServer[]>] [-VM]
<VirtualMachine[]> [<CommonParameters>]
```

The -VM parameter is required.

In the next example, the resource configuration of virtual machine VM1 is retrieved and piped to the Format-List -Property * command to list all of the property values. The output of the example is in the following screenshot:

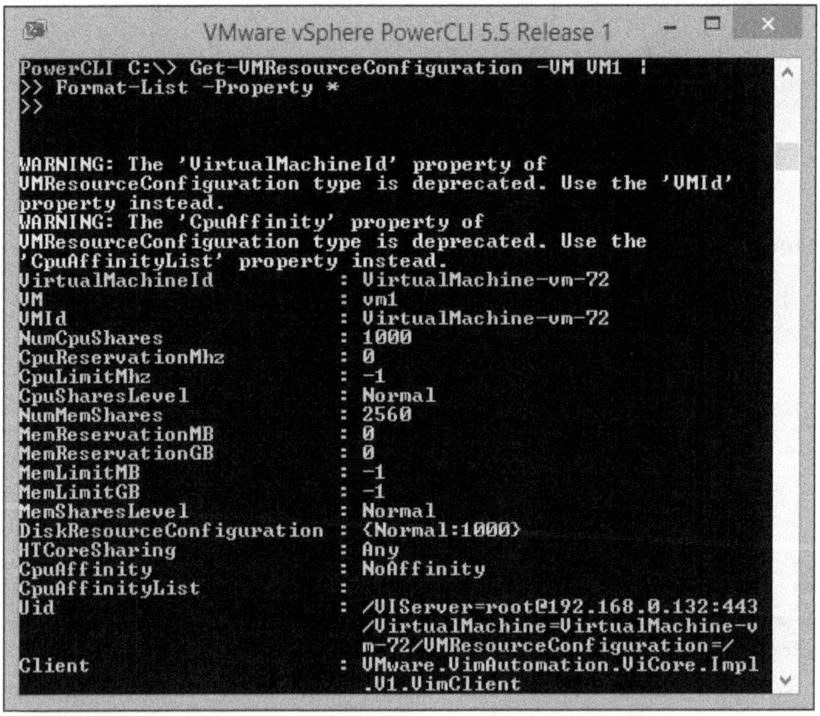

The `Set-VMResourceConfiguration` cmdlet can be used to modify the resource configuration of a virtual machine. The syntax of the `Set-VMResourceConfiguration` cmdlet is:

```
Set-VMResourceConfiguration [-Configuration] <VMResourceConfiguration[]>
[-HtCoreSharing <HTCoreSharing>] [-CpuAffinity <CpuAffinity>]
[-CpuAffinityList <Int32[]>] [-CpuReservationMhz <Int64>] [-CpuLimitMhz
<Int64>] [-CpuSharesLevel <SharesLevel>] [-NumCpuShares <Int32>]
[-MemReservationMB <Int64>] [-MemReservationGB <Decimal>] [-MemLimitMB
<Int64>] [-MemLimitGB <Decimal>] [-MemSharesLevel <SharesLevel>]
[-NumMemShares <Int32>] [-Disk <HardDisk[]>] [-NumDiskShares <Int32>]
[-DiskSharesLevel <SharesLevel>] [-DiskLimitIOPerSecond <Int64>]
[-WhatIf] [-Confirm] [<CommonParameters>]
```

The `-Configuration` parameter is the only required parameter. Most of the parameters are similar to the parameters of the `Set-ResourcePool` cmdlet. New parameters are `-Disk`, `-NumDiskShares`, `-DiskSharesLevel`, and `-DiskLimitIOPerSecond`. These parameters allow you to set a disk I/O limit, disk shares, and a disk shares level per disk.

In the following example, the CPU and memory shares level of virtual machine VM1 are set to high:

```
PowerCLI C:\> Get-VMResourceConfiguration -VM VM1 |
>> Set-VMResourceConfiguration -CpuSharesLevel High -MemSharesLevel High
>>

VM     NumCpuShares    CpuSharesLevel   NumMemShares    MemSharesLevel
--     ------------    --------------   ------------    --------------
VM1    2000            High             5120            High
```

Removing resource pools

The `Remove-ResourcePool` cmdlet will remove a resource pool for you. This cmdlet has the following syntax:

```
Remove-ResourcePool [-ResourcePool] <ResourcePool[]> [-Server
<VIServer[]>] [-WhatIf] [-Confirm] [<CommonParameters>]
```

The `-ResourcePool` parameter is required.

In the next example, the resource pool named `ResourcePool1` is removed:

```
PowerCLI C:\> Remove-ResourcePool -ResourcePool ResourcePool1
-Confirm:$false
```

Using Distributed Power Management (DPM)

The load of your virtual machines is probably not always the same. Sometimes they need more resources and sometimes they need fewer resources. **Distributed Power Management** (DPM) will use DRS to consolidate virtual machines on fewer ESXi hosts during periods of low resource utilization. The unused ESXi hosts will be powered off. If more resources are needed, DPM will power on ESXi hosts and DRS will move virtual machines to these hosts. DPM will save you or your company money in power and cooling costs.

 VMware has created a fling called "Proactive DRS" that uses the historical data gathered by VMware vCenter Operations Manager to proactively power on hosts before a predicted increase in resource demands. You can find Proactive DRS at: http://labs.vmware.com/flings/proactive-drs

Enabling DPM

DPM has two modes: manual and automatic. In manual mode, DPM will give recommendations to evacuate virtual machines from hosts and power off or power on the hosts. You will have to apply the recommendations manually. In the automatic mode, DPM will automatically apply DPM recommendations above a certain threshold.

In the next screenshot of the vSphere Web Client, you will see the DPM settings of a cluster with **Automation Level** set to **Manual** and **DPM Threshold** set in the middle:

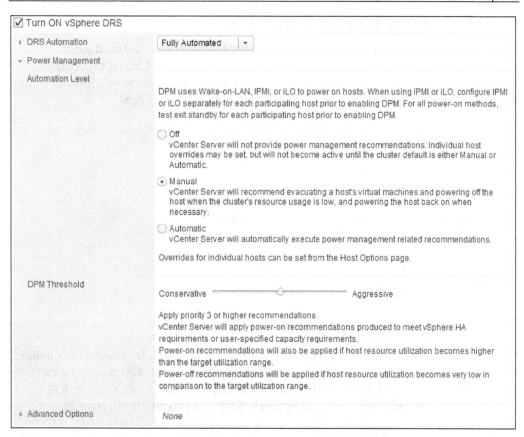

There are no cmdlets to configure DPM, so you have to use the vSphere
API again. You start with creating a ClusterConfigSpecEx object. Assign
a new ClusterDpmConfigInfo object to the dpmConfig property of the
ClusterConfigSpecEx object. Assign $true to the enabled property, and assign
manual or automated to the defaultDpmBehavior property. If you choose automated,
you can assign an integer value from 1 to 5 to the hostPowerActionRate property,
where 1 is the most aggressive threshold and 5 is the most conservative threshold:

```
# Enabling Distributed Power Management
$Cluster = Get-Cluster -Name Cluster01
$spec = New-Object VMware.Vim.ClusterConfigSpecEx
$spec.dpmConfig = New-Object VMware.Vim.ClusterDpmConfigInfo
$spec.dpmConfig.enabled = $true
$spec.dpmConfig.defaultDpmBehavior = "manual"
$spec.dpmConfig.hostPowerActionRate = 3
$Cluster.ExtensionData.ReconfigureComputeResource_Task($spec, $true)
```

Configuring hosts for DPM

For DPM to be able to power on hosts, you have to configure the **Intelligent Platform Management Interface (IPMI) / Integrated Lights-Out (iLO)** settings for power management. You have to specify the username, password, BMC IP address, and BMC MAC address of the IPMI interface in your host.

The next example will configure the IPMI information for host `192.168.0.133` using the `UpdateIpmi()` method:

```
# Updating IPMI info
$VMHost = Get-VMHost -Name 192.168.0.133
$ipmiInfo = New-Object VMware.Vim.HostIpmiInfo
$ipmiInfo.bmcIpAddress = "192.168.0.201"
$ipmiInfo.bmcMacAddress = "d4:85:64:52:1b:49"
$ipmiInfo.login = "IPMIuser"
$ipmiInfo.password = "IPMIpassword"
$VMHost.ExtensionData.UpdateIpmi($ipmiInfo)
```

Testing hosts for DPM

Before enabling DPM on a cluster or before adding a host to a DPM-enabled cluster, it is a good practice to test the IPMI settings of all of the hosts. You would be in trouble if DPM stopped a host and couldn't start it, wouldn't you? You can test a host for IPMI by putting it in standby mode first and starting it afterwards.

Putting hosts in standby mode

You can use the `Suspend-VMHost` cmdlet to put a host in standby mode. The syntax of the `Suspend-VMHost` cmdlet is:

```
Suspend-VMHost [-VMHost] <VMHost[]> [-TimeoutSeconds <Int32>]
[-Evacuate] [-Server <VIServer[]>] [-RunAsync] [-WhatIf] [-Confirm]
[<CommonParameters>]
```

The `-VMHost` parameter is required.

In the next example, host `192.168.0.133` will be put into standby mode:

```
PowerCLI C:\> Get-VMHost -Name 192.168.0.133 |
>> Suspend-VMHost -Confirm:$false
>>
```

Starting hosts

To start a host in the standby mode, you can use the `Start-VMHost` cmdlet. The syntax of this cmdlet is:

```
Start-VMHost [-VMHost] <VMHost[]> [-TimeoutSeconds <Int32>] [-Server
<VIServer[]>] [-RunAsync] [-WhatIf] [-Confirm] [<CommonParameters>]
```

The `-VMHost` parameter is required.

The host `192.168.0.133` that was put in standby mode in the preceding example will be started in the next example:

```
PowerCLI C:\> Get-VMHost -Name 192.168.0.133 |
>> Start-VMHost -Confirm:$false
>>
```

After a successful start from standby mode, your host is ready for DPM.

Retrieving the DPM configuration of a cluster

To check if DPM is enabled on a cluster and to see the DPM settings, you can look at the `ExtensionData.ConfigurationEx.DpmConfigInfo` property of the cluster.

In the next example, the DPM configuration of `Cluster01` is retrieved:

```
PowerCLI C:\> Get-Cluster -Name Cluster01 |
>> ForEach-Object {$_.ExtensionData.ConfigurationEx.DpmConfigInfo}
>>

Enabled             : True
DefaultDpmBehavior  : automated
HostPowerActionRate : 5
Option              :
DynamicType         :
DynamicProperty     :
```

Disabling DPM

To disable DPM, you can use almost the same script as to enable DPM. Just modify `$spec.dpmConfig.enabled = $true` into `$spec.dpmConfig.enabled = $false`.

You don't have to specify values for the `defaultDpmBehavior` or `hostPowerActionRate` properties.

```
# Disabling Distributed Power Management
$Cluster = Get-Cluster -Name Cluster01
$spec = New-Object VMware.Vim.ClusterConfigSpecEx
$spec.dpmConfig = New-Object VMware.Vim.ClusterDpmConfigInfo
$spec.dpmConfig.enabled = $false
$Cluster.ExtensionData.ReconfigureComputeResource_Task($spec, $true)
```

Removing clusters

The `Remove-Cluster` cmdlet will remove a cluster from your vSphere inventory. The `Remove-Cluster` cmdlet has the following syntax:

```
Remove-Cluster [-Cluster] <Cluster[]> [-Server <VIServer[]>] [-RunAsync]
[-WhatIf] [-Confirm] [<CommonParameters>]
```

The next example will remove the `Cluster02` cluster that was created at the beginning of this chapter:

```
PowerCLI C:\> Remove-Cluster -Cluster Cluster02 -Confirm:$false
```

 Be careful. Removing a cluster will also remove all of the hosts and virtual machines in the cluster!

Summary

In this chapter, you learned all about managing vSphere HA and DRS clusters, retrieving HA master or primary hosts, retrieving cluster configuration issues, disabling HA, disabling or enabling host monitoring, associating a host profile with a cluster, enabling VM and Application Monitoring, configuring the heartbeat datastore selection policy, moving hosts to clusters, moving clusters, using DRS rules and DRS groups, using resource pools, configuring resource allocation between virtual machines, and using DPM.

The next chapter will be about managing vCenter from PowerCLI.

9

Managing vCenter with PowerCLI

If you have more than one ESXi server, a vCenter Server will make your ESXi servers much easier to manage. A vCenter Server will also add a lot of additional features, such as HA and DRS clusters, to your vSphere environment,. In this chapter, we will discuss some topics that will help you manage your vSphere environment.

The following topics are covered in this chapter:

- Working with roles and permissions
- Managing licenses
- Configuring alarms
- Retrieving events

Working with roles and permissions

In a VMware vSphere environment, you might want to give certain **permissions** to users or administrators, who are not a part of the vSphere administrator's team, to perform specific tasks. For example, you might want to give the administrators of a server the permission to power on and off the server. You don't want to give these administrators all of the privileges in your environment because then you will lose control over it. There are many privileges you can give to somebody, and you probably want to give only a few. If you assigned privileges to users directly, it would be hard to see who has which privileges.

VMware vSphere has a nice feature called **roles**. Roles are a collection of privileges that you will need to perform a certain task. You can create a role called `Server administrator` and assign the `Power On` and `Power Off` privileges to this role. Every time you want to give an administrator the rights to power on and off a server, you can assign the `Server administrator` role to the administrator.

Permissions can be granted for every object in your vSphere environment, such as the root of your vSphere environment, datacenters, folders, clusters, and virtual machines. Permissions can be propagated to child objects of the main object to which you added a permission.

In the previous `Server administrator` example, you might want to create a folder for all of the servers assigned to the administrator. You can grant the `Server administrator` role to the administrator in the folder and propagate this permission to all of the child objects of the folder. This will give the administrator power on and off privileges for all of the servers in the folder.

Retrieving privileges

At the time of writing this book, using vSphere 5.5, there are 319 different privilege items you can grant to somebody. These privileges are arranged in 46 privilege groups. To get a list of all the privilege items or the privilege groups and their descriptions, you can use the `Get-VIPrivilege` cmdlet. This cmdlet has the following syntaxes:

```
Get-VIPrivilege [-PrivilegeGroup] [-PrivilegeItem] [[-Name]
<String[]>] [-Id <String[]>] [-Server <VIServer[]>]
[<CommonParameters>]


Get-VIPrivilege [[-Name] <String[]>] [-Role] <Role[]>
[-Id <String[]>] [<CommonParameters>]


Get-VIPrivilege [[-Name] <String[]>] [-Group] <PrivilegeGroup[]>
[-Id <String[]>] [<CommonParameters>]
```

The `Get-VIPrivilege` cmdlet without parameters will retrieve all of the privilege items and the privilege groups.

In the first example, we will retrieve all of the privilege items that have a name starting with `Power`:

```
PowerCLI C:\> Get-VIPrivilege -Name "Power*" -PrivilegeItem
```

The output of the preceding command is as follows:

```
Name               Description                           Server
----               -----------                           ------
Power              Power system operations               192.168.0.132
Power On           Power On or resume a virtual machine   192.168.0.132
Power Off          Power Off a virtual machine            192.168.0.132
Power On           Power On a vApp                        192.168.0.132
Power Off          Power Off a vApp                       192.168.0.132
```

In the second example, we will use the `Get-VIPrivilege -Role` cmdlet to retrieve the privileges of the `ReadOnly` role:

```
PowerCLI C:\> Get-VIPrivilege -Role ReadOnly
```

The output of the preceding command is as follows:

```
Name       Description                              Server
----       -----------                              ------
Anonymous  The only privilege held by sessions which  ... 192.168.0.132
View       Visibility without read access to an entity... 192.168.0.132
Read       Grants read access to an entity          192.168.0.132
```

In the third example, we will retrieve a list of the privilege groups using the following command:

```
PowerCLI C:\> Get-VIPrivilege -PrivilegeGroup
```

The output of the preceding command is too long to show in this book. Try the command yourself and see what it does.

In the fourth and last example of the `Get-VIPrivilege` cmdlet, we will use the `-Group` parameter to retrieve all of the privilege items of the `Alarms` group:

```
PowerCLI C:\> Get-VIPrivilege -Group Alarms
```

The output of the preceding command is as follows:

```
Name                 Description               Server
----                 -----------               ------
Create alarm         Create an alarm           192.168.0.132
Remove alarm         Remove an alarm           192.168.0.132
Modify alarm         Modify an alarm           192.168.0.132
Acknowledge alarm    Acknowledge an alarm      192.168.0.132
Set alarm status     Set status for an alarm   192.168.0.132
Disable alarm action Disable actions for an alarm  192.168.0.132
```

Using roles

Now that you know how to retrieve the vSphere privilege items and groups, you can start using the predefined roles or creating custom roles.

Creating roles

You can use the `New-VIRole` cmdlet to create a new role. The syntax of the `New-VIRole` cmdlet is as follows:

```
New-VIRole [-Name] <String> [[-Privilege] <Privilege[]>]
[-Server <VIServer[]>] [-WhatIf] [-Confirm] [<CommonParameters>]
```

The `-Name` parameter is required to create a new role.

In the following example, you will create the `Server administrator` role with the `Power on` and `Power off` privileges:

```
PowerCLI C:\> $Privileges = Get-VIPrivilege -Name "Power On","Power Off"
PowerCLI C:\> New-VIRole -Name "Server administrator" -Privilege
$Privileges
```

The output of the preceding commands is as follows:

```
Name                    IsSystem
----                    --------
Server administrator    False
```

In the next screenshot of the vSphere Web Client, you will see the privileges of the **Server administrator** role under **Privileges** after executing the preceding PowerCLI commands to create the role:

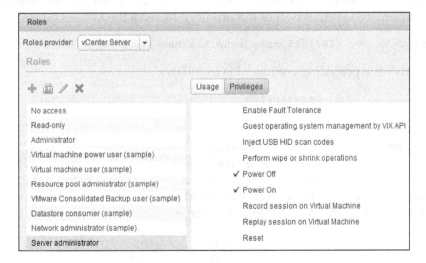

Retrieving roles

The `Get-VIRole` cmdlet retrieves all the roles on your server. The syntax of this cmdlet is as follows:

```
Get-VIRole [[-Name] <String[]>] [-Id <String[]>]
[-Server <VIServer[]>] [<CommonParameters>]
```

The `Get-VIRole` cmdlet without parameters retrieves all of the roles in your environment:

```
PowerCLI C:\> Get-VIRole
```

The output of the preceding command is as follows:

```
Name                         IsSystem
----                         --------
NoAccess                     True
Anonymous                    True
View                         True
ReadOnly                     True
Admin                        True
VirtualMachinePowerUser      False
VirtualMachineUser           False
ResourcePoolAdministrator    False
VMwareConsolidatedBack...    False
DatastoreConsumer            False
NetworkConsumer              False
Server administrator         False
```

You can also use the `-Name` parameter to retrieve specific roles:

```
PowerCLI C:\> Get-VIRole -Name "Server administrator"
```

The output of the preceding command is as follows:

```
Name                         IsSystem
----                         --------
Server administrator         False
```

If you combine the `Get-VIRole` and `Get-VIPrivilege` cmdlets, you will get the privileges of a role. If you look at the privileges of the `Server administrator` role, you will see that it has not only the `Power On` and `Power Off` privileges, but also the `Anonymous`, `View`, and `Read` privileges. These three privileges are added to all of the roles you create and cannot be removed from the created roles.

```
PowerCLI C:\> Get-VIRole -Name "Server administrators" | Get-VIPrivilege
```

The output of the preceding command is as follows:

```
Name       Description                                  Server
----       -----------                                  ------
Anonymous  The only privilege held by sessions which ... 192.168.0.132
View       Visibility without read access to an entit... 192.168.0.132
Read       Grants read access to an entity              192.168.0.132
Power On   Power On or resume a virtual machine          192.168.0.132
Power Off  Power Off a virtual machine                   192.168.0.132
Power On   Power On a vApp                               192.168.0.132
Power Off  Power Off a vApp                             192.168.0.132
```

Modifying roles

You can use the Set-VIRole cmdlet to give a new name to a role, add privileges to a role, or remove privileges from a role. The syntaxes of the Set-VIRole cmdlet are as follows:

```
Set-VIRole [-Role] <Role[]> [-Name <String>] [-AddPrivilege
<Privilege[]>] [-Server <VIServer[]>] [-WhatIf] [-Confirm]
[<CommonParameters>]


Set-VIRole [-Role] <Role[]> [-Name <String>] [-RemovePrivilege
<Privilege[]>] [-Server <VIServer[]>] [-WhatIf] [-Confirm]
[<CommonParameters>]
```

The -Role parameter is required to modify a role. The Set-VIRole cmdlet has two parameter sets, one for the -AddPrivilege parameter and one for the -RemovePrivilege parameter. This means that you can't use the -AddPrivilege and -RemovePrivilege parameters in the same command.

In the next example, you will modify the Server administrator role into an Alarm operator role. The name will be changed, the power privileges will be removed, and the alarms privileges will be added using the following commands:

```
PowerCLI C:\> Get-VIRole -Name "Server administrator" |
>> Set-VIRole -Name "Alarm operator" -RemovePrivilege (Get-VIPrivilege
-Name "Power On","Power Off") |
>> Set-VIRole -AddPrivilege (Get-VIPrivilege -Group Alarms)
>>
```

The output of the preceding command is as follows:

```
Name                    IsSystem
----                    --------
Alarm operator          False
```

Removing roles

The `Remove-VIRole` cmdlet can be used to remove roles. This cmdlet has the following syntax:

```
Remove-VIRole [-Role] <Role[]> [-Force] [-Server <VIServer[]>]
[-WhatIf] [-Confirm] [<CommonParameters>]
```

The `-Role` parameter is required to remove a role. By default you cannot remove a role that is associated with a permission. The `-Force` parameter indicates that you want to remove the role even if it is associated with a permission.

In the following example, we will remove the `Alarm operator` role:

```
PowerCLI C:\> Remove-VIRole -Role "Alarm operator" -Confirm:$false
```

Using permissions

Now that you know how to create and use roles in PowerCLI, you can start creating permissions. A vSphere permission grants the privileges in a role to users or groups of users on a vSphere inventory item.

Creating permissions

The `New-VIPermission` cmdlet creates new permissions. The `New-VIPermission` cmdlet has the following syntax:

```
New-VIPermission [-Entity] <VIObject[]> [-Principal] <VIAccount[]>
[-Role] <Role> [-Propagate [<Boolean>]] [-Server <VIServer[]>]
[-WhatIf] [-Confirm] [<CommonParameters>]
```

The `-Entity`, `-Principal`, and `-Role` parameters are required to create a new permission.

By default, new permissions are propagated to child objects in the vSphere inventory. If you just want to create a permission for an inventory item and not for its child objects, you have to use the `-Propagate` parameter with the `$false` value.

It is not possible to create new permissions for the following objects:

- Direct child folders of a datacenter
- Root resource pools of clusters and standalone hosts

These objects always inherit the permissions of their parent.

 VMware vCenter **Single Sign-On (SSO)** was first introduced in vSphere 5.1. In vSphere 5.5, the default Single Sign-On domain is named `vsphere.local` and the default Single Sign-On administrator account is `administrator@vsphere.local`. In vSphere 5.1, the default Single Sign-On domain is named `System-Domain` and the default Single Sign-On administrator account is `admin@System-Domain`.

In the next example, the vCenter Single-Sign On account `VSPHERE.LOCAL\Administrator` is granted the `Admin` role for the `New York` datacenter:

```
PowerCLI C:\> New-VIPermission -Entity (Get-Datacenter -Name 'New
York') -Principal VSPHERE.LOCAL\Administrator -Role Admin
```

The output of the preceding command is as follows:

```
Role                    Principal          Propagate IsGroup
----                    ---------          --------- -------

Admin                   VSPHERE.LOCA... True      False
```

In the following screenshot of vSphere Web Client, you will see the permissions of the **New York** datacenter under the **Permissions** tab after executing the preceding PowerCLI command to grant the **Admininistrator** role to the **VSPHERE.LOCAL\ Administrator** account for the **New York** datacenter:

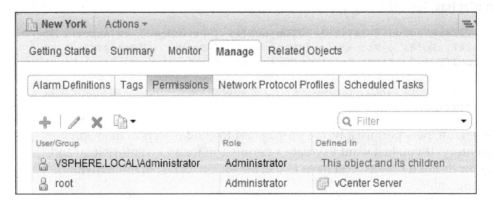

Retrieving permissions

The `Get-VIPermission` cmdlet retrieves the permissions defined for inventory objects. The syntax of this cmdlet is as follows:

```
Get-VIPermission [[-Entity] <VIObject[]>] [-Principal <VIAccount[]>]
[-Server <VIServer[]>] [<CommonParameters>]
```

The cmdlet will retrieve all of the permissions in your environment if you don't specify parameters. You can use the `-Entity` parameter to retrieve only the permissions for the specified inventory objects. Use the `-Principal` parameter to retrieve permissions for certain users or groups.

In the following example, we will retrieve all of the permissions of the `New York` datacenter:

```
PowerCLI C:\> Get-VIPermission -Entity (Get-Datacenter -Name 'New
York')
```

The output of the preceding command is as follows:

Role	Principal	Propagate	IsGroup
Admin	VSPHERE.LOCA...	True	False
Admin	root	True	False

If you retrieve the permissions, the default output doesn't show you the vSphere object for the permission. You can add this object by piping the output to the `Format-Table` cmdlet. Use the `-Property` parameter and specify all of the properties you want to retrieve, as shown in the following command line. The vSphere object is in the `Entity` property.

```
PowerCLI C:\> Get-VIPermission | Format-Table -Property Entity,Role,Princ
ipal,Propagate,IsGroup -AutoSize
```

The output of the preceding command is as follows:

Entity	Role	Principal	Propagate	IsGroup
New York	Admin	VSPHERE.LOCAL\Administrator	True	False
Datacenters	Admin	VSPHERE.LOCAL\Administrator	True	False
Datacenters	Admin	root	True	False

Modifying permissions

You can use the `Set-VIPermission` cmdlet to change the role of a permission or to modify a permission if it propagates to child objects or vice versa. The `Set-VIPermission` cmdlet has the following syntax:

```
Set-VIPermission [-Permission] <Permission[]> [-Role <Role>]
[-Propagate [<Boolean>]] [-Server <VIServer[]>] [-WhatIf] [-Confirm]
[<CommonParameters>]
```

The `-Permission` parameter is required to modify permissions.

In the following example, the permission of the account `VSPHERE.LOCAL\Administrator` on datacenter `New York` is changed into `ReadOnly` and the propagation of the permission to child objects is disabled:

```
PowerCLI C:\> Get-VIPermission -Entity (Get-Datacenter -Name 'New
York') -Principal VSPHERE.LOCAL\Administrator |
>> Set-VIPermission -Role ReadOnly -Propagate:$false
>>
```

The output of the preceding command is as follows:

```
Role                    Principal          Propagate IsGroup

----                    ---------          --------- -------

ReadOnly                VSPHERE.LOCA... False      False
```

Removing permissions

The `Remove-VIPermission` cmdlet will remove the specified permissions from your inventory. The syntax of this cmdlet is as follows:

```
Remove-VIPermission [-Permission] <Permission[]> [-WhatIf] [-Confirm]
[<CommonParameters>]
```

In the following example, the permission for `VSPHERE.LOCAL\Administrator` is removed from the `New York` datacenter:

```
PowerCLI C:\> Get-VIPermission -Entity (Get-Datacenter -Name 'New York')
-Principal VSPHERE.LOCAL\Administrator |
>> Remove-VIPermission -Confirm:$false
>>
```

Managing licenses

While writing this book, there are no PowerCLI cmdlets to add, retrieve, update, or remove licenses. You have to use the vSphere API to manage licenses in PowerCLI. There is only one cmdlet in PowerCLI for license management, `Get-LicenseDataManager`, and the only thing this cmdlet does is expose a hidden vSphere API.

You will use the vSphere API objects `LicenseManager`, `LicenseAssignmentManager`, and the hidden `LicenseDataManager` object to manage licenses.

You need to use `LicenseManager` to manage licenses in the license inventory on your vCenter Server. You can use `LicenseAssignmentManager` to manage the assignment of licenses to the ESXi servers. You use `LicenseDataManager` to associate licenses with containers in your vSphere environment and enable automatic license assignment to hosts that are added to a container.

The following three commands will give you hooks to the vSphere API license objects:

```
PowerCLI C:\> $LicenseManager = Get-View -Id 'LicenseManager-
LicenseManager'
PowerCLI C:\> $LicenseAssignmentManager = Get-View -Id
'LicenseAssignmentManager-LicenseAssignmentManager'
PowerCLI C:\> $LicenseDataManager = Get-LicenseDataManager
```

> You can get a list of all of the methods and properties of PowerShell objects by piping an object to the `Get-Member` cmdlet. For example:
>
> `PowerCLI C:\>$LicenseManager | Get-Member`

Adding license keys to the license inventory

To add a license to your vSphere license inventory, you have to use the `Licensemanager.AddLicense()` method. This method has two parameters. The first parameter is the license key that is to be added to your license inventory. The second parameter, called labels, is a pair of key-value labels that are ignored by the ESXi servers. You can use `$null` as the second parameter.

In the following example, you will add the license 00000-00000-00000-00000-00000 to your license inventory:

```
PowerCLI C:\> $LicenseManager = Get-View -Id 'LicenseManager-
LicenseManager'
PowerCLI C:\> $LicenseManager.AddLicense('00000-00000-00000-00000-
00000',$null)
```

 You can also work with a real license key instead of 00000-00000-00000-00000-00000. This is the Product Evaluation license key used for the 60-day evaluation period of new ESXi servers.

Retrieving license keys from the license inventory

To retrieve license keys from your license inventory, you just have to query the Licenses property of the LicenseManager object, as shown in the following commands:

```
PowerCLI C:\> $LicenseManager = Get-View -Id 'LicenseManager-
LicenseManager'
PowerCLI C:\> $LicenseManager.Licenses
```

The output of the preceding commands is as follows:

```
LicenseKey       : 00000-00000-00000-00000-00000
EditionKey       : eval
Name             : Product Evaluation
Total            : 0
Used             : 2
CostUnit         :
Properties       : {Localized}
Labels           :
DynamicType      :
DynamicProperty  :
```

Removing license keys from the license inventory

You can use the `LicenseManager.RemoveLicense()` method to remove a license from your license inventory. The `RemoveLicecense()` method has only one parameter: the license key. In the following example, you will remove the license key `00000-00000-00000-00000-00000` from your inventory:

```
PowerCLI C:\> $LicenseManager = Get-View -Id 'LicenseManager-
LicenseManager'

PowerCLI C:\> $LicenseManager.
RemoveLicense('00000-00000-00000-00000-00000')
```

Assigning licenses to hosts

Before PowerCLI 5.5 Release 1, in order to assign a license to a host you would have to use the `LicenseAssignmentManager.UpdateAssignedLicense()` method. This method has three parameters: the ID of the host, the license key, and the display name of the host. You don't have to specify the display name, so you can use `$null` for this parameter.

In the following example, you will assign the license key `00000-00000-00000-00000-00000` to the host `192.168.0.133`:

```
PowerCLI C:\> $VMHost = Get-VMHost -Name '192.168.0.133'
PowerCLI C:\> $LicenseKey = '00000-00000-00000-00000-00000'
PowerCLI C:\> $LicenseAssignmentManager = Get-View -Id
'LicenseAssignmentManager-LicenseAssignmentManager'
PowerCLI C:\> $LicenseAssignmentManager.UpdateAssignedLicense($VMHost.Id,
$LicenseKey, $null)
```

The output of the preceding commands is as follows:

```
LicenseKey       : 00000-00000-00000-00000-00000
EditionKey       : eval
Name             : Product Evaluation
Total            : 0
Used             : 2
CostUnit         :
Properties       : {Localized}
Labels           :
DynamicType      :
DynamicProperty  :
```

PowerCLI 5.5 Release 1 introduced a new parameter named -LicenseKey to the Set-VMHost cmdlet. You can use this parameter to assign a license key to a host using the following command:

```
PowerCLI C:\> Get-VMHost -Name '192.168.0.133' |
>> Set-VMHost -LicenseKey '00000-00000-00000-00000-00000'
>>
```

The output of the preceding command is as follows:

```
Name                ConnectionState PowerState NumCpu CpuUsageMhz
----                --------------- ---------- ------ -----------
192.168.0.133       Connected       PoweredOn       2        1035
```

Retrieving assigned licenses

The LicenseAssignmentManager.QueryAssignedLicenses() method retrieves the licenses assigned to a host. The method has only one parameter: the ID of the host. After running the method, you will find the license in the AssignedLicense property.

```
PowerCLI C:\> $VMHost = Get-VMHost -Name '192.168.0.133'

PowerCLI C:\> $LicenseAssignmentManager = Get-View -Id
'LicenseAssignmentManager-LicenseAssignmentManager'

PowerCLI C:\> $LicenseAssignmentManager.QueryAssignedLicenses
($VMHost.Id).AssignedLicense
```

The output of the preceding commands is as follows:

```
LicenseKey       : 00000-00000-00000-00000-00000
EditionKey       : eval
Name             : Product Evaluation
Total            : 0
Used             : 2
CostUnit         :
Properties       : {Localized}
Labels           :
DynamicType      :
DynamicProperty  :
```

Since PowerCLI 5.5 Release 1, the VMHost object has a LicenseKey property. You can now retrieve the license key of a host with the following command:

```
PowerCLI C:\> Get-VMHost -Name '192.168.0.133' |
>> Select-Object -Property Name,LicenseKey
>>
```

The output of the preceding command is as follows:

```
Name              LicenseKey
----              ----------
192.168.0.133     00000-00000-00000-00000-00000
```

Removing assigned license keys from hosts

The LicenseAssignmentManager.RemoveAssignedLicense() method will remove all of the assigned license keys from a host. This method has one parameter: the ID of the host.

In the following example, you will remove all of the licenses from the host 192.168.0.133:

```
PowerCLI C:\> $VMHost = Get-VMHost -Name '192.168.0.133'
PowerCLI C:\> $LicenseAssignmentManager = Get-View -Id
'LicenseAssignmentManager-LicenseAssignmentManager'
PowerCLI C:\>
$LicenseAssignmentManager.RemoveAssignedLicense($VMHost.Id)
```

Using the LicenseDataManager

With the automated deployment of the ESXi hosts by using Auto Deploy, you will also want to automate the assignment of vSphere license keys to hosts. PowerCLI provides an object called LicenseDataManager that you can use to associate license keys with host containers, such as clusters, datacenters, and datacenter folders. The presence of license keys that are associated with host containers makes it possible to automatically assign a license key to a host when an unlicensed host is added to a host container or is reconnected to the vCenter Server. If a host is already licensed, the host keeps the license key it already had.

You have to use the Get-LicenseDataManager cmdlet to get an instance of the LicenseDataManager object. The Get-LicenseDataManager cmdlet is supported only by vCenter Server 5.0 or higher. The use of the Get-LicenseDataManager cmdlet is different from what you are used to in PowerCLI. You have to use this cmdlet to retrieve a LicenseDataManager object, and then use the methods of this object to associate the licenses to the inventory nodes.

The syntax of the Get-LicenseDataManager cmdlet is as follows:

```
Get-LicenseDataManager [[-Server] <VIServer[]>] [<CommonParameters>]
```

Be warned that the Get-LicenseDataManager cmdlet is defined in the VMware.VimAutomation.License snap-in. If you use PowerCLI by starting PowerShell and adding the PowerCLI snap-ins, don't forget to add the VMware.VimAutomation.License snap-in if you want to use the Get-LicenseDataManager cmdlet.

Associating license keys with host containers

To associate license keys with host containers, you have to use the LicenseDataManager.UpdateAssociatedLicenseData() method. This method needs two parameters: the Managed Object Reference of the container and a LicenseData object. The LicenseData object contains a LicenseKeyEntry object consisting of methods named TypeId and LicenseKey. The only valid TypeId that I know of is vmware-vsphere.

In the next example, we will associate a license key to the New York datacenter:

```
$LicenseDataManager = Get-LicenseDataManager
$LicenseData = New-Object Vmware.VimAutomation.License.Types.
LicenseData
$LicenseKeyEntry = New-Object Vmware.VimAutomation.License.Types.
LicenseKeyEntry
$LicenseKeyEntry.TypeId = 'vmware-vsphere'
$LicenseKeyEntry.LicenseKey = '00000-00000-00000-00000-00000'
$LicenseData.LicenseKeys += $LicenseKeyEntry
$HostContainer = Get-Datacenter -Name 'New York'
$LicenseDataManager.UpdateAssociatedLicenseData($hostContainer.Uid
, $LicenseData)
```

Applying the associated license key to all the hosts in the container

After associating a license key to a host container, the hosts that were already in the container before the license key was associated will not automatically get the associated license keys applied. You have to use the `LicenseDataManager.ApplyAssociatedLicenseData()` method to apply the license key to the hosts.

In the following example, we will apply the license key associated with the `New York` datacenter to all of the hosts in the datacenter:

```
$LicenseDataManager = Get-LicenseDataManager
foreach ($VMHost in (Get-Datacenter -Name 'New York' | Get-
VMHost))
{
   $LicenseDataManager.ApplyAssociatedLicenseData($VMHost.Uid)
}
```

Retrieving license key associations

There are three possible ways to retrieve license key associations. You can do one of the following:

- Retrieve all of the license key associations to the host containers in your environment
- Retrieve the license keys associated with a specific host container
- Retrieve the effective license key of a host container.

In the following three sections, you will see examples of all the three possibilities.

Retrieving all of the license key associations to the host containers in your environment

To retrieve all of the license key associations to the host containers, you can use the `LicenseDataManager.QueryEntityLicenseData()` method. Before running the next example, I also associated a license to the cluster `Cluster01`. This cluster is in the `New York` datacenter.

The following example retrieves all of the license key associations in your environment:

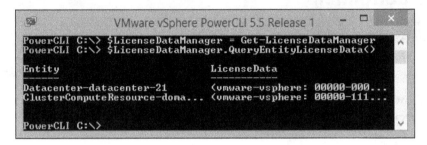

If you want to know the name of the entity `Datacenter-datacenter-39` or `ClusterComputeResource-domain-c52`, you can use the `Get-VIObjectByVIView` cmdlet to convert the `MoRef` parameter into a PowerCLI object. For example, to get the name of `Datacenter-datacenter-21`, you can use the command shown in the following screenshot:

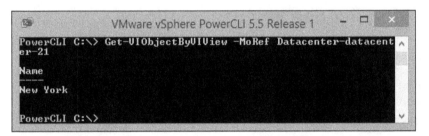

Retrieving the license keys associated with a specific host container

To retrieve the license keys associated with a specific host container, you have to use the `LicenseDataManager.QueryAssociatedLicenseData()` method. In the following example, we will retrieve the license keys associated with the `New York` datacenter:

```
PowerCLI C:\> $LicenseDataManager = Get-LicenseDataManager
PowerCLI C:\> $HostContainer = Get-Datacenter -Name 'New York'
PowerCLI C:\>
$LicenseDataManager.QueryAssociatedLicenseData($HostContainer.Uid)
```

The output of the preceding commands is as follows:

```
LicenseKeys
-----------
{vmware-vsphere: 00000-00000-00000-00000-00000}
```

Retrieving the effective license key of a host container

It is possible to associate a license key with a parent container and not with a child container. The license key associated with the parent container is also effective on the child container. If you want to know which is the effective license key of a host container, you have to use the `LicenseDataManager.QueryEffectiveLicenseData()` method. In the following example, we will retrieve the effective license key associated with the cluster `Cluster02`. The cluster `Cluster02` belongs to the `New York` datacenter and does not have a license key associated with it:

```
PowerCLI C:\> $LicenseDataManager = Get-LicenseDataManager
PowerCLI C:\> $HostContainer = Get-Cluster -Name Cluster02
PowerCLI C:\> $LicenseDataManager.QueryEffectiveLicenseData($HostContain
er.Uid)
```

The output of the preceding commands is as follows:

```
LicenseKeys
-----------
{vmware-vsphere: 00000-00000-00000-00000-00000}
```

As you can see in the output of the preceding example, the license key associated with the `New York` datacenter is effective on the `Cluster02` cluster.

Modifying license key associations

To associate another license key with a host container, you just have to replace the license key associated with the host container with a new license key. The PowerCLI code that you have to use to associate a new license key is exactly the same as what we used to associate a license key with a host container, as you saw earlier in the *Associating license keys with host containers* section. After modifying a license key association, you have to apply the new license key to all of the hosts in the container, as shown in the *Applying the associated license key to all the hosts in the container* section.

Removing license key associations

To remove the association of a license key with a host container, you have to use the `LicenseDataManager.UpdateAssociatedLicenseData()` method with $null as the second parameter. In the following example, we will remove the association of the license key with the datacenter `New York`:

```
$LicenseDataManager = Get-LicenseDataManager
$HostContainer = Get-Datacenter -Name 'New York'
$LicenseDataManager.UpdateAssociatedLicenseData($HostContainer.Uid,
$null)
```

Configuring alarms

In a vSphere environment, there are conditions (such as datastores running out of space) that you want to know about before things run out of control. In the "datastores running out of space" example, you would want to be warned before the datastore is full, so you can move some disks to another datastore to create extra free space on the datastore that is running out of space.

VMware vSphere provides alarms that trigger warnings and alerts when certain conditions are met. There are a lot of predefined alarms for almost every condition possible in vCenter Server. For example, there is the `Datastore usage on disk` alarm for datastores that will, by default, give you a warning if a datastore usage is above 75 percent and give you an alert if a datastore usage is above 85 percent. It is also possible to define actions such as `Send a notification email` that are executed when an alarm is triggered.

In PowerCLI, there are various cmdlets to modify alarm definitions and to create and modify alarm action triggers and alarm actions.

In the following screenshot of the vSphere Web Client, you will see the **Trigger states** notification of the **Datastore usage on disk** alarm:

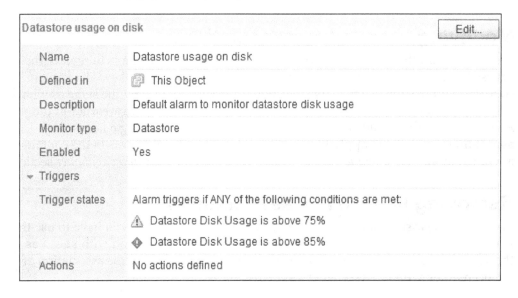

Retrieving alarm definitions

You can use the `Get-AlarmDefinition` cmdlet to retrieve the available alarm definitions. The syntax of this cmdlet is as follows:

```
Get-AlarmDefinition [-Id <String[]>] [[-Name] <String[]>] [[-Entity]
<VIObject[]>] [-Enabled [<Boolean>]] [-Server <VIServer[]>]
[<CommonParameters>]
```

There are three possible ways to retrieve alarm definitions. You can do one of the following:

- Get a list of all the available alarm definitions
- Filter the alarm definitions by name or entity
- Retrieve only the enabled alarm definitions

In the following example, we will retrieve the `Datastore usage on disk` alarm:

```
PowerCLI C:\> Get-Alarmdefinition -Name 'Datastore usage on disk'
```

The output of the preceding command is as follows:

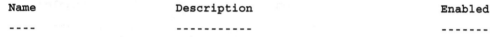

```
Name                      Description                            Enabled

----                      -----------                            -------

Datastore usage on disk Default alarm to monitor datastore... True
```

In the following screenshot of the vSphere Web Client, you will see the alarm definition for the **Datastore usage on disk** alarm:

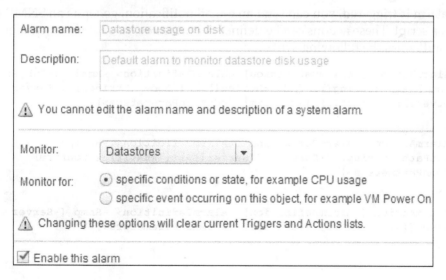

Modifying alarm definitions

To modify alarm definitions, you can use the Set-AlarmDefinition cmdlet that gives the ability to change the name and description of an alarm definition, specify how often the alarm actions repeat if the alarm is active, and enable or disable the alarm. The Set-AlarmDefinition cmdlet has the following syntax:

```
Set-AlarmDefinition [-AlarmDefinition] <AlarmDefinition[]>
[-ActionRepeatMinutes <Int32>] [-Description <String>] [-Enabled
[<Boolean>]] [-Name <String>] [-Server <VIServer[]>] [-WhatIf]
[-Confirm] [<CommonParameters>]
```

The -AlarmDefinition parameter is required to modify an alarm definition.

In the following example, we will disable the Datastore usage on disk alarm:

```
PowerCLI C:\> Get-AlarmDefinition -Name 'Datastore usage on disk' |
>> Set-AlarmDefinition -Enabled $false
>>
```

The output of the preceding command is as follows:

```
Name                        Description                         Enabled

----                        -----------                         -------

Datastore usage on disk Default alarm to monitor datastore... False
```

Creating alarm actions

If an alarm is triggered, you can send an e-mail notification, generate an SNMP trap, or run a script. These actions can be defined with the New-AlarmAction cmdlet. This cmdlet has the following syntaxes:

```
New-AlarmAction [-AlarmDefinition] <AlarmDefinition> -Email [-Subject
<String>] -To <String[]> [-Cc <String[]>] [-Body <String>] [-Server
<VIServer[]>] [-WhatIf] [-Confirm] [<CommonParameters>]


New-AlarmAction [-AlarmDefinition] <AlarmDefinition> -Script
-ScriptPath <String> [-Server <VIServer[]>] [-WhatIf] [-Confirm]
[<CommonParameters>]


New-AlarmAction [-AlarmDefinition] <AlarmDefinition> -Snmp [-Server
<VIServer[]>] [-WhatIf] [-Confirm] [<CommonParameters>]
```

As you can see, the `New-AlarmAction` cmdlet has three parameter sets, one for each type of alarm action you can define. The `-AlarmDefinition` parameter is always required to create an alarm action. To create a `Send a notification email` alarm action, the `-Email` and `-To` parameters are also required. To create a `Send a notification trap` alarm action, the `-Snmp` parameter is required. To create a `Run a command` alarm action, the `-Script` and `-ScriptPath` parameters are required.

In the first example, we will create a `Send a notification e-mail` alarm action for the `Datastore usage on disk` alarm:

```
PowerCLI C:\> Get-AlarmDefinition -Name 'Datastore usage on disk' |
>> New-AlarmAction -Email -To user@domain.com -Subject 'Datastore usage
on disk alarm' -Body 'Datastore {targetName} usage is over its alarm
limits'
>>
```

The output of the preceding command lines is as follows:

```
ActionType      Trigger
----------      -------
SendEmail       ...
```

The `{targetName}` variable in the preceding example will substitute the name of the datastore in the subject and body of the e-mail. The variables that you can use are shown in the following table. The table is copied from the vSphere 5.5 documentation's *Alarm Command-Line Parameters* section at `http://pubs.vmware.com/vsphere-55/topic/com.vmware.vsphere.monitoring.doc/GUID-B8DF4E10-89E3-409D-9111-AE405B7E5D2E_copy.html`:

Variable	Description
{eventDescription}	The text of the `alarmStatusChange` event. The {eventDescription} variable is supported only for the Condition and State alarms.
{targetName}	The name of the entity on which the alarm is triggered.
{alarmName}	The name of the alarm that is triggered.
{triggeringSummary}	A summary of the alarm trigger values.
{declaringSummary}	A summary of the alarm declaration values.
{oldStatus}	The alarm status before the alarm is triggered.
{newStatus}	The alarm status after the alarm is triggered.
{target}	The inventory object on which the alarm is set.

In the second example, we will create a `Send a notification trap` alarm action for the `Datastore usage on disk` alarm:

```
PowerCLI C:\> Get-AlarmDefinition -Name 'Datastore usage on disk' |
>> New-AlarmAction -Snmp
>>
```

The output of the preceding command is as follows:

```
ActionType        Trigger
----------        -------

SendSNMP          ...
```

In the third example, we will create a `Run a command` alarm action for the `Datastore usage on disk` alarm. The `c:\Scripts\DatastoreAlarm.cmd` script has to run when the alarm is triggered.

 `c:\scripts` is a location on the vCenter Server and not on your local PC.

In the following screenshot of the vSphere Web Client, you will see the actions that can be taken under the **Action** column when the state of the **Datastore usage on disk** alarm changes from warning to alert:

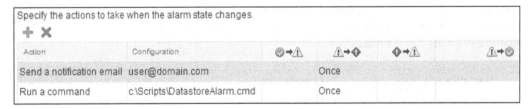

As mentioned earlier, use the following command to create a `Run a command` alarm action for the `Datastore usage on disk` alarm:

```
PowerCLI C:\> Get-AlarmDefinition -Name 'Datastore usage on disk' |
>> New-AlarmAction -Script -ScriptPath c:\Scripts\DatastoreAlarm.cmd
>>
```

The output of the preceding command is as follows:

```
ActionType        Trigger
----------        -------
ExecuteScript     ...
```

You cannot specify a PowerShell or PowerCLI script as the value of the `-ScriptPath` parameter. Rather, you have to specify a batch file. Of course you can call PowerShell from inside the batch file. For example, you can call the script `c:\scripts\AlarmAction.ps1` from a batch file with the following command:

`echo.| powershell -command "&{c:\scripts\AlarmAction.ps1}"`

You can find more information in the VMware Knowledge Base article *Unable to invoke PowerShell scripts as alarm action on vCenter Server 5.0 (2039574)* at `http://kb.vmware.com/kb/2039574`.

Configuring the vCenter Server mail server and sender settings

Before you can send an e-mail as an alarm action, you have to specify an SMTP server and the e-mail address that will be used as the sender's address in the e-mails sent by vCenter Server. There are no PowerCLI cmdlets to do this. You have to use the vSphere API.

In the next example, we will configure the vCenter Server with `smtpserver.blackmilktea.com` as the address of the SMTP server and `vcenter@blackmilktea.com` as the sender's e-mail address. The following script uses the `VpxSettings UpdateOptions()` method to configure the SMTP server and the sender's e-mail address:

```
$OptionValue = New-Object VMware.Vim.OptionValue[] (2)
$OptionValue[0] = New-Object VMware.Vim.OptionValue
$OptionValue[0].key = 'mail.smtp.server'
$OptionValue[0].value = 'smtpserver.blackmilktea.com'
$OptionValue[1] = New-Object VMware.Vim.OptionValue
$OptionValue[1].key = 'mail.sender'
$OptionValue[1].value = 'vcenter@blackmilktea.com'
$VpxSettings = Get-View -Id 'OptionManager-VpxSettings'
$VpxSettings.UpdateOptions($OptionValue)
```

In the following screenshot of the vCenter Server **Mail** settings (in the vSphere Web Client), you will see the defined SMTP server address and the sender's e-mail address in the **Mail server** and **Mail sender** text fields after executing the preceding PowerCLI script:

Mail

Enter the settings that vCenter Server uses for sending email alert.

| Mail server | smtpserver.blackmilktea.com |
| Mail sender | vcenter@blackmilktea.com |

Retrieving alarm actions

The Get-AlarmAction cmdlet will retrieve the alarm actions of the specified alarm definitions. The syntax of the Get-AlarmAction cmdlet is as follows:

```
Get-AlarmAction [[-AlarmDefinition] <AlarmDefinition[]>] [-ActionType
<ActionType[]>] [-Server <VIServer[]>] [<CommonParameters>]
```

In the following example, we will retrieve the alarm actions of the Datastore usage on disk alarm definition. Because the default output shows only the ActionType and Trigger properties, the output is piped to the Format-List -property * command to show all of the properties.

```
PowerCLI C:\> Get-AlarmDefinition -Name 'Datastore usage on disk' |
>> Get-AlarmAction | Format-List -Property *
>>
```

The output of the preceding command is as follows:

```
Body            : Datastore usage is over its alarm limits
Cc              : {}
To              : {user@domain.com}
Subject         : Datastore usage on disk alarm
ActionType      : SendEmail
AlarmDefinition : Datastore usage on disk
Trigger         : {Yellow -> Red (Once)}
Uid             : /VIServer=root@192.168.0.132:443/Alarm=Alarm-alarm-8/
SendEmailAction=1049345814/
AlarmVersion    : 59
Client          :
```

```
ActionType       : SendSNMP
AlarmDefinition  : Datastore usage on disk
Trigger          : {Yellow -> Red (Once)}
Uid              : /VIServer=root@192.168.0.132:443/Alarm=Alarm-alarm-8/
SendSNMPAction=-1381748622/
AlarmVersion     : 59
Client           :

ScriptFilePath   : c:\Scripts\DatastoreAlarm.cmd
ActionType       : ExecuteScript
AlarmDefinition  : Datastore usage on disk
Trigger          : {Yellow -> Red (Once)}
Uid              : /VIServer=root@192.168.0.132:443/Alarm=Alarm-alarm-8/
RunScriptAction=307617281/
AlarmVersion     : 59
Client           : Client          :
```

Removing alarm actions

You can use the `Remove-AlarmAction` cmdlet to remove an alarm action. The `Remove-AlarmAction` cmdlet has the following syntax:

```
Remove-AlarmAction [-AlarmAction] <AlarmAction[]> [-WhatIf]
[-Confirm] [<CommonParameters>]
```

The `-AlarmAction` property is required to remove an alarm action.

In the following example, we will remove the `SendSNMP` alarm action from the `Datastore usage on disk` alarm definition:

```
PowerCLI C:\> Get-AlarmDefinition -Name 'Datastore usage on disk' |
>> Get-AlarmAction -ActionType SendSNMP |
>> Remove-AlarmAction -Confirm:$false
>>
```

Creating alarm action triggers

Every new alarm action will be triggered once the alarm state changes from warning (yellow) to alert (red). If you want to create additional alarm action triggers, you can use the `New-AlarmActionTrigger` cmdlet to create a new action trigger for the specified alarm action. The syntax of this cmdlet is as follows:

```
New-AlarmActionTrigger [-StartStatus] <InventoryItemStatus>
[-EndStatus] <InventoryItemStatus> -AlarmAction <AlarmAction>
[-Repeat] [-WhatIf] [-Confirm] [<CommonParameters>]
```

The -StartStatus, -EndStatus, and –AlarmAction parameters are required to create an alarm action trigger.

In the next example, we will create a new alarm action trigger for the SendEmail alarm action of the Datastore usage on disk alarm definition. The trigger is started when the alarm state changes from normal (green) to warning (yellow). The alarm action will be repeated once every hour until the alarm is acknowledged.

```
PowerCLI C:\> Get-AlarmDefinition -Name 'Datastore usage on disk' |
>> Get-AlarmAction -ActionType SendEmail |
>> New-AlarmActionTrigger -StartStatus 'Green' -EndStatus 'Yellow'
-Repeat
>>
```

The output of the preceding command lines is as follows:

```
StartStatus      EndStatus        Repeat
-----------      ---------        ------
Green            Yellow           True
```

Now, use the following command to set the time intervals between the occurrence of the alarms:

```
PowerCLI C:\> Set-AlarmDefinition 'Datastore usage on disk'
-ActionRepeatMinutes 60
```

The output of the preceding command is as follows:

```
Name                      Description                      Enabled
----                      -----------                      -------
Datastore usage on disk Default alarm to monitor datastore... True
```

Retrieving alarm action triggers

To retrieve alarm action triggers, you can use the Get-AlarmActionTrigger cmdlet. This cmdlet has the following syntax:

```
Get-AlarmActionTrigger [[-AlarmAction] <AlarmAction[]>]
[<CommonParameters>]
```

In the next example, we will retrieve the alarm action triggers of the SendEmail alarm action of the Datastore usage on disk alarm definition.

```
PowerCLI C:\> Get-AlarmDefinition -Name 'Datastore usage on disk' |
>> Get-AlarmAction -ActionType SendEmail |
>> Get-AlarmActionTrigger
>>
```

The output of the preceding command is as follows:

```
StartStatus      EndStatus      Repeat
-----------      ---------      ------
Yellow           Red            False
Green            Yellow         True
```

In the next screenshot of the vSphere Web Client, you will see the **Trigger states** and **Alarm actions** notifications for the **Datastore usage on disk** alarm:

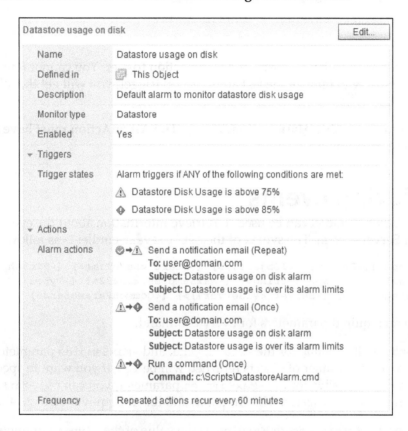

Removing alarm action triggers

We can remove alarm action triggers using the Remove-AlarmActionTrigger cmdlet. The syntax of the Remove-AlarmActionTrigger cmdlet is as follows:

```
Remove-AlarmActionTrigger [-AlarmActionTrigger]
<AlarmActionTrigger[]> [-WhatIf] [-Confirm] [<CommonParameters>]
```

The -AlarmActionTrigger parameter is required to remove an alarm action trigger.

In the following example, the alarm action trigger with the start status `Green` will be removed from the `SendEmail` alarm action of the `Datastore usage on disk` alarm definition:

```
PowerCLI C:\> Get-AlarmDefinition -Name 'Datastore usage on disk' |
>> Get-AlarmAction -ActionType SendEmail |
>> Get-AlarmActionTrigger |
>> Where-Object {$_.StartStatus -eq 'Green'} |
>> Remove-AlarmActionTrigger -Confirm:$false
>>
```

An alarm action must have at least one alarm action trigger. You cannot remove the last one. If you try to remove the last alarm action trigger, you will get the following error message:

You cannot remove this AlarmActionTrigger. The AlarmAction must have at least one AlarmActionTrigger.

Retrieving events

The `Get-VIEvent` cmdlet can be used to retrieve information about the events on a vCenter Server system. The syntax of the `Get-VIEvent` cmdlet is as follows:

```
Get-VIEvent [[-Entity] <VIObject[]>] [-Start <DateTime>] [-Finish
<DateTime>] [-Username <String>] [-MaxSamples <Int32>] [-Types
<EventCategory[]>] [-Server <VIServer[]>] [<CommonParameters>]
```

There are no required parameters for every command.

If you don't specify a value for the `-Start`, `-End`, and `-MaxSamples` parameters, the default maximum number of objects returned will be `100`. If you want to specify the maximum value possible for the `-MaxSamples` parameter, you can use `-MaxSamples` (`[int]::MaxValue`). This is a .NET notation and it is the equivalent of 2,147,483,647.

You can specify `Error`, `Info`, or `Warning` as the value of the `-Types` parameter in order to retrieve the events of the specified types only. For example, to retrieve a maximum of 50 error events from the error events of the last 24 hours, you can use the following command:

```
PowerCLI C:\> $StartDate = (Get-Date).AddDays(-1)
PowerCLI C:\> Get-VIEvent -Start $StartDate -Types Error -MaxSamples 50 |
>> Select-Object -Property CreatedTime,FullFormattedMessage
>>
```

The output of the preceding command lines is as follows:

```
CreatedTime              FullFormattedMessage
-----------              --------------------
1/19/2014 8:45:54 AM Host 192.168.0.133 in New York is not responding
1/20/2014 9:39:40 PM Cannot login root@192.168.0.133
```

The events returned by the Get-VIEvent cmdlet are of different types, depending on the type of the event. To get a sorted list of some of the names of the event types in your environment, you can use the following command lines:

```
PowerCLI C:\> Get-VIEvent -MaxSamples 500 |
>> Select-Object -Property @{
>>     Name = "TypeName"
>>     Expression = {$_.GetType().Name}
>> }|
>> Sort-Object -Property TypeName -Unique |
>> Format-Wide -Property TypeName -Column 2
>>
```

The output of the preceding command is as follows:

```
AlarmAcknowledgedEvent                    AlarmStatusChangedEvent
DatastoreFileDeletedEvent                 DatastoreIORMReconfiguredEvent
DrsVmMigratedEvent                        DrsVmPoweredOnEvent
DvsPortLinkDownEvent                      DvsPortLinkUpEvent
EventEx                                   NoAccessUserEvent
NonVIWorkloadDetectedOnDatastoreEvent     ScheduledTaskCompletedEvent
ScheduledTaskStartedEvent                 TaskEvent
UserLoginSessionEvent                     UserLogoutSessionEvent
VmAcquiredTicketEvent                     VmBeingHotMigratedEvent
VmDasResetFailedEvent                     VmEmigratingEvent
VmMessageEvent                            VmPoweredOnEvent
VmReconfiguredEvent                       VmRemoteConsoleConnectedEvent
VmResettingEvent                          VmResourceReallocatedEvent
VmStartingEvent
```

Play with the value of the -MaxSamples parameter to get a large or small number of event type names.

You can use the names of the event types to filter for certain events. For example, to retrieve events related to the creation of a virtual machine, you can filter for the VmBeingDeployedEvent, VmCreatedEvent, VmRegisteredEvent, or VmClonedEvent event type names.

You can use these event type names, to find the person who created the virtual machine. In this case, you have to specify the virtual machine as the value of the -Entity parameter. You have to use the -MaxSamples parameter with a large value, otherwise you might not find the event if the virtual machine was not created recently. The output of the Get-VIEvent cmdlet must be piped to the Where-Object cmdlet to filter for the events related to the creation of the virtual machine. In the following example, the event related to the creation of the virtual machine VM1 will be retrieved:

```
PowerCLI C:\> $VM = Get-VM -Name VM1
PowerCLI C:\> Get-VIEvent -Types Info -Entity $VM -MaxSamples
([int]::MaxValue) |
>> Where-Object {
>>    $_.Gettype().Name -eq "VmBeingDeployedEvent" -or
>>    $_.Gettype().Name -eq "VmCreatedEvent" -or
>>    $_.Gettype().Name -eq "VmRegisteredEvent" -or
>>    $_.Gettype().Name -eq "VmClonedEvent"
>> }
>>
```

The output of the preceding command is as follows:

```
SrcTemplate        : VMware.Vim.VmEventArgument
Template           : True
Key                : 2652
ChainId            : 2649
CreatedTime        : 12/11/2013 6:00:28 PM
UserName           : root
Datacenter         : VMware.Vim.DatacenterEventArgument
ComputeResource    : VMware.Vim.ComputeResourceEventArgument
Host               : VMware.Vim.HostEventArgument
Vm                 : VMware.Vim.VmEventArgument
Ds                 :
Net                :
```

```
Dvs                     :
FullFormattedMessage : Deploying VM5 on host 192.168.0.134 in New York
from template Windows2012Template
ChangeTag               :
DynamicType             :
DynamicProperty         :
```

Now, you know that the virtual machine VM1 was created by the user root on December 11, 2013, at 6:00:28 P.M.

Summary

In this chapter, you learned how to use PowerCLI to manage your vSphere environment with vCenter Server. Topics such as retrieving privileges, using roles, using permissions, managing licenses, using the LicenseDataManager object, modifying alarm definitions, creating alarm actions, creating alarm action triggers, retrieving events, and configuring the vCenter Server mail server and sender settings were discussed.

In the next chapter, we will learn how to report with PowerCLI.

10
Reporting with PowerCLI

Creating reports is the task that most new PowerCLI users start with. Your boss wants a report of all the new virtual machines created last month or a list of all the datastores that are over 90 percent full. PowerCLI will make it easy for you to create such a report and save it as a CSV or HTML file. In this chapter, you will learn some techniques to create reports.

The following topics are covered in this chapter:

- Retrieving log files
- Creating log bundles
- Performance reporting
- Exporting reports to CSV files
- Generating HTML reports
- Sending reports by e-mail
- Reporting the health of your vSphere environment with vCheck
- Using PowerGUI

Retrieving log files

ESXi servers and vCenter Servers generate log files. Some of these log files can be retrieved using PowerCLI. The Get-LogType cmdlet can be used to retrieve information about the available log file types on a virtual machine host or vCenter Server. The syntax of the Get-LogType cmdlet is as follows:

```
Get-LogType [[-VMHost] <VMHost[]>] [-Server <VIServer[]>]
[<CommonParameters>]
```

There are no required parameters. If you specify a value for the –VMHost parameter, the available log types on the host will be retrieved. If you omit the –VMHost parameter, the available log types on the default vCenter Server will be retrieved.

In the first example, we will retrieve the available log types on the vCenter Server:

```
PowerCLI C:\> Get-LogType
```

The output of the preceding command is as follows:

```
Key                                Summary
---                                -------
vpxd:vpxd-23.log                   vCenter server log in 'plain' format
vpxd:vpxd-alert-21.log             vCenter server log in 'plain' format
vpxd:vpxd-alert.log                vCenter server log in 'plain' format
vpxd:vpxd-profiler-46.log          vCenter server log in 'plain' format
vpxd:vpxd-profiler.log             vCenter server log in 'plain' format
vpxd:vpxd.log                      vCenter server log in 'plain' format
vpxd:vpxd_cfg.log                  vCenter server log in 'plain' format
vpxd-profiler:vpxd-profiler-4...   vpxd-profiler
vpxd-profiler:vpxd-profiler.log    vpxd-profiler
```

In the second example, we will retrieve the available log types on the ESXi server 192.168.0.133:

```
PowerCLI C:\> Get-LogType -VMHost 192.168.0.133
```

The output of the preceding command is as follows:

```
Key            Summary
---            -------
hostd          Server log in 'plain' format
vmkernel       Server log in 'plain' format
vpxa           vCenter agent log in 'plain' format
```

Now that you know the available log types, you can use them as input for the Get-Log cmdlet and retrieve entries from these logs or the entire bundle of log files. The Get-Log cmdlet has the following syntaxes:

```
Get-Log [-Key] <String[]> [[-VMHost] <VMHost[]>] [[-StartLineNum]
<Int32>] [[-NumLines] <Int32>] [-Server <VIServer[]>]
[<CommonParameters>]
```

```
Get-Log [[-VMHost] <VMHost[]>] [-Bundle] [-DestinationPath] <String>
[-Server <VIServer[]>] [-RunAsync] [<CommonParameters>]
```

The -Key or -DestinationPath parameter is required to retrieve the log files.

In the next example, we will retrieve the vmkernel log file from the host
192.168.0.133:

```
PowerCLI C:\> Get-Log -Key vmkernel -VMHost 192.168.0.133 |
>> Select-Object -ExpandProperty Entries
>>
```

The output of the preceding command is as follows:

```
2014-01-27T17:52:56.774Z cpu1:32881)ScsiDeviceIO: 2337:
Cmd(0x412e8089cf00) 0x1a, CmdSN 0x2f0f from world 0 to dev
"mpx.vmhba1:C0:T1:L0" failed H:0x0 D:0x2 P:0x0 Valid sense data:
0x5 0x24 0x0.

2014-01-27T17:52:56.777Z cpu0:32783)NMP:
nmp_ThrottleLogForDevice:2321: Cmd 0x1a (0x412e8089cf00, 0) to dev
"mpx.vmhba32:C0:T0:L0" on path "vmhba32:C0:T0:L0" Failed: H:0x0
D:0x2 P:0x0 Valid sense data: 0x5 0x20 0x0. Act:NONE
```

VMware Knowledge Base article *Interpreting SCSI sense codes in VMware ESXi
and ESX (289902)* at http://kb.vmware.com/kb/289902 will give you a detailed
explanation on the SCSI code that are in the output of the preceding command.

If you want to search a log file for certain strings or patterns, you can use the
PowerShell Select-String cmdlet to do so. The syntax of this cmdlet is given
as follows:

```
Select-String [-Pattern] <String[]> [-Path] <String[]> [-AllMatches]
[-CaseSensitive] [-Context <Int32[]>] [-Encoding <String>] [-Exclude
<String[]>] [-Include <String[]>] [-List] [-NotMatch] [-Quiet]
[-SimpleMatch] [<CommonParameters>]


Select-String [-Pattern] <String[]> [-AllMatches] [-CaseSensitive]
[-Context <Int32[]>] [-Encoding <String>] [-Exclude <String[]>]
[-Include <String[]>] [-List] [-NotMatch] [-Quiet] [-SimpleMatch]
-InputObject <PSObject> [<CommonParameters>]


Select-String [-Pattern] <String[]> [-AllMatches] [-CaseSensitive]
[-Context <Int32[]>] [-Encoding <String>] [-Exclude <String[]>]
[-Include <String[]>] [-List] [-NotMatch] [-Quiet] [-SimpleMatch]
-LiteralPath <String[]> [<CommonParameters>]
```

The -InputObject parameter is required in order to search a log file, and it accepts input from the pipeline **ByValue**. The -Pattern or -SimpleMatch parameter is also required. If you want to specify a filename to search through the content of the file, you have to use the -Path or -LiteralPath parameter. If you want to use **wildcards**, you have to use the -Path parameter. The value of the -LiteralPath parameter is used exactly as it is typed. No characters are interpreted as wildcards.

As an example of the preceding Select-String cmdlet syntax, you can use the following command to retrieve all of the lines from the vmkernel log file in the host 192.168.0.133 that contain the word WARNING:

```
PowerCLI C:\> Get-Log -Key vmkernel -VMHost 192.168.0.133 |
>> Select-Object -ExpandProperty Entries |
>> Select-String -SimpleMatch 'WARNING'
>>
```

In the preceding example, the command uses the -SimpleMatch parameter to search for a string. If you want to search for a **regular expression**, you should use the -Pattern parameter instead.

If you want to retrieve a specific number of lines from the log file, you can use a combination of the -StartLineNum and -NumLines parameters. First you might want to know how many lines the log file contains. This number is easily retrieved using the following command:

```
PowerCLI C:\> Get-Log -Key vmkernel -VMHost 192.168.0.133 |
>> Select-Object -Property StartLineNum,LastLineNum
>>
```

The output of the preceding command is as follows:

```
StartLineNum            LastLineNum
------------            -----------
           1                   3365
```

To retrieve only the last 100 entries of the log file, you can now use the following command:

```
PowerCLI C:\> Get-Log -Key vmkernel -VMHost 192.168.0.133
-StartLineNum 3266 -NumLines 100 |
>> Select-Object -ExpandProperty Entries
>>
```

If you omit the –VMHost parameter, you will retrieve vCenter Server log files. In the following example, we will retrieve the contents of the vpxd.log file:

```
PowerCLI C:\> Get-Log -Key vpxd:vpxd.log |
>> Select-Object -ExpandProperty Entries
>>
```

Creating log bundles

VMware Technical Support might ask for a log bundle when you submit a support request. You can create a log bundle from the vCenter Server's log files with the following command:

```
PowerCLI C:\> Get-Log -Bundle -DestinationPath c:\
```

The output of the preceding command is as follows:

```
Data
----
C:\vcsupport-52387fc8-52de-113b-7f28-1908e9ffa0d7.zip
```

In the following command, we will create a log bundle from the log files on the host 192.168.0.133:

```
PowerCLI C:\> Get-Log -VMHost 192.168.0.133 -Bundle -DestinationPath
c:\
```

The output of the preceding command is as follows:

```
Data
----
C:\vmsupport-52348fab-b7a7-97f1-bf2a-719b91ab84b3.tgz
```

Performance reporting

If your users complain that their virtual machines are running slow, you may want to find the reason for their complaints. You also want to know how your vSphere environment is performing, to see if additional hosts are necessary to keep your systems running smoothly. In PowerCLI, you can use the Get-Stat cmdlet to retrieve statistical information that is available on the ESXi hosts and vCenter Servers.

VMware vCenter Servers keep statistical information about the performance of the virtual machines, hosts, resource pools, and so on. This statistical information is retrieved by the hosts in real time and aggregated in four **statistical intervals** on the vCenter Servers. The real-time information is collected by the hosts with a collection frequency of 20 seconds and kept for 1 hour. The aggregated information is stored in the database of the vCenter Server.

Retrieving the statistical intervals

Information about the statistical intervals can be retrieved using the Get-StatInterval cmdlet. The syntax of this cmdlet is as follows:

```
Get-StatInterval [[-Name] <String[]>] [[-SamplingPeriodSecs]
<Int32[]>] [-Server <VIServer[]>] [<CommonParameters>]
```

There are no required parameters; without parameters, the Get-StatInterval cmdlet gives information about all of the four statistical intervals. The default output is in seconds. To make the output more useful, we can use calculated properties to convert the output Sampling Period to Minutes and Storage Time to Days using the following command lines:

```
PowerCLI C:\> Get-StatInterval |
>> Select-Object -Property Name,
>> @{Name="Sampling Period (Minutes)"
>>    Expression={($_.SamplingPeriodSecs)/60}},
>> @{Name="Storage Time (Days)"
>>    Expression={$_.StorageTimeSecs/(60*60*24)}}
>>
```

The output of the preceding command is as follows:

Name	Sampling Period (Minutes)	Storage Time (Days)
Past day	5	1
Past week	30	7
Past month	120	30
Past year	1440	365

The sampling period for the real-time interval is 20 seconds. As you can see in the preceding output, the sampling periods for the statistical intervals increase from 5 minutes in Past day to 30 minutes in Past week, 2 hours in Past month, and 1 day in Past year. This means that, if you retrieve an average CPU usage value in the past day's statistical interval, the value is an average of 5 minutes.

During the aggregation process, the data from the previous statistical interval is taken to create the data for the next statistical interval. For example, to calculate an average value for the past week's statistical interval, the average value calculated is an average of the six average values from the same time period in the past day's statistical interval.

Performance data is retrieved for **metric groups** such as CPU, datastore, disk, memory, network, power, and system.

Depending on the **statistics level** of a statistical interval, the approximate number of metrics is aggregated and stored in the vCenter Server database. Statistics Level 4 stores all metrics, while statistics Level 1 stores the least metrics.

The following screenshot shows the **Statistics intervals** settings in **vCenter Server Settings**, with a different **Statistics Level** for each statistics interval:

vCenter Server Settings				Edit...
▾ Statistics				
Statistics intervals	Enabled	Interval Duration	Save For	Statistics Level
	Yes	5 minutes	1 day	Level 4
	Yes	30 minutes	1 week	Level 3
	Yes	2 hours	1 month	Level 2
	Yes	1 day	1 year	Level 1

A statistics level must have the same value as the statistics level of the previous interval, or a lower one.

> The statistics levels in the screenshot are just an example and are not recommended values! Try to keep the statistics levels low, otherwise your vCenter Server database will grow larger and the aggregation rollup jobs will take a lot of time to complete. The default setting is 1 for every statistics level interval! Higher levels include more metrics. Each statistics level includes all of the metrics of the lower statistics levels and includes additional metrics. Statistics Level 4 contains all metrics that are supported by the vCenter Server. More information about the statistics levels and the metrics included in each level can be found in the VMware vSphere documentation at the following link:
>
> http://pubs.vmware.com/vsphere-55/topic/com.vmware.vsphere.monitoring.doc/GUID-25800DE4-68E5-41CC-82D9-8811E27924BC.html

Retrieving performance statistics

The Get-Stat cmdlet retrieves the statistical information available on a vCenter Server system. The syntax of this cmdlet is as follows:

```
Get-Stat [-Entity] <VIObject[]> [-Common] [-Memory] [-Cpu] [-Disk]
[-Network] [-Stat <String[]>] [-Start <DateTime>] [-Finish
<DateTime>] [-MaxSamples <Int32>] [-IntervalMins <Int32[]>]
[-IntervalSecs <Int32[]>] [-Instance <String[]>] [-Realtime]
[-Server <VIServer[]>] [<CommonParameters>]
```

The -Entity parameter is required. The value of this parameter must be the object whose performance statistics you want to retrieve.

In the following example, we will retrieve the performance statistics for the host 192.168.0.133 and for every metric ID only one sample is shown:

```
PowerCLI C:\> Get-Stat -Entity (Get-VMHost -Name 192.168.0.133)
-MaxSamples 1
```

The output of the preceding command is as follows:

MetricId	Timestamp	Value	Unit	Instance
cpu.usage.average	12/14/2013 1:00:00 AM	2.9	%	
cpu.usagemhz.average	12/14/2013 1:00:00 AM	132	MHz	
mem.usage.average	12/14/2013 1:00:00 AM	49.5	%	
disk.usage.average	12/14/2013 1:00:00 AM	54	KBps	
net.usage.average	12/14/2013 1:00:00 AM	91	KBps	
sys.uptime.latest	12/14/2013 1:00:00 AM	646483	second	

In the next example, three samples of the real-time values for the cpu.usage. average metric are shown for the host 192.168.0.133. This host has two CPUs, Instance 0 and Instance 1. The rows in the following output where the instance is empty are average values of the two instances:

```
PowerCLI C:\> Get-Stat -Entity (Get-VMHost -Name 192.168.0.133) -Stat
cpu.usage.average -Realtime -MaxSamples 3 |
>> Sort-Object -Property Timestamp -Descending
>>
```

The output of the preceding command is as follows:

```
MetricId              Timestamp                    Value Unit    Instance
--------              ---------                    ----- ----    --------
cpu.usage.average     12/14/2013 12:29:40 PM       72.88 %       1
cpu.usage.average     12/14/2013 12:29:40 PM        3.78 %       0
cpu.usage.average     12/14/2013 12:29:40 PM        8.33 %
cpu.usage.average     12/14/2013 12:29:20 PM       38.65 %       0
cpu.usage.average     12/14/2013 12:29:20 PM       10.27 %       1
cpu.usage.average     12/14/2013 12:29:20 PM       24.46 %
cpu.usage.average     12/14/2013 12:29:00 PM       39.86 %       0
cpu.usage.average     12/14/2013 12:29:00 PM        8.44 %       1
cpu.usage.average     12/14/2013 12:29:00 PM       24.15 %
```

The preceding output shows a time difference of 20 seconds between the intervals. The times in the `Timestamp` column are the times when the interval finishes.

The following screenshot shows a Realtime Summary performance graph report from the vSphere Web Client for the CPU usage of the host `192.168.0.133`:

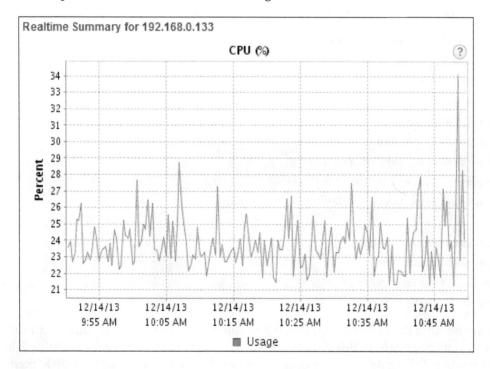

Retrieving metric IDs

If you want to know which metric IDs are available for an object in a certain statistical interval, you can use the Get-StatType cmdlet to retrieve them. The syntax of the Get-StatType cmdlet is as follows:

```
Get-StatType [[-Name] <String[]>] [-Entity] <InventoryItem[]> [-Start
<DateTime>] [-Finish <DateTime>] [-Interval <StatInterval[]>]
[-Realtime] [-Server <VIServer[]>] [<CommonParameters>]
```

The -Entity parameter is required to retrieve metric IDs.

In the next example, we will retrieve the available metric IDs for the host 192.168.0.133 in the real-time statistical interval and return them after sorting:

```
PowerCLI C:\> Get-StatType -Entity (Get-VMHost -Name 192.168.0.133)
-RealTime |
>> Sort-Object
>>
```

The output of the preceding command is as follows:

```
cpu.coreUtilization.average
cpu.costop.summation
cpu.demand.average
cpu.idle.summation
cpu.latency.average
cpu.ready.summation
cpu.reservedCapacity.average
cpu.swapwait.summation
cpu.totalCapacity.average
cpu.usage.average
cpu.usagemhz.average
cpu.used.summation
cpu.utilization.average
cpu.wait.summation
```

I have aborted the output of the preceding command after the CPU counter group (or the metric group) in this chapter because the command returned 168 metric IDs in total. The following are other counter groups besides CPU: datastore, disk, mem, net, power, rescpu, storageAdapter, storagePath, and sys.

Exporting reports to CSV files

If your boss asks for a report, he probably wants it in the form of a spreadsheet. The easiest way to create a spreadsheet from a PowerCLI report is to export it to a CSV file. This CSV file can be imported in a spreadsheet. Another use case for CSV files is creating export files of one system that you can use later to import into another system. For example, you can use CSV files to export the settings of vCenter Server and import them in another vCenter Server. PowerShell contains the `Export-CSV` cmdlet to create CSV files.

The syntax of the `Export-CSV` cmdlet is as follows:

```
Export-Csv [[-Path] <String>] [[-Delimiter] <Char>] [-Append]
[-Encoding <String>] [-Force] [-LiteralPath <String>] [-NoClobber]
[-NoTypeInformation] -InputObject <PSObject> [-Confirm] [-WhatIf]
[<CommonParameters>]
```

```
Export-Csv [[-Path] <String>] [-Append] [-Encoding <String>] [-Force]
[-LiteralPath <String>] [-NoClobber] [-NoTypeInformation]
[-UseCulture] -InputObject <PSObject> [-Confirm] [-WhatIf]
[<CommonParameters>]
```

The `-InputObject` parameter is required and it accepts input from the pipeline ByValue and ByPropertyName. The first parameter set is for the `-Delimiter` parameter. The second parameter set is for the `-UseCulture` parameter.

In the following example, we will create a CSV file containing the virtual machines in your environment. The output of this script has some problems that will be discussed later in this section.

```
PowerCLI C:\> Get-VM | Export-CSV -Path c:\VMs.csv
```

If you open the `c:\VMs.csv` file in `Notepad` or with the `Get-Content` cmdlet, you will see that the first line contains the type of the objects in the file:

```
#TYPE
VMware.VimAutomation.ViCore.Impl.V1.Inventory.VirtualMachineImpl
```

Your boss doesn't want to know this. You can prevent the creation of this first line by using the `Export-CSV -NoTypeInformation` parameter.

The second problem is the comma that is used as a delimiter between the columns in the CSV file. In a lot of cultures, the default delimiter for a CSV file is another character. For example, the default CSV file delimiter in the Netherlands, where I live, is a semicolon. There are two possible solutions for this problem:

- You can use the `-Delimiter` parameter and specify the delimiter character as a value. For example:

```
PowerCLI C:\> Get-VM |
>> Export-CSV -Path c:\VMs.csv -Delimiter ';'

>>
```

- Another and in my opinion better solution is to use the `-UseCulture` parameter. This creates the CSV file with the correct delimiter for the current culture on the system where the script is running. Combined with the `-NoTypeInformation` parameter, the command becomes something like this:

```
PowerCLI C:\> Get-VM |
>> Export-CSV -Path c:\VMs.csv -UseCulture -NoTypeInformation
>>
```

The last problem with the `Export-CSV` cmdlet is that the values of properties that contain array objects are not shown in the CSV file. The file only shows the type of the property. For example, the column `HardDisks` is filled with the following value:

```
VMware.VimAutomation.ViCore.Types.V1.VirtualDevice.HardDisk[]
```

You can use the .NET `[string]::Join()` method to solve this problem. This method requires two parameters. The first parameter is a character used as a delimiter. The second parameter is the array of objects you want to join.

The next example shows you how to get the names of the hard disks in the CSV file. You now have to use the `Select-Object` cmdlet to specify all of the objects that you want to return in the CSV file. For the `HardDisks` column, you have to create a calculated property. The following example will only return the name of the virtual machines and the hard disks:

```
PowerCLI C:\> Get-VM |
>> Select-Object -Property Name,
>> @{Name="HardDisks";Expression={[string]::
Join(',',$_.HardDisks)}} |
>> Export-CSV -Path c:\VMs.csv -UseCulture -NoTypeInformation
>>
```

The next screenshot shows the exported CSV file after it's imported into a spreadsheet. The virtual machines are from my home lab that I used to write this book:

	A	B
1	Name	HardDisks
2	DC1	Hard disk 1
3	DNS1	Hard disk 1
4	test2	Hard disk 1
5	vCenter Mobile Access	Hard disk 1
6	VM1	Hard disk 1
7	VM2	Hard disk 1,Hard disk 2
8	VM4	
9	VM7	
10	WindowsServer2012	Hard disk 1

Generating HTML reports

CSV files are nice, but HTML files are more impressive. This section will show you how to create nice looking HTML files from your reports. PowerShell gives you the `ConvertTo-Html` cmdlet to do this. The syntax of this cmdlet is as follows:

```
ConvertTo-Html [[-Property] <Object[]>] [[-Head] <String[]>]
[[-Title] <String>] [[-Body] <String[]>] [-As <String>] [-CssUri
<Uri>] [-InputObject <PSObject>] [-PostContent <String[]>]
[-PreContent <String[]>] [<CommonParameters>]


ConvertTo-Html [[-Property] <Object[]>] [-As <String>] [-Fragment]
[-InputObject <PSObject>] [-PostContent <String[]>] [-PreContent
<String[]>] [<CommonParameters>]
```

There are no required parameters. The first parameter set creates an entire HTML page. The second parameter set creates an HTML fragment.

In the first example, you will create a report about the connection state of the hosts. The `ConvertTo-Html` cmdlet doesn't have a `-Path` parameter to specify a filename. This problem can be solved by piping the output to the `Out-File` cmdlet, as shown in the following code:

```
Get-VMHost |
Select-Object -Property Name,ConnectionState |
Sort-Object -Property Name |
ConvertTo-Html |
Out-File -FilePath c:\VMHosts.html
```

You can open the `c:\VMHosts.html` file in a browser using the following command:

```
PowerCLI C:\> Start-Process -FilePath c:\VMHosts.html
```

 Be warned that the first time you use the `ConvertTo-Html` cmdlet, you might be disappointed because the output doesn't look nice by default.

The following screenshot shows the output of the preceding command:

Name	ConnectionState
192.168.0.133	Connected
192.168.0.134	Maintenance

To make the output look nicer, it is better to create an HTML fragment from the script and make the HTML header yourself. To make an HTML fragment, you have to use the `ConvertTo-Html -Fragment` parameter. To create the HTML header, you can use a PowerShell `here-string`.

In the next example, an HTML header and tail are created with `here-string` cmdlets. The table is created using `ConvertTo-Html -Fragment`. If the host's connection state is `Connected`, the color of the text is changed to `green`. If the connection state is `Disconnected`, the color is changed to `red`. A **Cascading Style Sheet** or **CSS** is used to provide the background and foreground colors for the HTML body and table. After creating the HTML page, a web browser is started to display the page.

```
# The path to the HTML file
$FilePath = 'c:\VMHostsConnectionState.html'

# Create the HTML header
$Header = @"
<!DOCTYPE html PUBLIC "-//W3C//DTD XHTML 1.0 Strict//EN"
"http://www.w3.org/TR/xhtml1/DTD/xhtml1-strict.dtd">
<html xmlns="http://www.w3.org/1999/xhtml" xml:lang="en"
lang="en">
<head>
<title>VMware vSphere Hosts ConnectionState Report</title>
<style type="text/css">
<!--

body {
  background-color: lightgray
```

```
}
table {
  background-color: white
}
th {
  color: white;
  background-color: darkgray
}
tr {
  background-color: white
}

</style>
</head>
<body>
<h2>VMware vSphere Hosts ConnectionState Report</h2>
"@

# Create the VMHost ConnectionState report table
$Fragment = Get-VMHost |
Select-Object -Property Name,ConnectionState |
Sort-Object -Property Name |
ConvertTo-Html -Fragment

# Create the tail of the HTML page
$Tail = @"
</body>
</html>
"@

# Combine all of the pieces into one HTML page
# Color Connected green and Disconnected red
$HTML = $Header
$HTML += $Fragment.Replace('<td>Connected</td>',
  '<td style="color: green">Connected</td>').
Replace('<td>Disconnected</td>',
  '<td style="color: red">Disconnected</td>')
$HTML += $Tail
$HTML | Out-File -FilePath $FilePath

# Open a web browser and display the page
Start-Process -FilePath $FilePath
```

The following screenshot shows the output of the preceding script. Do you agree that it looks much better than the first HTML report?

Using fragments, you can easily create one report with different segments for hosts, virtual machines, networks, and so on.

Sending reports by e-mail

After creating a report, you might want to send it to your boss or to yourself. The PowerShell `Send-MailMessage` cmdlet can send e-mail messages using an SMTP server. The syntax of this cmdlet is as follows:

```
Send-MailMessage [-To] <String[]> [-Subject] <String> [[-Body]
<String>] [[-SmtpServer] <String>] [-Attachments <String[]>] [-Bcc
<String[]>] [-BodyAsHtml] [-Cc <String[]>] [-Credential
<PSCredential>] [-DeliveryNotificationOption
<DeliveryNotificationOptions>] [-Encoding <Encoding>] [-Port <Int32>]
[-Priority <MailPriority>] [-UseSsl] -From <String>
[<CommonParameters>]
```

The `-From`, `-To`, and `-Subject` parameters are required to send a report by e-mail. You can use the PowerShell `$PSEmailServer` preference variable for the SMTP server. If the `$PSEmailServer` variable is not set, you have to use the `-SmtpServer` parameter.

You can send a report by putting it in the body of the e-mail or as an attachment. If the report is an HTML document and you want to send it in the body of the e-mail, you have to use the `-BodyAsHtml` parameter.

In the first example, the HTML report file that was created in the previous section is sent in the body of an e-mail. In this example, we will use splatting to specify the parameters. The PowerShell `Out-String` cmdlet is used to create a single string from the HTML content.

The SMTP server used in this environment does not require authentication or SSL and uses the default port 25. Additional parameters may be required in some environments.

```
$Parameters = @{
  From = 'admin@blackmilktea.com'
  To = 'manager@blackmilktea.com'
  Subject = 'VMware vSphere hosts Connection State report'
  Body = Get-Content -Path 'c:\VMHostsConnectionState.html' | Out-
String
  BodyAsHtml = $true
  SmtpServer = 'smtpserver.blackmilktea.com'
}
Send-MailMessage @Parameters
```

You don't have to create a file before you can send an e-mail. You can also use the content of a variable. In the second example, we will use the content of the $HTML variable (created in the previous section of this chapter) as the body of the e-mail:

```
$Parameters = @{
  From = 'admin@blackmilktea.com'
  To = 'manager@blackmilktea.com'
  Subject = 'VMware vSphere hosts Connection State report'
  Body = $HTML
  BodyAsHtml = $true
  SmtpServer = 'smtpserver.blackmilktea.com'
}
Send-MailMessage @Parameters
```

In the third example, we will send the HTML report created in the previous section as an attachment:

```
$Parameters = @{
  From = 'admin@blackmilktea.com'
  To = 'manager@blackmilktea.com'
  Subject = 'VMware vSphere hosts Connection State report'
  Body = 'VMware vSphere hosts Connection State report is attached to
this email.'
  Attachment = 'c:\VMHostsConnectionState.html'
  SmtpServer = 'smtpserver.blackmilktea.com'
}
Send-MailMessage @Parameters
```

Reporting the health of your vSphere environment with vCheck

In this section of the book *Learning PowerCLI*, I want to introduce a PowerCLI script that every vSphere admin should use. The **vCheck** script written by Alan Renouf can check your vSphere environment for various configuration issues and report them in an HTML format. The vCheck script reports several issues such as VMs having CD-ROMs connected, VMs with CPU or memory reservations configured, VMs ballooning or swapping, VMs with less than 100 MB free space on a disk, VMs with an old hardware version, and VMs that have no VMware Tools installed. These are just a few examples. The script reports many more issues.

The script is written in a modular way, and it uses a plugin for every check it performs. It is very easy to write your own plugins and add them to the script. There are plugins created to check other technologies such as Microsoft Exchange. Reading the vCheck plugins is a good way to see how the checks are implemented and learn from PowerCLI scripts created by other people in the community. The vCheck script is meant to run daily as a scheduled task so that you can receive the results in your mailbox.

You can find Alan's blog post about vCheck at the following link:

`http://www.virtu-al.net/vcheck-pluginsheaders/vcheck/`

The vCheck script is now maintained at GitHub and can be downloaded from the following link:

`https://github.com/alanrenouf/vCheck-vSphere`

In the next screenshot, you will find some of the issues the vCheck script in my home lab found:

VMs in Inconsistent folders 4	
The Following VM's are not stored in folders consistent to their names, this may cause issues when trying to locate them from the datastore manually	
VM	Path
VM7	[Datastore2] VM3
VM1	[Datastore2] VM5
DNS1	[Datastore2] vm7
test2	[Cluster01_Vmfs01] test1

NO VM Tools: 7	
The following VMs have No VMTools installed, for optimal configuration and performance these should be installed	
Name	Status
DC1	toolsNotInstalled
VM2	toolsNotInstalled
DC1	toolsNotInstalled
VM4	toolsNotInstalled
VM1	toolsNotInstalled
DNS1	toolsNotInstalled
WindowsServer2012	toolsNotInstalled

Using PowerGUI

PowerGUI is a combination of **PowerGUI Script Editor** and **PowerGUI Administrative Console**. You can use the PowerGUI Script Editor to edit your PowerCLI scripts. The script editor will give you syntax highlighting and tab completion features. The PowerGUI Administrative Console is a graphical user interface for running your PowerCLI scripts. You can create your own PowerCLI scripts and add them to the PowerGUI Administrative Console. Also, there are **PowerPacks** that you can download from the PowerGUI website, and they will extend the PowerGUI Administrative Console. For VMware, PowerPacks are already there for VMware vSphere Management, Image Builder and Auto Deploy, and VMware LabManager Administration. These PowerPacks can be used to create a lot of different reports and to perform actions on vSphere objects just as in the vSphere Client. You can examine the PowerCLI code that is behind a report or an action. So, if you want to know how things work, you can easily find out. You can download PowerGUI for free from http://www.powergui.org/.

The next screenshot shows the **PowerGUI Administrative Console** window:

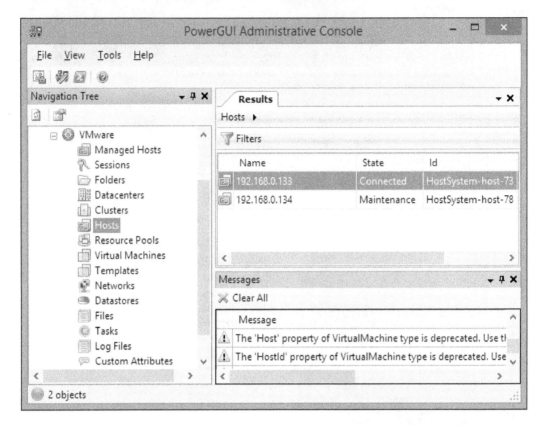

Summary

In this chapter, you learned techniques to create reports with PowerCLI. You saw how to create log files and log bundles using the Get-Log cmdlet. Performance reporting using the Get-Stat cmdlet was discussed. CSV files and HTML reports were created using the Export-CSV and ConvertTo-Html cmdlets, and they were sent by e-mail using the Send-MailMessage cmdlet. Then you were introduced to the vCheck script to report common issues in your vSphere environment, and finally, you learned how to use PowerGUI.

This was the last chapter of the book *Learning PowerCLI*. I hope that you enjoyed reading this book, and I hope that you will use PowerCLI to make your job as a vSphere administrator easier.

If you have questions about PowerCLI or PowerCLI scripts that you are writing, the best place to ask your questions is the PowerCLI community in the VMware VMTN Communities at `http://www.vmware.com/go/powercli`.

Go to the **Discussions** tab and click on **Start a discussion** in the **Actions** section, or use the PowerCLI command `Get-PowerCLICommunity` to open the PowerCLI community from your PowerCLI session. You may get an answer in a few minutes.

You can also help other people by answering their questions. Answering questions is a great way to improve your own PowerCLI skills.

Index

D

dasConfig property 255, 259
Datastore Cluster
  creating 240
  datastores, adding 243
  datastores, removing 244
  datastores, retrieving 243
  modifying 241, 242
  removing 244
  retrieving 241
Datastore heartbeating 258
Datastore Maintenance Mode 240
datastores
  adding, to Datastore Cluster 243
  creating 228
  NFS datastores, creating 229
  removing 247
  removing, from Datastore Cluster 244
  retrieving 233
  retrieving, in Datastore Cluster 243
  upgrading, to VMFS-5 245, 246
DefaultParameterSet parameter set 140
devices
  adding, to virtual machine 153
devices, adding to virtual machine
  CD drive, adding 158, 159
  CD drive, modifying 164, 165
  floppy drive, adding 157, 158
  floppy drive, modifying 164
  hard disk, adding 154
  hard disk, modifying 159, 160
  hard disk, moving to another datastore 161
  modifying 159
  network adapter, adding 156
  network adapter, modifying 162, 163
  SCSI controller, adding 155
  SCSI controller, modifying 161, 162
devices, removing from virtual machine
  CD drive, modifying 165
  CD drive, removing 167
  floppy drive, removing 166
  hard disk, removing 165
  network adapter, removing 166
Disconnect-VIServer cmdlet 22
**Distributed Management Task Force, Inc.
    (DMTF) 102**

Distributed Power Management (DPM)
  cluster configuration, retrieving 285
  disabling 286
  enabling 282, 283
  hosts, configuring for 284
  hosts, putting in standby mode 284
  hosts, starting 285
  hosts, testing for 284
  using 282
Distributed Resources Scheduler (DRS) 249
distributed virtual port groups
  configuration, exporting 219
  configuration, restoring 218
  configuration, rolling back 218
  configuring 216
  creating 214
  creating, from export 215, 216
  creating, from reference group 215
  host network adapter, migrating to 220
  Network I/O Control, configuring 219
  removing 220
  renaming 217
DRS clusters
  creating 250
DRS groups
  removing 270
DRS recommendations
  using 275
DRS rules
  modifying 274
  removing 274
  retrieving 272, 273
  using 263
Dynamic Resource Scheduling (DRS) 97

E

**EnableNetworkResourceManagement()
    method 219**
esxcli
  using, from PowerCLI 125-128
esxcli command
  $esxcli.hardware.cpu command 127
  about 125-129
  using, from PowerCLI 125-127
events
  retrieving 316-319

J

jumbo frames 190

L

Length property 66
LicenseAssignmentManager.Query
        AssignedLicenses() method 300
LicenseAssignmentManager.Remove
        AssignedLicense() method 301
LicenseAssignmentManager.Update
        AssignedLicense() method 299
LicenseDataManager
    associated license keys, applying to hosts in
        container 303
    effective license key of host container,
        retrieving 305
    license key associations, retrieving 303
    license key associations, retrieving to host
        containers in environment 303
    license key associations, retrieving with
        specific host container 304
    license keys, associating with host contain-
        ers 302
    using 301
LicenseDataManager.ApplyAssociated
        LicenseData() method 303
LicenseDataManager.QueryEffective
        LicenseData() method 305
LicenseDataManager.UpdateAssociated
        LicenseData() method 302
license inventory
    license keys, adding 297, 298
    license keys, removing from 299
    license keys, retrieving from 298
license key associations
    modifying 305
    removing 305
    retrieving 303
    retrieving, to host containers in
        environment 303
    retrieving, with specific host container 304
LicenseManager.RemoveLicense()
        method 299
licenses
    assigned license keys, removing from
        hosts 301

assigned licenses, retrieving 300
assigning, to hosts 299
keys, adding to license inventory 297
keys, removing from license inventory 299
keys, retrieving from license inventory 298
managing 297
list() method 127
log bundles
    creating 325
log files
    retrieving 321-324
Logical Unit Number (LUN) 228

M

maintenance mode
    about 100
    cluster DRS automation levels 100
    disabling 100
    enabling 100
    host putting, Set-VMHost cmdlet used 100
Managed Object References
    using 55
Master Boot Record (MBR) 245
Math.Round method 84
maxFailureWindow 256
maximum transmission unit (MTU) 188
Measure-Object cmdlet
    using 82, 83
    value, rounding 84
methods 67, 68
metric IDs
    retrieving 330
minUpTime 256
Move-Cluster cmdlet 263
Move-VMHost cmdlet 262
multipathing policy
    setting 233, 234
multiple servers
    connecting to 19, 20

N

network adapter
    adding 156
    modifying 162, 163
    removing 166
Network File System (NFS) 227

Thank you for buying
Learning PowerCLI

About Packt Publishing

Packt, pronounced 'packed', published its first book "Mastering phpMyAdmin for Effective MySQL Management" in April 2004 and subsequently continued to specialize in publishing highly focused books on specific technologies and solutions.

Our books and publications share the experiences of your fellow IT professionals in adapting and customizing today's systems, applications, and frameworks. Our solution based books give you the knowledge and power to customize the software and technologies you're using to get the job done. Packt books are more specific and less general than the IT books you have seen in the past. Our unique business model allows us to bring you more focused information, giving you more of what you need to know, and less of what you don't.

Packt is a modern, yet unique publishing company, which focuses on producing quality, cutting-edge books for communities of developers, administrators, and newbies alike. For more information, please visit our website: www.packtpub.com.

About Packt Enterprise

In 2010, Packt launched two new brands, Packt Enterprise and Packt Open Source, in order to continue its focus on specialization. This book is part of the Packt Enterprise brand, home to books published on enterprise software – software created by major vendors, including (but not limited to) IBM, Microsoft and Oracle, often for use in other corporations. Its titles will offer information relevant to a range of users of this software, including administrators, developers, architects, and end users.

Writing for Packt

We welcome all inquiries from people who are interested in authoring. Book proposals should be sent to author@packtpub.com. If your book idea is still at an early stage and you would like to discuss it first before writing a formal book proposal, contact us; one of our commissioning editors will get in touch with you.

We're not just looking for published authors; if you have strong technical skills but no writing experience, our experienced editors can help you develop a writing career, or simply get some additional reward for your expertise.

VMware vSphere 5.1 Cookbook

ISBN: 978-1-84968-402-6   Paperback: 466 pages

Over 130 task-oriented recipes to install, configure, and manage various vSphere 5.1 components

1. Install and configure vSphere 5.1 core components

2. Learn important aspects of vSphere such as administration, security, and performance

3. Configure vSphere Management Assistant (VMA) to run commands/scripts without the need to authenticate every attempt

vSphere High Performance Cookbook

ISBN: 978-1-78217-000-6   Paperback: 240 pages

Over 60 recipes to help you improve vSphere performance and solve problems before they arise

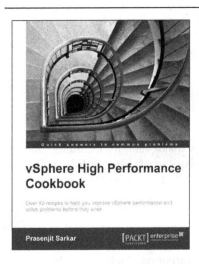

1. Troubleshoot real-world vSphere performance issues and identify their root causes

2. Design and configure CPU, memory, networking, and storage for better and more reliable performance

3. Comprehensive coverage of performance issues and solutions including vCenter Server design and virtual machine and application tuning

Please check **www.PacktPub.com** for information on our titles

Instant VMware vCloud Starter

ISBN: 978-1-84968-996-0   Paperback: 76 pages

A practical, hands-on guide to get started with
VMware vCloud

1. Learn something new in an Instant! A short, fast,
   focused guide delivering immediate results

2. Deploy and operate a VMware vCloud in your
   own demo kit

3. Understand the basics about the cloud in general
   and why there is such a hype

4. Build and use templates to quickly deploy
   complete environments

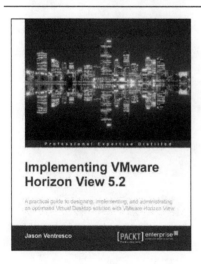

Implementing VMware Horizon View 5.2

ISBN: 978-1-84968-796-6   Paperback: 390 pages

A practical guide to designing, implementing, and
administrating an optimized Virtual Desktop solution
with VMware Horizon View

1. Detailed description of the deployment
   and administration of the VMware Horizon
   View suite

2. Learn how to determine the resources your
   virtual desktops will require

3. Design your desktop solution to avoid
   potential problems, and ensure minimal
   loss of time in the later stages

Please check **www.PacktPub.com** for information on our titles

www.ingramcontent.com/pod-product-compliance
Lightning Source LLC
Chambersburg PA
CBHW062049050326
40690CB00016B/3033